HIGH-LEVEL
RESUMES

HIGH-POWERED TACTICS
FOR HIGH-EARNING
PROFESSIONALS

Marshall A. Brown
and
Annabelle Reitman

CAREER
PRESS

Franklin Lakes, NJ

HIGH-LEVEL RESUMES
EDITED BY CLAYTON W. LEADBETTER
TYPESET BY KATE HENCHES
Cover design by Mada Design, Inc. / NYC
Printed in the U.S.A. by Book-mart Press

To order this title, please call toll-free 1-800-CAREER-1 (NJ and Canada: 201-848-0310) to order using VISA or MasterCard, or for further information on books from Career Press.

The Career Press, Inc., 3 Tice Road, PO Box 687,
Franklin Lakes, NJ 07417
www.careerpress.com

Library of Congress Cataloging-in-Publication Data

Brown, Marshall A., 1956-
    High-level resumes : high-powered tactics for high-earning professionals / by
Marshall A. Brown and Annabelle Reitman.
        p. cm.
    Includes index.
    ISBN 1-56414-780-0
    1. Résumés (Employment) 1. Reitman, Annabelle. II. Title.

HF5383.B74 2005
650.14′2—dc22

2004059450

DEDICATION

To my parents,
Florence and Morry, for teaching me important lessons in life.
To Judith and John for their love, support, and encouragement along the way.
—Marshall A. Brown

To Rachael
who thinks it's "a hoot" and is very proud of having a mother
in the third phase of her career, going into her fourth and most creative one.
—Annabelle Reitman

ACKNOWLEDGMENTS

Contributors

This book was made possible by the generous time and effort of the individuals who assisted us in the writing, as well as our clients and peers who provided us with good and bad examples of resumes. We would like to thank:

Seth Kahn—author of *Creating Beehives: Building Communities that Generate Returns*, organizational community specialist, conference speaker, and executive strategy consultant in Washington, D.C.

James P. Dittbrenner and Harvey T. Kaplan, Ph.D—K&D Associates in Rockville, Maryland.

Deb Rollison—Rollison & Associates in Silver Spring, Maryland.

Cory Edwards, CRW, CCMC, CECC—president, Partnering For Success, LLC, in Sterling, Virginia.

Nancy Abramson—career coach, Whole Life Transitions in Potomac, Maryland.

Alesia Benedict, CPRW, JCTC—executive director, Getinterviews.com in Rochelle Park, New Jersey.

Jan Boxer—principal, Strategic Partners, Inc., in Potomac, Maryland.

Linda Finkle, CCG, PCC, CDMP—CEO, Incedo Group, LLC, in Potomac, Maryland.

Louise Garver, CPRW, JCTC, CMP, CEIP, MCDP—professional resume writer and career coach, Career Directions, LLC, in Enfield, Connecticut.

L. Jeannette Mobley—principal, The JPM Group in Washington, D.C.

Priscilla D. Nelson—senior partner, Nelson & Associates in Reston, Virginia.

Walter J. O'Neill—senior vice president, The Ayers Group in Princeton, New Jersey.

Larry Slesinger—founder and CEO, Slesinger Management Services in Bethesda, Maryland.

Ken Soha—career management consultant, Soha & Associates in Fairfax, Virginia.

And thanks to Dawn Hatzer and Jeffrey Shields, who were brave enough to provide their own resumes.

Appreciations

We are extremely grateful to the following individuals who helped to make this book a reality. Their support and energy is greatly appreciated:

Sharon Armstrong, of Human Resources 911, for introducing us to Marilyn Allen.

Marilyn Allen, of Allen O'Shea Literary Agency, LLC, for being our literary agent.

Beth McFarland, of Society for Human Resource Management, for connecting us with a great group of human resource professionals.

The human resource professionals and executive recruiters who took the time to be interviewed and who provided us with quotes: Sam Bresler, SPHR; Joan Gotti; Sylvia Gray; R. Gregory Green, SPHR; Michael Hoagland, CAE; Pamela Kaul; Suzanne Lulewicz; Leonard Pfeiffer IV; Libby Sartain, SPHR; Jackie Silver; and Larry Slesinger.

Annette Summers, executive director of the Association of Career Professionals, International, for helping us gather resumes.

Peter Fox, for his administrative support and "timeliness."

I would also like to personally thank Susan Sarfati, for showing me what determination and leadership is all about, and Kevin Nourse, for his humor and guidance. And a special thanks to Eric Scharf, for his friendship and patience.

—*Marshall A. Brown*

CONTENTS

PREFACE

Our Story, as Told by Marshall A. Brown and Annabelle Reitman

It was a winter Sunday afternoon. We had accepted the offer to write a senior-level resume book. We thought long and hard; how were we going to make this resume book different from the hundreds of resume books already out there? How was this going to be unique? What "great words of wisdom" could we provide to our readers? And we wanted to write the book in a creative and powerful manner.

Then it hit us. We did not know of any senior-level resume books that identified storytelling as a means of writing a resume and searching for a new job or career. Just as we tell our clients that the uniqueness of their resumes is what separates them from the stack that hiring directors receive, so do their unique stories.

Don't you want your resume to be talked about? Don't you want your experience and accomplishments to be remembered by hiring directors? Of course you want your skills and knowledge to be told in a manner that is authentic and unique to you.

Throughout this book, you will hear different stories being reported. All of these are true, real-life stories that we have been privileged to have heard in our many years of career coaching.

We would like to encourage you to think about your uniqueness—what experience and qualifications you bring to the table—and to tell your story. No one else has the same story. Our hope is that this story engages, energizes, and inspires you. We wish you much success in the telling of *your* story.

Once you have your story developed, then it's all about marketing yourself... marketing Brand You! According to Tom Peters, marketing and leadership guru,

"We believe that in today's world you gotta be *distinct*—distinctly talented—or you are in danger of rapidly becoming *extinct!*"

Employers pay for results and what you can produce for them. And job seekers who succeed are the ones who know what they have to offer and what they are capable of doing better than some of their competition. It's also about taking charge of your own career and knowing your marketable and transferable skills.

It is imperative in today's competitive job market to know *you*! Knowing what you have to offer and then marketing and branding yourself as the person with that information will help to separate you from your competition. Your marketability will depend on your ability to demonstrate, on paper and verbally, your skills (even if within the same organization).

To help you understand storytelling, Seth Kahan, storyteller and organizational community specialist in Washington, D.C., who integrates his storytelling expertise in his organizational consulting practice, identifies the art of storytelling as follows:

> Storytelling has been around for centuries and is a powerful form of communication. Everyone remembers certain stories—stories that have been passed down from one generation to another. Human beings remember stories.

> Since the mid-1990s, storytelling has been a fruitful topic of discussion in organizations that include Harvard, Walt Disney, Hewlett-Packard, IBM, MIT, Eastman Chemical, the U.S. Army, the World Bank, Royal Dutch Shell, and the Center for Association Leadership. This ancient human phenomenon has been in the spotlight, because its potency is being plumbed for gold.

> Leaders, and anyone who wants to influence, learn quickly that storytelling is a skill they must master. "The age-old practice of storytelling is one of the most effective tools leaders can use," says the *Harvard Business Review* ("Telling Tales" by Stephen Denning in *Harvard Business Review*, May 2004). Everyone agrees that, following a presentation, stories are what people remember. Listeners may not be able to recount the details of charts and graphs, but they always remember the tale that caught the point and drove it home. They remember it so well, in fact, that it is this story they are most likely to relay to their colleagues. In the process, they pass along valuable information that can be reexamined and applied anew.

> A story can be thought of as *the smallest portable context*. It does more than transport the listener. Embedding itself in memory, the story attaches to all related information and brings it to bear on interpretation. This quality of association, it turns out, is incredibly valuable. Information out of context is, at best, transactional and, at worst, misinforming. But stories come with their own built-in circumstances and situational nuances that clarify, highlight, dramatize, and accentuate. This context assists the listener in understanding the information and storing it so it can be recalled and reapplied in new situations.

> What does this have to do with resumes? Everything! With stories, you can build a resume that influences, takes the reader out of his dreary world, and paints a picture of *his* organization's rosy future complete with *your* presence. Now, that's influence!

"Transformation is the result of a well-told story," says the Massachusetts Institute of Technology (*The Four Elements of Every Successful Story* by Robert Dickman, Society of Organizational Learning and Massachusetts Institute of Technology, in *Reflections*, Volume 4, Number 3). When being considered for a senior position, nothing short of transforming the selection committee will do. If your resume does not gel into a coherent story, creating a vision of your capacity, potential, and contribution, then it will drift through fingers and join the piles of meaningless data they are burdened with combing. As *CIO Magazine* has said, "Numbers aren't everything. Don't underestimate the importance of weaving a good story into your business case" ("ROI's Secret Ingredient" by Jack Keen, in *CIO Magazine*, June 15, 2003).

I rely on the transformational power of storytelling in my work with CEOs. For example, rolling out a new strategy is a complex process that relies on the CEO being able to engage stakeholders. It is not just a matter of sharing information, but garnering the goodwill and commitment of everyone required to shepherd the new strategy into success. If people choose to support the strategy only because they are being ordered, their follow-up behavior will be weak and can even sabotage new directions. However, if they *identify* with the new direction the organization is taking on, their follow-up actions will be thoughtful and appropriately responsive to circumstances.

I convene stakeholders, including employees and CEO, and everyone tells stories from their personal lives, exploring critical aspects of the new strategy. Together we examine these stories and discover what is most important about them. This material—from *their* lives—is then associated with the organization's strategy and objectives. Through this process, people come to identify with the new strategy and take personal accountability for seeing it through to fruition. By telling stories and listening to each other's, the personal relationship to the organization's strategy is strengthened, creating a bond that comes from a high level of commitment. It is no wonder that organizations are beginning to appreciate the value of a well-told story.

From an organization's perspective, having the right people in the right positions is critical. When they are looking for leaders, they choose people whose stories mesh with their organization's needs. Telling your story in a way that it is easy for people to grasp, hear, and see has never been more critical to successful professional development.

This is where Marshall A. Brown and Annabelle Reitman's *High-Level Resumes* comes in. Here you will find a well-defined process that will guide you on this critical journey. If you are looking for a guide on how to create the executive resume, you have found the master key. In the pages ahead, you can expect to find techniques to build your story, develop the hook that will grab your intended audience, include all relevant experience to land your intended position, and market your story to those who best match the future you are pursuing. You are in tremendously good hands here. Follow their advice, and yours is one story that will have a happy ending.

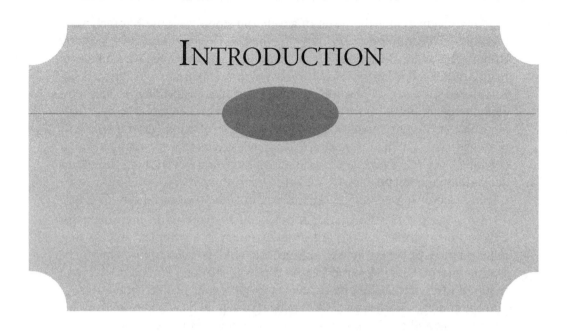

INTRODUCTION

"The greater thing in this world is not so much where we stand as in what direction we are going."

—*Oliver Wendell Holmes*

Individuals in hiring positions, whether they are human resource professionals, search committees, or recruiters, have little time to figure out how a candidate's skills and experience relate to their needs. *High-Level Resumes* provides practical guidelines and a step-by-step process for telling your unique work story effectively and efficiently. Professionals have told us what they look for when they review resumes and how they go about separating the yeses from the nos. Therefore, we also included real-life interviews from recruiters and human resource professionals who actually review resumes on a day-to-day basis.

Read and follow through on their excellent words of advice.

Our vision in writing *High-Level Resumes* was to provide you the necessary tools to develop a customized, targeted document to achieve the following:

- Bring your background and experience to the attention of hiring authorities.
- Showcase your relevant, in-depth, and extensive work background.
- Demonstrate that you have the right qualifications for the job.
- Illustrate how you can benefit the organization.
- Increase your chances to make the first selection cut.

This book was designed for use by senior-level executives. We have identified our audience as having a minimum of 10 years' experience, higher than average compensation for their industry/profession, and some managerial responsibilities. We did not define "senior level" based solely on specific dollar amounts, because different industries have different compensation ranges. For example, typically, the financial profession salary range is higher than in the nonprofit professional's range.

We have included some other unique features to assist senior-level executives in creating the resumes that will get them hired for their desired positions:

- **Special Markets**—Examine three select working environments (associations, military to civilian, and federal government) that require distinct resume treatment not always covered in other resume books.

- **Electronic Formatting**—Review the most up-to-date information regarding using your resume electronically.

- **Customized Appendixes**—Assess your skills, personal attributes, achievements, and resume headings.

- **Up-to-Date Print and Web Resources**—Refer to the newest print and Web resources available to you for developing your job search strategy.

- **Worksheets**—Plan and design your resume with 11 detailed worksheets.

Now let's get started creating the targeted resume to tell *your* story!

CHAPTER

1

Review of
Resume Basics

"And if not now, when?"
—Talmud

Chapter Overview

When was the last time you looked at and updated your resume? If you are like most senior-level professionals, that was quite a long time ago—perhaps as long as eight to 10 years. It is possible that you think your resume is not very outdated (about two to three years old), and that all you need to do is to add your latest responsibilities and achievements and/or continued education activities. In fact, your resume may actually require a complete overhauling. Additionally, the reasons for needing one now may differ from the last time you used a resume. As a successful, motivated, competent, and experienced professional, your resume should always be current and available. Do not be caught unprepared and in a spot where you quickly have to put together a resume without careful thought and attention. You never know when an unexpected opportunity could arise or when you might receive a call from a head-hunter. For all these reasons plus others, you should always have an up-to-date resume in your computer, and this chapter is your starting point.

Consider this chapter as your own "resume refresher course," and tackling the problem of where and how to begin preparing a resume will be much easier and smoother. A reexamination will quickly bring you up to speed on resume fundamentals and the latest thinking about resume development, setup, and applications. By the time you have finished reading this chapter and sit down to actually begin drafting the document, you will have gained a better understanding of basic resume fundamentals including (1) types of information and data you need to gather and organize,

(2) decisions you need to make regarding element design and arrangement, and (3) determining who your audiences will be and how and where to carry out distribution activities.

This chapter covers the essential fundamentals of:

+ Resume purposes and objectives.
+ Resume content and information.
+ Resume format options.
+ Resume style.
+ Additional resume technical pointers.
+ Preparing to gather needed information.

Resume Purposes and Objectives

What exactly is a resume suppose to accomplish? Is there more than one use for a resume? Should I have more than one version of my resume? A resume is not only required but also very much a multipurpose tool for carrying out your job search action plan. A resume is no longer just utilized in response to specific job openings. Additionally, the days of doing a job search via a "gunshot" approach (sending out the resume indiscriminately, hoping it will land on the desk of someone who is hiring) are over. People have learned that this approach is ineffective, resulting in a waste of time, energy, and money. The way successful job seekers view how and when a resume is used has changed within the last seven to 10 years. In today's highly competitive market, you need to take a proactive approach in your job search for a new and/or better work opportunity. Consequently, a marketing mindset and attitude is required for a successful job campaign.

A resume's overall purpose is to serve as your marketing tool. It is your advertising piece (think "company fact sheet"), designed to attract a predetermined targeted audience. As Leonard Pfeiffer, managing director of Leonard Pfeiffer Co. in Washington, D.C., states, "Always remember, you are the product, which you are selling, and this is your marketing and advertising material! What is the buyer looking for? How can I package and present myself to fulfill his or her needs?" A highly effective resume showcases your qualifications, thereby accomplishing your primary goal—presenting yourself and making a case for being selected to continue on to the next level of the screening and hiring process.

A resume's primary marketing objectives are to present you in a powerful, targeted, and concise manner in order to:

+ Grab a reviewer's attention quickly and to sustain the interest in you.
+ Demonstrate that you have the experience and background they need.
+ Show in an easy-to-read manner how and why you can be an asset to an employer.
+ Create a professional image so that you stand out from your competition.
+ Enable you to make the first cut and to remain on the short list for a first-level interview.

- Guide an interview, keeping it focused on your expertise, successes, and the data supporting your case for being hired.

A resume's secondary marketing objectives are to enhance your level of awareness, learn of opportunities, and increase your circle of contacts by:

- Getting you an introduction to specific people.
- Having people make referrals that they feel can be helpful to you.
- Enabling you, in a networking situation, to learn of opportunities and organizations that maybe of interest to you.
- Introducing, in an informational interview, a person to your background and give them some time to think about how they can be of most help to you.
- Allowing someone, in your absence, to share information about you that is objective, complete, and correct.

Leonard Pfeiffer summarizes it quite well: "Resumes do not get jobs—the objective of a resume is to get you an interview! It is a marketing piece to gain their attention, to attract their curiosity, and to assist you in the door."

It should be noted that very often the initial reviewer and the initial interviewer are not necessarily the same person. Most likely, a headhunter or an HR specialist will receive all the resumes submitted and select those to be forwarded to the person conducting the first round of interviews. That said, it would not be unusual for a professional at your level of experience to know the hiring VP or director and submit your resume directly to that person or to be able to bypass the in-house HR recruiter by obtaining a direct referral or recommendation from a fellow colleague.

Resume Content and Information

As a seasoned professional, your background and experience are quite extensive and it can be hard to decide what to include and what to omit. The information selected to place in your resume should project a professional picture that presents you as a strong, capable candidate and/or match the requirements of a particular job opening.

All resume content items can be categorized as either *required information*, which is basic and essential, or *elective information*, to be include if it is relevant and/or enhances your position.

Following are the types of required resume data and facts to include.

Contact Information

In addition to your name and full address, this section should only include the phone number, cell phone number, and e-mail address where you want them to reach you—that is, do not include a work phone number or e-mail address if you need to be discreet. You can list a Web page URL if you have one and it showcases pertinent consulting or entrepreneurial experience and skills.

Objective/Goal

The more traditional approach has been to write one of two types of objective/goal:

+ A general job or career statement, such as "Seeking an HR management position with opportunities for growth and career advancement."
+ A specific job title or position sought, such as "To obtain a position as a corporate learning officer, utilizing seven years in training and development."

Today's more acceptable way of handling this section is as a concise description of the responsibilities being sought with reference to your qualifications and how your actions affected former employers' bottom lines. In fact, most candidates use the heading of "Professional Summary" or "Qualifications Highlights." This approach—focused on your successes rather than capabilities—is especially appropriate for a senior-level professional and is a great marketing strategy. Save the drafting of this statement for last, as it represents the highlights of the resume's content.

For one job opening, a recruiter or interviewer may read up to 100 resumes from which they may only select a maximum of 20 candidates for the first round of interviews. You may only have 10 to 30 seconds to grab their interest and give more attention to your resume and qualifications. Write an introductory statement from the perspective of what the organization requires—a brief statement of two or three sentences directed toward the organization's needs. For example, Nancy, an HR generalist, wrote this summary statement for a specific job listing:

"Distinctive mid-level HR administrator with strong and diversified background in strategic planning, team leadership, curriculum development and delivery, needs assessment, and employee supervision. Achieved within two years an increase in staff performance by 12% and staff work satisfaction by 18%."

Professional Work Experience

This section contains a listing of your employers, positions, responsibilities, and/or assignments. If you have been self-employed, include services or products provided and the client base.

Accomplishments and Successes

Include those accomplishments and successes achieved as an individual and as a team member, specifically giving detailed accounts for those that provide validation for qualifications and job responsibilities listed previously.

Licenses and Certificates

When listing licenses and certificates, spell out any acronyms and include initials in parentheses behind the title or name.

Education

The education section includes all activities that were part of your professional development and growth: academic degrees, certifications, CEUs, additional specialized training, and ongoing learning courses. Classes could have been in-house, at a campus or conference center, or Web-based.

Following are some types of elective resume data and information you may wish to include.

Security Clearances

When noting security clearances, include the level of clearance and date granted.

Affiliations

This section includes a listing of membership in professional, civic, and community service organizations. Write out the complete names of the organizations, because you cannot assume everyone is familiar with a group's acronym. Do not include any political, religious, racial, or ethnic affiliations, unless you think it would be beneficial in your marketing campaign or are interested in obtaining a position in a related association or nonprofit organization. If you belong to a number of organizations, group them by type of affiliation, with a listing of all positions held and descriptions of involvement. Providing the details gives a greater impact and dimension to your volunteerism as well as illustrates your leadership abilities in a different context than work.

Publications, Presentations, and/or Patents

This listing indicates your level of commitment and contribution to your profession or industry. Depending on the extent of your activities you may want to break this section into more than one category.

Awards and Honors

The order of listing awards and honors should be those received (1) from employers, (2) from professional associations, (3) in recognition of community service, and (4) for academic achievements. Where appropriate, include a very brief explanation of its significance or importance.

Other Information

Sometimes, there are specific personal highlights that would help the reader to remember you, enhance the picture of who you are, and/or identify with you, and this section can act as the resume closing. Such items can include military service, foreign languages, mentoring, competitive or avid athletic/sport interests, extensive global travel, volunteerism, and/or other unique personal history items.

Resume Format Options

The traditional chronological and functional resume formats are not usually the most efficient and effective ways for senior-level professionals to present their various specialized, in-depth experiences and qualifications. A quick review of the descriptions of these types of resumes will indicate why. In today's highly competitive job market, where there are more candidates than positions, you do not want the reader to have to take too long to figure out who you really are and what you have to offer. Many reviewers take only 10 to 30 seconds to scan a resume and decide whether to place it in the "call in for an interview" or "reject" pile.

Chronological Resume

A chronological resume takes a historical approach by outlining your work history, starting with the most recent position and ending with the oldest. Most reviewers and hiring agents prefer this format because it is the easiest one to follow and find needed information. Your career progression is shown over time by linking together a detailed job description of responsibilities with employer data. Additionally, if the organizations you have worked for, particularly your most recent employer, are well-known and have excellent reputations, they will be more visible in a chronological resume format.

Disadvantages of a chronological resume for a senior-level professional:

- Your age is more obvious.
- It is not particularly imaginative, allowing you to stand out.
- It is not selective and does not allow for highlighting specific qualifications up front.
- A reader cannot quickly see the overall picture of the extent of your background.

Functional Resume

A functional resume presents skills and experiences and stresses accomplishments and strengths rather than a progressive career history. One of its main features is a background summary statement. This synopsis section, one or two short paragraphs, highlights experience and expertise, specializations, and competitive edge, including both work content specific and transferable skills. This format is particularly useful when making a career change, and you may need to pull up experiences from several years ago to a more frontline placement.

Disadvantages of a functional resume for a senior-level professional:

- It does not naturally highlight details of promotions and career growth.
- The details of employment information are de-emphasized and minimized.
- It does not necessarily contain all the information required for a particular defined work opportunity.
- It is not, as a matter of course, results- or outcome-oriented.
- It could seem as if you have an erratic work history or gaps of unemployment.

Targeted Resume Format

If traditional resume formats do not work for senior-level professionals, what will? A targeted resume configuration is one that is really quite appropriate for people in this category. This is one version of what many people refer to as a combination resume format, because it has elements of both chronological and functional resumes. Basically, you are extracting selected information and arranging the facts and data in blocks, thereby bringing it to the forefront. This is quite different from showing your capabilities in the traditional resume manner of listing information in sequential time order.

For a highly experienced professional, a targeted resume setup works best because experiences, savvy, and competencies that have produced measurable results are highlighted. Skills, knowledge, and most importantly, your successes in using or applying the competencies listed reflect your creditability. Aptitudes in high demand are clearly seen for solving problems with effective outcomes; providing leadership to an organization, a work unit, or a project team; seeing the big picture; and having a package of other strengths and expertise that is an added value to the employer. A targeted resume can bundle qualifications and achievements in a way that directs your story towards the specific needs and culture of a potential employer.

As a successful, seasoned professional with an in-depth and varied work history, you have more than one avenue of employment to consider in your job search efforts. With a targeted resume, you can more easily and readily rebundle your qualifications and customize your experiences to match different types of job specifications and employer's requirements.

Resume Style

The design of a resume reflects your creativity and demonstrates your personal style and individuality, allowing the reader to feel they are truly getting to know you as a multidimensional person. A resume document should not be boring, only concentrating on credentials and data, appearing detached and cold. What you want to do is set up a visual pattern that is pleasing, interesting, and inviting to the reader. Think about how you want the overall look and form to project your professional image. R. Gregory Green, SPHR, president of HRx-Human Resource Remedies in Santa Fe, New Mexico, stresses, "Your resume should give a glimpse of your personality. It should reflect not only what you have to offer, but also, through its language and focus, give a sense of how you have approached your work and what results you have achieved."

You have a number of decisions to make as you consider content, layout, and design of your resume. Be consistent in the use of tabs, fonts, point size, bullet settings, and line and paragraph constructs. Think carefully about your choice of section and subsection headings to use, as well as your selection of specific verbs and adverbs that best reflect your specific skills, knowledge, strengths, and experiences. Green reiterates: "A resume should be easy to read, using a simple and direct format, in a clear and presentable typeface and font, and on quality white paper. Colored paper or small typefaces do not reproduce well, if they are later faxed or duplicated for internal distribution. Do not use an unusual or heavy typeface, which may create the impression of flamboyance or extravagance."

Your resume's maximum impact on a reader is more likely to occur when you are in control and orchestrate the development of the resume from start to finish. One way to accomplish this is by drafting the resume in your own words, phrases, etc., and deciding on the placement of information to reflect not only your skills and knowledge, but also your personality, enthusiasm, and commitment. It is essential that you feel an ownership of your resume—that is, you are comfortable and confident that it truly represents your professional self. Consequently, your response to a request for a copy of your resume is done with poise and ease that is reflected in your voice when stating, "I believe that I have the background and experience that will be of interest to you." Furthermore, having created a resume that you are proud of, you are more apt to voluntarily give out copies.

Resume Technical Pointers

A reviewer not only looks for reasons to select a resume for the short initial interview pile, but also looks for reasons to reject a resume. When a document has a "high polish," clarity, balance, and "togetherness" look to it, the hiring agent receives the message that you are a consummate professional. This is particularly true when a person who has never met you uses the resume as their main tool for selecting candidates for the initial interview invite.

Frequently, a resume is rejected simply because of typos, grammar errors, or just not being easy to read. Therefore, it is essential to pay close attention to the required or preferred resume technical points. Some of the rules are just standard English and writing usage, and others are good resume development procedures.

Fifteen accepted guidelines to follow as you develop your resume are:

1. Be accurate; check and, if necessary, double check all dates and figures.
2. Omit jargon and other language that is organization- or industry-specific—particularly when making a career change or professional shift to another field and/or industry—such as acronyms, titles, phrases, and so forth.
3. Try not to repeat or overuse the same professional skill word, action verb, or other characterizing words in describing your background and experiences.
4. Do not abbreviate to save space, other than the usual accepted abbreviations such as state names, academic degrees, part of an organization's name, and those commonly used in a specific field or industry.
5. Use white space and wide margins to make the resume visually appealing.
6. Keep the language simple, easy to read, clear, concise, and brief; keep statements brief, crisp, and succinct.
7. Review for grammar, spelling of formal names/titles, and correct English usage.
8. Avoid gender-specific words such as "manpower" and "salesman."
9. Be consistent in verb tenses, abbreviations, formatting, headings, design, style, fonts, and spacing.
10. Omit the use of "I" (first person), "he" or "she" (third person), and "a," "an," or "the" (unnecessary articles).

11. Use short sentences, paragraphs, or bullets, and start each opening sentence with an action verb or professional skill word.

12. For a resume that is more than one page, put your name at the top of any following pages, in case they become separated from each other, and clip the pages together—do not staple.

13. Keep your resume to two pages in length, unless you have an unusual background or extensive experiences that need to be included or unless more is necessary for meeting the job qualifications.

14. Choose high-quality paper stock that says "this is a successful senior-level professional."

15. Proofread word by word at least twice, then have a couple of colleagues (your fresh eyes) do the final critique and proof with complete objectivity and neutrality, providing you with their impressions and recommendations.

Preparing to Gather Needed Information

Prior to beginning the actual drafting of your resume, some fundamental questions that need to be asked include:

♦ What specific professional skills, knowledge, and/or competencies do I want to include and how do I want to prioritize them?

♦ What achievements and successes document my background and experiences?

♦ How do I want to project my credibility, motivation, and confidence?

♦ As people conduct their 10 to 30 seconds of scanning my resume, what are the ideal descriptive image words I want to surface in their minds about me?

♦ Where will I market myself, network, and/or apply for a job and how does this affect what is showcased in the resume?

Your responses to these questions are the basic resources for creating an ideal professional image and keeping you focused and on track in the development of your targeted resume. As you plan and continue to draft your resume, keep in mind that your goal for the finished document is to ask yourself, "Am I pleased with the results and ready to have my resume read by others?" and be able to answer a resounding yes!

As you read through the following two chapters, you will find 11 practical worksheets designed to help you undertake the somewhat laborious task of resume creation. These worksheets will help you consider your options and decide what the "right" and satisfactory responses to the previously listed questions are for you at this point in time.

In the future, as additional experience and knowledge are gained, professional interests shift, or events in your personal life impact your professional life, the answers to the same questions may change and your resume will need to be reviewed and revised. In fact, it is a good practice to reassess your resume and its contents once a year, so that you are always ready for that unexpected great opportunity.

With the creation of a high-level resume, you have a powerful and persuasive resource that will help you move forward in your chosen profession or industry. By introducing your background and experience exactly to your liking and priorities, you will be moving closer to achieving your ideal career goal.

Chapter Highlights

Recapping Chapter 1, the key concepts for guiding and shaping a targeted resume are:

1. First and foremost, a resume is your most important marketing tool.

2. The primary purpose of a resume is creating a tailor-made image that says you are the best person who can be hired to accomplish the job in a very professional and proficient manner.

3. Required resume information and data include name, contact information, objective/goals, professional work experiences/history, accomplishments and successes, licenses/certificates, and education.

4. Elective resume information and data include security clearances; affiliations/memberships; publications, presentations, or patents; and awards and honors.

5. The traditional chronological and functional resume formats are not usually the most efficient and effective for senior-level professionals with their various specialized, in-depth experiences and qualifications. Instead, a customized, targeted resume emphasizing skills and achievements is more appropriate for this type of job seeeker.

6. For a highly experienced professional, a targeted resume configuration works best to spotlight your savvy and competencies producing results through your abilities to solve problems, provide leadership to an organizational unit or team, and see the big picture, as well as to have a package of skills and expertise that are an added value to the employer.

7. The style of a resume reflects your creativity, demonstrating your personal flair and individuality, thereby allowing the reader to feel he has truly come to know you as a real, multidimensional person..

8. Paying close attention to the required or preferred resume technicalities is essential to your resume's marketability and improves your chances of making it to the initial interview.

9. It is important for you to feel you have ownership of your resume—to be comfortable and confident, because you have responsibility for its content and style and it truly represents your professional self.

"Knowing what you want is the first step in getting it."
—Louise Hart

CHAPTER

2

Prepare to Tell Your Story

"If opportunity doesn't knock, build a door."
—*Milton Berle*

Chapter Overview

In reality, all job search strategies center around telling your story—who you are professionally, what you can do, what you would like to do. However, most importantly, your story relates what it is unique about your background and experience, setting you apart from and above other candidates. More than your job titles and where you worked, employers are interested in your skills, strengths, and results. What will you accomplish and how will you meet their needs? The presentation of your resume is the first opportunity to tell your professional story to individuals who have access to your targeted market.

In Chapter 1, reference was made to thinking of yourself as the product to be marketed to the employer or the consumer. What will be your pitch? What will be your story? Will it always be the same story or will elements of it change or shift to fit different situations? And two or three years from now, how will your story be different—what items no longer relevant or current will be deleted, and what new pertinent facts will be integrated into your story?

A targeted resume focuses on your qualifications needed by an organization at this moment in time, thereby increasing your chances for a high-level match and being contacted for an interview. For this to happen, your resume needs to be exactly on the mark in introducing your story. Suzanne J. Lulewicz, president of SJL Associates in Mount Airy, Maryland, believes that "...well-told stories are outstanding

24

resume development tools for you. The stories you work with when planning to present yourself for potential organizations give prospective employers an opportunity to learn in-depth about your knowledge, skills, and talents, recreated in circumstances in which you actually used them. They also serve to identify for you whether the organization is a match for your creative talents."

This chapter deals with the essential resume elements of information and data, to help you:

- Set up a targeted resume.
- Organize work content skills and professional competencies.
- Organize transferable skills.
- Identify optional personal attributes.
- Identify accomplishments.
- Create a unique professional niche.

Set up a Targeted Resume

At this point do not worry about technical items such as resume format, style, headings, and specific wording. Concentrate on pulling together information and data that will become the elements for creating your professional story as a resume. As a senior-level professional, you have plenty of experiences and qualifications to choose from—in fact, there are probably too many. Start by retrieving files and records that contain information related to:

- **Work:** Job descriptions, performance evaluations, project reports, promotion confirmations, memos acknowledging your contributions, and a portfolio of work examples.
- **Education and Professional Development:** Diplomas, certificates, and transcripts.
- **Professional and Community Service:** Memberships, board and committee positions held, and awards received.

Once all relevant information has been gathered, you face two challenges in trying to assess, select, and organize the facts that will best convey and validate the professional story you want to tell today:

- Paring down and pinpointing the specific information and data that is not only important and significant, but also will project your desired professional identity.
- Arranging the selected information and data in a unified, condensed, and directed manner, pulling everything together in a single, powerful, professional image.

Unfortunately, there are no shortcuts to creating an outstanding targeted resume to help you achieve your work or job objectives. It does take an investment of time and energy. However, there are some preliminary steps you can follow in order to organize the information and data efficiently and effectively, to keep you centered on your task. As a senior-level professional, it is critical that the decisions you make, regarding which background items to include in your targeted resume and which to leave out, are done systematically and in priority order. Otherwise, it is easy to become mired down in the piles of information and data that are the result of your many years of diversified and multileveled work history.

Seeking a new position, whether voluntarily or involuntarily, should be looked upon as a great opportunity to obtain a job that brings you closer to your ideal work situation and your passion. But when was the last time you even thought about what would be your perfect work situation? In today's hectic and sometimes frantic world of work and personal responsibilities, most people feel they cannot afford or are too tired to think about the "what ifs." Now that you are taking the first step in a job search campaign by putting together your resume, take some time and think about your "what ifs." Set this dream job as the goal to reach, and see how close you can come to achieving this position.

Forget job titles and formal descriptions of your dream job for now. In your mind, can you picture what kind of work you are doing, what type of problems or projects you are dealing with, where you are doing it, whom you are working with, etc.? Would you be able to describe it accurately and with detail to another person? You may even surprise yourself in what you dream up as your ideal work situation. Nothing is impossible.

For example, Robert's partial description of his ideal work situation includes: "Working for a major international consulting firm, using my HR, communications, and marketing background, involved in new business development, facilitating organizational change, and leadership coaching, both here and abroad. In addition, develop proposals and arrange contracts and agreements. Travel frequently to Europe and Asia. My workspace back at corporate headquarters is a top floor corner office with wide windows overlooking the city and facing west towards the river and sunsets. It is decorated with antique pottery pieces acquired in my travels."

Please note that the examples used in this chapter through Chapter 4 are from the human resources field, making it easier for the reader to see and understand how the various aspects of a professional's background fit together.

To help you develop this image with details, complete Worksheet #1 on page 27.

WORKSHEET #1: DESCRIPTION OF IDEAL JOB/CONSULTING ASSIGNMENT

Instructions: Be as creative and as detailed as possible to provide a complete picture of this dream situation. Have some fun with this activity and let your imagination take hold. The goal is that when the description is read, a person can visualize the work situation and see you in this ideal job or consulting assignment. Describe each item using words and phrases that are meaningful and desirable to you at this present time in your professional life. There are no right, wrong, or "off the wall" responses. If the description feels right to you, then it is the right response. Give as many details as possible. In outlining your ideal job/consulting assignment, think about the following characteristics:

1. Professional/work skills, knowledge, and abilities you want to use.
2. Type and size of organization.
3. Work role and responsibilities.
4. Work environment, structure, and culture.
5. Geographic location.
6. Compensation and benefits.
7. Client/customer.
8. Other characteristics important to you.

Ideal Job/Consulting Assignment Statement: _____

_____

_____

_____

Note: Ask some of your colleagues who know you quite well to read this ideal job description and provide some feedback on whether or not they can truly see you in this work situation. Brainstorm further with them about how the match can be improved.

Keep this ideal job or consulting assignment before you as you start gathering, selecting, and organizing information and data for integration into a resume. Ask yourself, "What facts in my background and work history do I think support the abilities, competencies, and experience that would qualify me for this dream job/ assignment?" Also ask, "What can I mention that is unique or different about myself in order to make a lasting impression on a reviewer or interviewer?"

Note: The answers to these two questions are not necessarily one and the same.

Before opening your computer to begin gathering your needed information, return to Chapter 1 and quickly review how to organize your resume content and information sections. It is assumed that you know what to include in the contact information section. For the moment, skip the first section—qualifications or summary statement— as this section is really the last one created. This part of your resume serves as the introduction to your most important and impressive facts and statistics. Therefore, it is best to wait and decide what to include after your resume has been completed and you can make your selections from the other resume sections or elements. Consider this statement as the PR blurb or "elevator speech" for your story.

The following sections describe the four essential story elements of a targeted resume, with worksheets to take inventory of your work content and transferable skills, other personal attributes, and accomplishments. The last section presents a process for establishing your unique professional niche that is the basis for your qualifications or summary statement.

Organize Work Content Skills and Professional Competencies

The first group of professional skills are work content skills, often called "hard skills." These are individual proficiencies directly related to a person's ability to carry out the basic tasks and activities of a particular profession or industry. An experienced professional has a variety of work content skills. For example, as a learning and performance specialist, Emma's work content skills include instructional design planning and implementation, e-learning and platform delivery, as well as need assessment and facilitation skills.

When related or aligned skills are combined with the knowledge of a specialized vocabulary and subject matter into an integral whole, a professional competency or expertise has been acquired. Having a professional competency enables you to carry out the more complex functions of a field. For example, Emma's competency in the learning and performance field includes the work content skills listed previously, plus knowledge of learning styles, human performance improvement fundamentals, and adult learning.

As you begin to take inventory of the work content skills you have, write a brief description of its present and past applications. Be prepared that this can take some time to do, depending on the extent and diversity of your work experiences. For example a partial description of Emma's training skill is: "Created, wrote, and initiated training courses in the areas of leadership development, change management, team building, supervision skills, and diversity."

Then ask yourself, "How well do I use this skill? Is this a favorite skill of mine? Am I really interested in continuing to use or practice this skill? Is this skill essential to the position I would now like to have?" Depending on your responses, you may decide to omit a skill completely from your resume, as your interest or professional focus has changed and you really are not interested in using the skill at this time. On the other hand, you may have little experience in using a skill and realize that you have developed an interest in using it in your next position.

To help you to inventory your work content skills and choose those for highlighting in your story, complete Worksheet #2 on page 29.

WORKSHEET #2: IDENTIFY WORK CONTENT SKILLS

Instructions: As you read through your materials, identify a minimum of seven work content skills that you have performed in carrying out job responsibilities or have learned and believe you want to showcase in your targeted resume. Appendix A on page 116 can assist you with this step. For each work content skill identified, write one to three brief sentences regarding tasks or responsibilities involved, product(s) provided, customer and/or clients served, and content or subject matter of the activities.

Next, rank these work content skills from 1 to 5, according to:

1. Degree of proficiency in use of the skill.
2. Level of experience in use of the skill.
3. Desire to continue to use the skill.

The skills you have ranked high in the "desire to continue to use" category as well as in at least one other category become part of the essential information you want included in the first third of your target resume. The skills that have been ranked high in all three categories form your competencies or expertise and are highlighted in the qualifications or summary statement. Now compare these work content skills to those needed in your ideal job or consulting assignment. How closely aligned are they? If they are not closely aligned, do you know the reasons why?

Note: There may be work content skills you have ranked low in ability and in-depth experience but would like to strengthen and become part of your expertise. For these skills, consider enrolling in one or more professional development activities, such as a certificate or degree-granting program or obtaining CEUs through workshops and conferences.

Work Content Skill	Ability to Use	In-Depth Experience	Desire to Use
1.			
2.			
3.			
4.			
5.			
6.			
7.			
8.			
9.			
10.			

Note: List as many work content skills as needed.

Organize Transferable Skills

The second category of professional skills is transferable skills, also referred to as "soft skills." These proficiencies are used in a broad range of work functions. Common transferable skills include writing, interpersonal, and supervision skills and are required in the majority of middle and upper levels of responsibilities and across the board in all fields and industries. What does differ from position to position are the content, subject matter, or who is involved. As a senior-level professional looking for a new position, you need to be aware of your transferable skills and how and where they have been applied in various areas or functions of your field.

For example, Maria, an HR director, briefly describes one of her transferable skills this way:

Managed: "Supervised a staff of 12 human resource professionals, and administrative assistants, as well as five contracted trainers. Planned and administered a $1-million budget. Was responsible for the overall direction, planning, and development of training programs, personnel retention studies with recommendations, and equal opportunity compliance."

Knowing your transferable skills is critical to successfully making a career change into a different profession/industry or a professional shift in your specialization from one arena to another. Understanding how and where to apply and use these skills indicates your ability to quickly reposition yourself and transition with ease and success. Chapter 6 is devoted to this topic.

The most common and widely used transferable skills can be organized into various groupings, as explained in Appendix A:

* Administration/Management.
* Communication.
* Design/Planning.
* Human Relations/Interpersonal.
* Information Management.
* Leadership.
* Negotiations.
* Operations.
* Persuasion.
* Research/Analysis.

To help you inventory your transferable skills and chose those for highlighting in your story, complete Worksheet #3 on page 31.

WORKSHEET #3: IDENTIFY TRANSFERABLE SKILLS

Instructions: As you read through your papers, make a list of five to 10 transferable skills that you presently use, have used in carrying out job responsibilities, or have learned and want to showcase in your targeted resume. Appendix A on page 116 can be of assistance with this step. Write one to three brief sentences regarding tasks or responsibilities involved, product(s) provided, customer and/or clients served, and content or subject matter of the activities.

Next rank these transferable skills from 1 to 5, according to:

1. Degree of proficiency in use of the skill.
2. Level of experience in use of the skill.
3. Desire to continue to use the skill.

The skills you have ranked high in the "desire to continue to use" category as well as in at least one other category become part of the essential information you want included in the first third of your target resume. The skills that have been ranked high in all three categories form your transferable group sets and you want highlighted in the qualifications or summary statement. Now compare these transferable skills to those needed in your ideal job or consulting assignment. How closely aligned are they? If they are not closely aligned, do you know the reasons why?

Note: There may be transferable skills you have ranked low in ability and in-depth experience that you would like to continue to use or believe are necessary to the next step on your career ladder. For these skills, you may want to initiate some professional development activity for improvement, such as on-site training courses, off-site workshops, and continuing education courses.

Transferable Skills	Ability to Use	In-Depth Experience	Desire to Use
1. _____	_____	_____	_____
2. _____	_____	_____	_____
3. _____	_____	_____	_____
4. _____	_____	_____	_____
5. _____	_____	_____	_____
6. _____	_____	_____	_____
7. _____	_____	_____	_____
8. _____	_____	_____	_____
9. _____	_____	_____	_____
10. _____	_____	_____	_____

Note: List as many transferable skills as needed.

Identify Optional Personal Attributes

Along with identified work content and transferable skills pertinent to your story, you have other attributes that can be integrated into your story as well. These qualities enhance your story by putting a personality and individuality to your targeted resume, placing you in a better position for making the first cut. What constitutes a strength or asset that goes beyond your skill areas? The answer is any personal quality that can help to differentiate you from others in your field. How do you think of yourself? Are you multilingual? Do you consider yourself very imaginative? How about being quite adventurous? Do you see yourself as a risk-taker?

Now think of events or activities not related to work that can reflect these attributes and increase your chances to be remembered no matter how many resumes are received. You may be able to speak several languages fluently, have participated in the NYC and Boston marathons for the last four years, have an outstanding military service record, or initiated a volunteer community service project. Frequently, experiences can serve to delineate not only personal attributes, but transferable skills as well—initiating a community service project illustrates attributes such as commitment, service orientation, as well as leadership and management skills.

For example, Lisa illustrates her humor talent in the following ways: "Do stand-up comedy. Perform at various comedy clubs around the Washington, D.C. area. For the past three years have emceed the DC Professional Women's Network's Annual Breast Cancer Research Fund Raising Event. This year also served as the entertainment coordinator. Use humor in training workshops." With this descriptive statement, she has shown her sense of humor, commitment to a cause, and creativity, as well as her organizational and management skills.

To help you identify specific attributes and strengths that can be integrated into your story, complete Worksheet #4 on page 33.

WORKSHEET #4: IDENTIFY OPTIONAL PERSONAL ATTRIBUTES

Instructions: Do a mental review of your strongest personal attributes that you feel you can capitalize on for your story. Appendix B on page 122 can be of assistance with this step. Identify the events and activities not related to work that would illustrate these select personal qualities.

As you begin to identify those personal attributes and the events/activities appropriate for incorporation into your targeted resume, ask yourself the following questions:

1. In what ways do these personal attributes contribute to my professional story?
2. In what ways do these personal attributes relate to my ideal work situation?
3. In what ways do these personal attributes enhance my resume and make a lasting impression on a reviewer or interviewer?

Select five to seven incidents that you think best fit the above criteria and list them with one or two brief sentences regarding the main tasks or activities involved. For each incident, identify one to three important personal attributes involved. Next, rank these attributes from 1 to 5, according to:

1. Relationship to your ideal work situation.
2. Contribution to resume's impression on reviewer or interviewer.

Give serious consideration to the attributes that have ranked high on the two listed qualities regarding how and where they should be incorporated into your story for your targeted resume.

Nonwork Incident With Description	Identify Personal Attributes	Relationship to Ideal Work Situation	Contribution to Impression
1. _____	_____	_____	_____
_____	_____	_____	_____
2. _____	_____	_____	_____
_____	_____	_____	_____
3. _____	_____	_____	_____
_____	_____	_____	_____
4. _____	_____	_____	_____
_____	_____	_____	_____
5. _____	_____	_____	_____
_____	_____	_____	_____
6. _____	_____	_____	_____
_____	_____	_____	_____
7. _____	_____	_____	_____
_____	_____	_____	_____

Identify Accomplishments

Accomplishments are measurable quantitatively or qualitatively; they are results-oriented incidents that demonstrate, in a very specific and dramatic way, your outstanding proficiencies and personal characteristics. Listen to R. Gregory Green, who states, "I want to see facts! When you list your positions and experiences, always include your relevant accomplishments while in those positions. What have you done and what have you achieved while doing it? What were your special contributions? What results did you achieve in accomplishing your mission?"

Success examples come not only from your work experiences, but also from other areas of your life. Positioning yourself for advancement, a new job, a career change, or a professional shift is dependent on high-level quality of performance. As a senior-level professional, you will most likely find it difficult to sort out your many varied successes and select the ones you feel are the most meaningful, relevant, and likely have the greatest impact on a reader. As you review and determine which successes provide the best documentation for your qualifications, the following guidelines help carry out the selection process. Consider:

- How productive you really are at solving problems, reaching goals, and achieving set outcomes.
- How valuable you can be to a potential employer.
- How outstanding your competencies and skill sets are, as well as your personal attributes.
- How your story holds together, thereby giving validation to your qualifications.

Joan Gotti, senior vice president of a major financial institution in New York City, looks at the hard leadership components and proven statements of a candidate's experience. She says, "You must be able to anchor the generalizations made in your resume with specific examples and proven results. Don't just say that you have general management skills; list specific skills and back it up with the results of your action."

For example, Justin, a human performance specialist, cites as an accomplishment: "Developed, conducted, and evaluated employee-training programs on customer service and verbal communication for a call center staff of 60. This resulted in a 10% increase in customer satisfaction, a 12% increase in efficiency of handling called-in service requests, and a 20% improvement in staff's attitude about their jobs."

Although achievements are based in the past, they are really focused towards the future and what your potential and capabilities are for high performance. As you review your work, education, military, volunteer, and other activity files and records, start from the present and work backward in time. Just as one experience can illustrate both skills and personal attributes, so can one accomplishment be relevant to more than one proficiency or personal quality. Ten years is the usual acceptable amount of time to go back. However, if your interests and professional focus have changed, you may want to go back a bit in your past for an accomplishment that gives credibility to a skill or strength important to your present job search. Regardless, look for activities, projects, and tasks demonstrating accomplishments in such areas as:

- Providing leadership—day-to-day operations, team projects, reorganization activities, or crisis-oriented.
- Identifying a problem, presenting, resolving or implementing a solution.
- Proposing, planning, and initiating a new project, program policy/ procedures, initiative, system, manual, or service.
- Finding new funding sources, writing grant proposals, receiving total funding requests, or administration funding revenue.
- Increasing revenues sales volume or collections, ROI, decreasing costs or fees, expanding customer or client base.
- Consolidating/merging work sites, systems, procedures, forms, inventory.
- Improving staff/employee productivity, efficiency, morale, customer service or production; updating computer system/software, plant equipment, office forms, systems, manuals, procedures, or other technology systems.
- Opening new territories, outlets, stores, or branch offices.
- Writing and/or editing publications in print and on Websites; giving presentations, hearing testimonies, or making speeches at conferences or community meetings; or facilitating board meetings, workshops, or seminars.

Make special note if you have received a bonus, memos of appreciation, recognition certificate, etc., as an acknowledgement of a successful outcome.

To help you identify specific accomplishments illustrating your qualifications and individualization and to validate your story, complete Worksheet #5 on page 36.

Worksheet #5: Identify Accomplishments

Instructions: Before beginning the process of identifying accomplishments, take a second look at the results of worksheets 2, 3, and 4. Appendix C on page 124 can be of assistance with this step. Refer back to your records and files or do a mental review of your successes. Select 10 to 12 incidents that demonstrate or give evidence for your outstanding work content and transferable skills and personal attributes.

For each identified accomplishment, write about three brief sentences describing this accomplishment. Include its impact, and/or the quantified results or outcomes. Think of your identified work content, transferable skills, and personal attributes that can be linked to each listed accomplishment and indicate them in the appropriate column. Remember, an achievement can illustrate more than one qualification.

Accomplishment Incident With Description	Skills Related To	Personal Attributes Related To
1.		
2.		
3.		
4.		
5.		
6.		
7.		
8.		
9.		
10.		
11.		
12.		

Create Your Own Unique Professional Niche or Image

A professional niche is a customized bundling of your skills, knowledge, personal attributes, education, work history, and achievements that projects a unique professional image, or your "brand identity," to prospective recruiters, employers and clients. The information and data assembled in worksheets 2 through 5 constitute your basic story elements and will shape and provide the content for your customized professional niche statement. Think of your ideal work assignment and the qualifications and proficiencies required to turn your vision into reality. Developing a professional niche can be your most difficult task, as it involves:

+ Determining what items from the extensive information and data that you have established best illustrates your ideal professional self.

+ Prioritizing the skill sets, competencies, bodies of knowledge, and experiences that should be bundled to demonstrate that you are the best candidate for the job.

+ Writing a concise, succinct, and specific summary statement that markets your qualifications in a powerful and visible manner.

+ Having a crystal-clear image of your present professional self or "brand" and what qualities make you an unique and outstanding individual.

Putting it all together or packaging your story is the final step for getting ready to tell your story in a targeted resume format.

For example, Connie, an assistant HR manager, decides that the work content competency of training is priority #1 and management of an HR department is priority #2. The next paragraph illustrates Connie's created professional niche by the bundling of skills:

"Human resource specialist with over 10 years' diversified experience providing leadership in the areas of general human resources policies and procedures, training, recruitment, and affirmative action. Have in-depth expertise in curriculum development and implementation for the healthcare industry in the subject areas of leadership, diversity, communication skills, and supervision. Excel in leading project teams, developing strategies for change management and organizational development, as well as facilitating high-performance team building. An accomplishment most proud of is having proposed, developed, and initiated an ESL program that, as of June 2004, is a requirement for all INOVA Hospital's non-English speaking service workers."

To help you develop your unique professional niche, projecting an image with credibility and confidence to your chosen market, complete Worksheet #6 on page 38.

WORKSHEET #6: CREATE YOUR PROFESSIONAL NICHE STATEMENT

Instructions: Review the top work content skills, transferable skills, personal strengths, and accomplishments assembled from Worksheet #2 through #5. Reorganize as a single priority—listing work content skills/competencies, transferable skill sets, and optional personal attributes—that best supports your ideal professional image and work situation. Start with your top proficiency and place in its appropriate category column as priority #1.

Bundle the top three to five items established in this listing by writing a short descriptive summary statement of five to seven sentences of your customized professional niche. Ideally, include an achievement that is most compatible with the professional niche message.

After creating your customized professional niche statement, ask colleagues who know you quite well to read this paragraph and provide feedback regarding what they think about your "brand," as portrayed by the professional niche statement. How close do their impressions come to your ideal professional image? Edit the professional niche statement as needed.

Priority Ranking	Work Content Competencies	Transferable Skills Sets	Personal Attributes/Strengths
1.	_____	_____	_____
2.	_____	_____	_____
3.	_____	_____	_____
4.	_____	_____	_____
5.	_____	_____	_____

Drafted Professional Niche Statement: ―――――――――――――――
_____
_____
_____
_____

Revised Professional Niche Statement: ――――――――――――――
_____
_____
_____
_____

Chapter Highlights

To recap Chapter 2, the key concepts regarding the elements of your story, for guiding and shaping your ideal professional image as the foundation for a targeted resume are:

1. Look at the initiation of a job search campaign as a great opportunity to obtain a job that brings you closer to your ideal work situation and your passion.

2. Develop your ideal job or consulting assignment so that, when drafting your targeted resume, you will know what qualifications to stress in your story.

3. The first story element is work content skills, individual proficiencies directly related to a person's ability to carry out the basic tasks and activities of a particular profession or industry. Competencies are several related or aligned skills, plus knowledge of a specialized vocabulary and subject matter that makes up a professional competency, allowing more complex functions of that field.

4. The next story element is transferable skills, which are used in a broad range of work functions and are required in most middle and upper levels of responsibilities and across the board in all fields and industries.

5. The next story element is optional personal attributes, personal qualities that enhance your story by putting a personality and individuality to your targeted resume, placing you in a better position for making the first cut.

6. The fourth story element is achievements, which can be quantitatively or qualitatively measured. They are specific results-oriented incidents that demonstrate your proficiencies and personal characteristics in a very specific and dramatic way.

7. A unique professional niche is a customized bundling of your skills, knowledge, personal attributes, education, work history, and achievements that project a unique professional image, or your "brand identity," to prospective recruiters, employers, and clients.

Chapter 3 provides you with guidelines and strategies for creating a targeted resume efficiently and effectively.

> *"Your vision will become clear only when you can look into your own heart."*
> —*Carl Jung*

CHAPTER

3

Develop Your Story

*"To understand the heart and mind of a person, look not at what he has
already achieved, but at what he aspires to do."*
—Kahlil Gibran

Chapter Overview

At this point, it is time to put on your creativity hat and tell your story! Suzanne Lulewicz gives us her viewpoint of storytelling: "Our stories have in essence timeless motifs. While they are clearly structured with a beginning, middle, and end, embellished with action and meaning, and closed with a summary capturing the ultimate interpretation of the story, they carry with them the culture and value of who we are in a moment in time and depend on the audience to whom the story is told." With your ideal job and market in mind, think of how you are going to present yourself in your resume. Who will be your audience? What is the professional image you want to convey to them? What experiences and qualities are to be prioritized and highlighted?

Like a story, a targeted resume has a beginning (the lead-in to the story), the middle (the details of the story), and the ending (the final details and closing). Also like a story, a targeted resume needs to be consistent, having each section build on the previous one, resulting in an integrated, fully complete story. Furthermore, like a good story, a good targeted resume leaves a lasting impression.

As you know, the decision to offer one person a job over another is not a scientific process. If after the final round of interviewing you are one of two evenly matched candidates, it well may be that the one or two interesting, unique details in your resume are the deciding factor to make the offer to you rather than the other person. Consequently, your resume needs to be absolutely on-target and complete in telling your story.

How do you sort out all the information and data that has been generated from Worksheet #1 through #5? How do you identify what are the best and most relevant facts and information, giving you the chance to make that first screening cut? Once again, it is time to prioritize and decide what information is to be used and what is to be omitted. This time, however, you'll focus on those specific points within your background and experience to shape, channel, fill in, and expand your story into a fully developed targeted resume.

This chapter deals with strategies and guidelines for putting together the elements of your story as an integrated complete message with a specific hook (or hooks) to grab the reviewer's attention. The result: *your entire resume is read*. Particular consideration is given to the special features of your story and your powerful opening statement. Points that will be addressed include:

+ Setting aside prioritized key words/phrases for professional image.
+ Bundling qualifications to enhance competitiveness.
+ Drafting concise and accurate job descriptions.
+ Choosing optional nonwork experiences.
+ Selecting supportive accomplishments.
+ Creating a powerful declaration summary statement.
+ Pulling your story all together as a targeted resume.
+ A special note on resume length.
+ Alternative resumes and rebundling qualifications.
+ One very last resume check-up.

Set Aside Prioritized Key Words/Phrases for Professional Image

The first step is to select your key words/phrases as the basis for developing major sections of your resume, such as skill/competency highlights, job descriptions, and achievements. The final step is creating a qualification summary. This summary is your story synopsis and, therefore, needs to be a concise but powerful, dynamic, attention-grabbing declaration to draw the attention of the reader. In order for you to write this type of paragraph, your story needs to be laid out in front of you before selecting the appropriate information for inclusion.

Along the way you will need to make many decisions regarding the overall style and layout for the organization and actual placement of information within the body of the resume. Your desired result is to spotlight your most significant qualifications that answer the ultimate question, "Why should I hire you above anyone else?"

The confident and successful answer to this question depends on the selection and use of key words and phrases in your resume. Key words and phrases are descriptive image words that you want people to think of when reviewing your resume, to decide how closely you are a match to their needs. These are the words you are comfortable using when referring to yourself, your qualifications, and accomplishments, not only in your resume, but also in job and informational interviews. These are the words you integrate into the introduction of yourself at meetings, workshops, or networking events. You believe that they truly represent your professional self.

Key words and phrases enable the hiring agent with the means to:

* Scan your resume quickly, to form an immediate impression of your standing as a candidate.
* Assess your senior professional level by easily seeing a solid description of your work content skills/knowledge of a specialized field or industry.
* Total up your core qualifications for a maximum count and make a match.
* Expeditiously access your achievements that demonstrate your level and breadth of expertise.

For example, for Ralph, an instructional designer, this grouping of key words and phrases illustrates one of his basic HR competencies:

Training Competency: "Key words and phrases include: have knowledge of adult learning; four subject matter areas, training theories, techniques, and technology; assessment of employer and employee needs, design curricula techniques to deliver long-distance and online training, evaluate training outcomes."

In assembling your listing of key words and phrases, try to think about the number of relevant key words and phrase groupings you can organize. Grouping your proficiencies allows the reviewer to identify as many of your qualifications as possible that directly meet the requirements of an actual job listing. Additionally, when you do your homework and become better acquainted with the concerns of an organization, it will be much easier to emphasize your assets that can be an added value to them, thereby gaining another reason for being called in for an interview. As Sam Bresler, SPHR, of San Diego, California, states: "One of the first things I look for on a resume is whether I can easily understand the 'business value' the candidate has added to his/her previous employers. It needs to be succinct and contain real substance. Show what you have done to make the organization a better place."

It is to your advantage to have a diversity of qualifications, including some personal attributes, illustrated by specific key words and phrases in your resume. You want the flexibility and option to create somewhat different renditions of your story, depending on the situation and opportunity—that is, to have the means to move around your priority order of key words and phrases in your introductory summary statement, skills listings, job description, and achievements. (The rebundling of your skills is discussed later in the chapter.) This strategy strengthens the impact of your resume. As you apply for various job openings, you do not know exactly what the job qualifications and requirements are, what the recruiter's priorities for sorting resumes are, or what can grab someone's attention or interest.

You will return to this listing repeatedly as you put together not only your initial basic resume draft but any future versions, to ensure that all necessary and appropriate qualifications are included and validated with accomplishment statements. To help you identify and prioritize these descriptive words and phrases and put together a key word and phrase list supporting your resume's, professional image, complete Worksheet #7 that follows.

WORKSHEET #7: DEVELOPMENT OF KEY WORDS AND PHRASE LIST

Instructions: Reexamine your responses to all the previous worksheets. What skills, bodies of knowledge, and personal attributes are repeated throughout the materials and jump out at you? List these key words and phrases and identify frequency by checking off each time it is mentioned. Group the more frequently mentioned related words and phrases (a minimum of five checks) according to professional/industry qualifications and/or requirements for desired position. (You can refer to Appendix A on page 116 for suggested headings.) Review these groupings and prioritize the actual groups and the assembled key words and phrases within each group, according to their importance for your next job. These key words and phrases are the focal points of your targeted resume.

1. Identify descriptive words/phrases (check off each time it is mentioned.)

_____

_____

_____

2. Group key word/phrases. _____

_____

_____

_____

3. Prioritize groups and their key word/phrase. _____

_____

_____

_____

Note: Include as many key words and phrases as applicable.

Bundle Qualifications
to Enhance Competitiveness

We have continually emphasized the need to outshine your competitors and the importance of grabbing and retaining the reader's attention in order to make the first round of cuts for the interview invites. Use your identified key words and phrases for bundling your skills and experiences to create a basic targeted resume. Before doing this task, make sure you know:

- Who is your marketing audience—specific industries and potential employers within the industries?
- What individual responsibilities and functions are you interested in doing? (Do not be concerned with job titles, because titles are many times too general or vague to define specific work activities and qualifications.)
- If creating a resume for a specific job opening, what are the specific eligibility requirements?

The objective is to put together a marketing package that clearly defines the product—you! As a senior-level professional, you want your resume to have a sophisticated, accomplished look to it that is representative of your savvy, maturity, and experience.

The information in a resume is presented in a manner that is unified and complete, without any "out of kilter" facts or information to distract the reader. The resume's copy should flow smoothly and logically from one section to the next rather than jump from one subject to another. The desired effect is to have the reader's eye drawn along to the end of your resume, ensuring that a full reading is done of your qualifications and "added value" qualities. The practical step-by-step procedures laid out in the next four sections show the way to identify, organize, and prioritize your skills and experiences in order for your resume to reflect your ideal professional story.

Draft Concise and Accurate Job Descriptions

As a senior-level professional, it is quite important that each job listed in your resume is a clear, accurate, and comprehensible account of your responsibilities and functions. Job titles alone do not always reflect what was actually carried out or what you did in your role. Many titles are generic and usually mean different things to different employers, for example, "corporate director for learning and performance" or "vice president of human relations and development." What do these titles really mean in terms of precise and specific functions and roles? This is especially true for the more senior levels of the organizational structure where a position is more likely to have a number of different and complex responsibilities and functions. Additionally, because of your own special interests or abilities, you may have developed the position in ways that are not usually typical of your job title.

Recent Job History

All recent job descriptions include the following basic items:

- Employer name and address.
- Dates of employment.
- Job title.
- Responsibilities/functions.

However, depending on the situation or job opening, you need to think of how you want to lead off this section. Your decision about whether to place your job title or the name of your employer first depends on which one is (1) more relevant or related and/or (2) more impressive as a marketing image.

Employer Name and Address

Spell out full name of organization (no acronyms, unless universally recognized, such as IBM or UPS). Address includes only city and state. If not evident, from employer's name, include a brief one-sentence explanation of the purpose of the organization. For example:

Setefex International—A 4000M global consumer product company, Chicago, IL

Dates of Employment

You can list years only or months and years—your personal preference. However, be consistent throughout the resume, particularly in each subsection.

Job Title

Include full title with no abbreviations. It is important if you have been with an employer for a number of years and received one or more promotions to show career progression and development by changes in your job title. This is significant to the director of corporate staffing for Marriott International of Bethesda, Maryland, Jackie Silver: "I also look for career progression—how your positions string together. It needs to be a logical progression of responsibilities."

In the same employer subsection, start with your current or most recent position (include dates) and work backwards. For example:

Employer USA

Regional Manager	2001 to present
Branch Manager	1997-2001
Assistant Branch Manager	1995-1997

Sam Bresler explains what he wants to see regarding career development: "I look for the types of growth opportunities the candidate has had and in what period of time. Show your career progression and how you have developed your career....for more senior-level candidates, I like to see periods of long-term commitment to an organization."

Responsibilities/Functions

A senior-level professional faces a major dilemma: how to sort out the diverse and sometimes complex responsibilities or functions that they have and simplify so that they are easy to read and be understood by someone else. Furthermore, the description is of what you actually do, not the official issued HR job announcement.

Under each job title, spell out the day-to-day major tasks involved, in short paragraph or bullet format, making sure that each sentence includes key words and phrases from the listing you developed. You may want to review materials (journal, newsletter, Website) from your professional association to make sure that your job description reflects the latest terminology. Keeping in mind your prime targeted marketing audience and/or your ideal job assignment, arrange each sentence in priority order, reflecting the tasks most important or required in this arena. However, if there is a significant skill that you are not really interested in using, downplay it by placing it towards the end of the job description.

Do not confuse responsibilities and functions with achievements that are usually one-time incidents, reflecting exceptional outcomes or performance that is beyond expectations (as discussed and identified in Chapter 2 and further expanded on later in this chapter). Following is an example comparing a job description with an achievement that illustrates your ability to get the job done:

Director, Human Resources Department

Job Responsibilities: Manage all aspects of daily HR operations including training programs, employee recruitment, new employer orientation, for over 1,000 employees in six operational divisions. Coordinate grievances, regulatory compliance procedures, and worker's compensation program. Develop and track HR budget of 1M. Supervise a staff of eight professionals and four administrative assistants.

Achievement: Saved more than $500,000 in training costs over a three-year period by developing and initiating six in-house staff development curriculum in supervision, computer skills, time management, report writing, oral presentations, and customer service. Employee evaluation ratings of training courses indicated an overall satisfaction rating of 92%.

Earlier Work History

It is not necessary to provide a full-blown detailed employment history going back more than 15 years. In many instances, when you go back further than that, the tools, knowledge, and methods used to get the job done are outdated. The main function of the early part of your work experience is to account for time outside of full-time education and other planned nonworking periods. It shows that you do not have any questionable or unexplained gaps in your work history. This early employment can be presented in one of two ways:

1. As a summary statement. This is particularly useful if you have age-related concerns and feel that including dates will point out this fact. For example, set up a subsection like the following:

Prior Work History

Ten years prior experience in HR and compliance work as a general assistant and staff member.

2. As a listing of employers. This is a simple running list of employers' names and addresses, job titles, and dates. It is not necessary to include a description of work functions. For example, set up a subsection with the heading:

Additional Professional Experience

Employer One, Buffalo, NY, Assistant to the VP Human Relations, 1989–1994

Employer Two, Lennox, MA, Personnel Assistant, Compliance Department, 1985–1988

To help you organize your job description statement and place task sentences in priority order, complete Worksheet #8 on page 48.

WORKSHEET #8: DESCRIBE RESPONSIBILITIES AND FUNCTIONS

Instructions: For each job title included in the primary employment history section, write out your responsibilities. Review the drafted job description statement and underline the included key words and phrases (refer to Worksheet #7) skills/competencies, and transferable skill sets. For the second draft, note the sentences with the largest number of underlines, identifying the most significant job tasks. Rearrange these sentences in order of importance, time spent carrying out, and desire to use. Rewrite to edit words and to simplify information.

Job title: _____

Duties description with key words and phrases underlined: _____

_____

_____

Duties description rewritten: _____

Sentence 1: _____

Sentence 2: _____

Sentence 3: _____

Job title: _____

Duties description with key words and phrases underlined:

_____

_____

Duties description rewritten: _____

Sentence 1: _____

Sentence 2: _____

Sentence 3: _____

Job title: _____

Duties description with key words and phrases underlined: _____

_____

_____

Duties description rewritten: _____

Sentence 1: _____

Sentence 2: _____

Sentence 3: _____

Note: Include as many jobs with descriptions as needed. Enhance each job description statement as needed.

Choose Optional Nonwork Experiences

As discussed in Chapter 2, nonwork experiences add another dimension to your story and often are what give the individuality to your resume. More than your employment history, other life experiences—your volunteer and community service, military service, professional activities, awards, publications, etc.—give a multidimensional picture to your resume—both professional and personal. Trying to get a handle on who the candidate is as a person is important to Sam Bresler, when reviewing resumes: "I look for whether the applicant has accomplishments outside of the workplace. For leadership positions, I especially value volunteer leadership roles in professional associations. In my eyes, this type of experience does help to give a candidate a strong competitive edge."

Review those experiences listed on Worksheet #4 on page 33 and decide which nonwork experiences illustrate personal attributes that have the most meaning to you and that you feel can give you the edge in standing out from the crowd and being remembered. Though nonwork experiences usually serve the purpose of highlighting your personal attributes, if a specific work content or transferable skill was significantly developed or reinforced as part of a nonpaid/volunteer experience, then integrate it into your resume.

Upon completing the selection and writing of your nonwork experiences, decide how and where you will place these items within your resume. Do some of the experiences have enough details and/or importance to merit separate sections? For example:

PROFESSIONAL AFFILIATIONS

American Society for Training and Development (ASTD) activities include:
Washington, D.C. Chapter: President 2001–2002
Also served as Program Chair and headed committee that revised Chapter's Policy and Procedure Manual
ASTD National
Member of *Training and Development* Journal Review Board 2003–present
Member of Leadership Training Conference Committee 2000–2001

Or should all nonwork experiences be grouped under one section? For example:

ADDITIONAL INFORMATION AND EXPERIENCES

American Society for Training and Development, Washington, D.C. Chapter
Chair, Professional Development Day Committee, 2002
Society for Human Resources Management, Washington, D.C. Chapter
Member, Communications Committee, Member 2004
National Zoo, Washington, D.C.
Volunteer, Give presentations about pandas and help feed animals since 1998
Washington, D.C. Public Schools Mentor Program
Since 2000, have served as mentor to elementary school student

To help you choose and place in priority order those activities reflecting personal attributes and strengths that would enrich your story and professional image, complete Worksheet #9 that follows.

WORKSHEET #9: CHOOSE OPTIONAL NONWORK EXPERIENCES

Instructions: Transfer and expand on the nonwork experiences identified in Worksheet #4 on page 33. Underline your personal attributes and, if applicable, any work content/transferable skills mentioned. Review listed experiences and, in priority order, write down those nonwork experiences with the largest number of underlines in their descriptive paragraphs and that you believe have the greatest impact for your resume and professional image. Rewrite description to edit and simplify information as required.

Nonwork experiences statement with personal attributes (and if applicable, work content/transferable skills) underlined:

Experience 1: _____

_____

Experience 2: _____

_____

Experience 3: _____

_____

Experience 4: _____

_____

Experience 5: _____

_____

Prioritized nonwork experiences: _____

_____

Note: Include as many nonwork experiences as are needed.

Select Supportive Accomplishments

As a senior-level professional, hiring agents expect to see a number of accomplishments or achievements included in your resume. This is the validation they look for regarding your leadership, managerial skills, unique savvy, and specialized expertise. Libby Sartain, SPHR, senior VP human resources of Yahoo, Inc., in Sunnyvale, California, agrees: "Be sure to list REAL and authentic accomplishments."

As you review the accomplishments, ask yourself, "Of all the accomplishments listed, which ones best illustrate how I have..."

+ Added value to an organization?
+ Made a difference to an organization?
+ Used my skills, competencies, experience, and personal attributes and strengths?

On a personal note, also ask yourself, "What accomplishments am I the most proud of and/or are the most important to me—and why?"

The selections of accomplishments that give the most credibility to your story are those incidents that most frequently mention your key words and phrases. Accomplishment examples come not only from the work place but also from other parts of your life, such as volunteer work and professional activities. As you identify and separate them out, begin to edit and prune the descriptive statements into bullet format in preparation for inclusion in your resume.

For example, Sidney, a management/organization development specialist, lists these descriptive accomplishments:

- Coordinated a five-member team to develop and conduct a survey and analyze its results to improve shift production in five plants. Recommendations adopted leading to a reduction of operating costs by $150 million. Division awarded "Best management practice" out of 10 divisions.

- Facilitated evaluation of staff performance levels for four departments, resulting in the complete reorganization and goal setting strategies for these departments' training programs. Increased customer satisfaction from 70% to 87%.

To help you select your most relevant, powerful accomplishment occurrences, complete Worksheet #10 that follows.

WORKSHEET #10: SELECT SUPPORTIVE ACCOMPLISHMENTS

Instructions: Transfer the eight to 10 accomplishments identified in Worksheet #5, on page 36. Check off how frequently each prioritized key word and phrase from the listing you developed appears in each accomplishment occurrence. List as many occurrences and establish as many key word/phrase columns as needed. In priority order, put aside the accomplishments with the most frequently mentioned key words and phrases and the most impressive outcomes or results. Do a preliminary identification of specific qualifications illustrated by each achievement. Edit and simplify as required.

Accomp-lishment	Key Word/ Phrase	Key Word/ Phrase	Key Word/ Phrase	Key Word/ Phrase	Key Word/ Phrase	Key Word/ Phrase
1.						
2.						
3.						
4.						
5.						

Prioritized accomplishments, listing associated qualifications: _____

_____

Note: Include as many accomplishments and key words/phrases as needed.

Create a Powerful Declaration Summary Statement

The first item that is read by a reviewer scanning your resume is your "wow" statement. Your goal in creating this declaration is to have the reader focus in a definite and desired direction. This statement is comparable to the first impression made when you walk into an office or when you meet the interviewer. A declaration strongly announces that, although you have similar qualifications to other candidates, you measure up more and stand out from the other candidates because of specific details. It is very clear to the reader what type and level of job for which you are qualified. An example of a "wow" statement is from Carrie, an assistant VP HRD division:

> "Over 15 years experience as a human resource executive with international-based organizations. Expertise in policy formulation, strategic development, performance-based management systems, and succession planning. Initiated five executive development programs, one of which was awarded the ASTD "Best Practices Award in 2000." Speak three languages fluently and have worked in five countries."

As a senior-level professional, the use of a summary statement instead of a simple objective sentence or two is more appropriate. With your years of experience and depth and breadth of expertise, a story synopsis of your background and experience is justified. Furthermore, you have the capabilities and savvy to apply for more than one type of position or job title. An objective statement is too narrow and limiting for your status and situation.

The essence of this summary statement is in your professional niche statement that brings together your most important and relevant qualifications to set the stage and establish the theme of your story. A powerful declaration summary statement is composed of your four to five most significant and impressive qualifications. Reread the description of your created professional niche once again. However, this time read it from the perspective of: "When this professional niche statement is placed at the beginning of your resume, what impact does it have on the reader?" To help you edit and turn your professional niche into a powerful summary statement about you and your qualifications, complete Worksheet #11 on page 53.

WORKSHEET #11: CREATE A POWERFUL SUMMARY STATEMENT

Instructions: Review your professional niche statement from Worksheet #6 on page 38, considering the perspective of an employer's needs and evoking their desire to know more about you and your expertise. Identify the four or five most significant and impressive qualifications that immediately say to a reader, "call this candidate in for an interview." Rewrite the statement as a clear and compact paragraph (not more than four sentences), declaring to a reader that you have what is required and desired in a candidate. Edit and cut as needed.

Identified qualifications from professional niche statement:

1. _____
2. _____
3. _____
4. _____
5. _____

My powerful summary statement: _____

_____

_____

_____

Pull Your Story All Together as a Targeted Resume

As you begin to put together the pieces of your story and create a targeted resume, keep in mind that to some extent your professional image is projected through the styling and formatting of your resume. This is your opportunity to showcase your individuality, personality, and creativity. If you are in communications, the arts, entertainment, advertising/PR, and other related fields or industries, this is a great way to show off your flair and talent for originality and attention-getting design work.

For your targeted resume to be effective, you need to make decisions regarding the items that follow.

Name and Contact Info Set-up

How do you want to place this information—each line centered, set up in two columns, or spread out across the page? Your name—should it be in a different font than the resume itself, and in what size font? Be sure to include your e-mail address and cell phone number. If you have a Website that contains a portfolio of samples of your design work that is pertinent to the job, include the address as part of your contact information. (**Note:** In your cover letter, mention where the reader can view your work.) You may want to set the contact section apart from the body of the resume by a graphic line.

Resume Section and Headings

How do you want to organize your story? What is the best way to present information and experience validating your professional image and qualifications? Individual sections help to define groups of similar information with headings as the guide to what a section contains. One general rule to follow pertaining to resume sections is that there should not be more than five major sections. Too many major sections makes it harder for a reviewer to locate the information being sought, as well as giving the resume the appearance of being complicated. Instead, if a resume section looks too cumbersome or long, break it out with subsections.

Headings are a major design element of your resume. You have a number of options for section heading titles, depending upon how you want to organize your information and the ideal professional image you want to project. To help you with this task, see Appendix D on page 126.

Paragraph vs. Bullet Set-up

To an extent, this is a design issue. You want the reader to be continually drawn to the next sentence, the next section. Paragraphs are used when more than one or two sentences are required to communicate a clear understanding of the information or details needed to complete a description. On the other hand, bullets are a shorthand way to highlight or emphasize information succinctly and crisply. Draft the information in both formats and see what works best for you and the situation. This is particularly true regarding job and achievement descriptions.

Specific Accomplishment(s) to Illustrate Specific Qualification(s)

How will you decide which accomplishment, incident, or aspect best illustrates a qualification? What are your criteria for the placement of these incidents within your story? Accomplishments can be situated within the body of a job description, set up as a subsection to showcase competencies, or grouped as a separate section for a dramatic solid effect.

Education

If your academic degrees or certificates are more than 10 years old, omit dates. Depending on the extent of your professional development or continuing education coursework, you may want to make this a separate subheading or just have one grouping, "Education and Training."

Other Information

Other experiences from your life add more dimension to your professional and personal character. Refer back to "Optional Nonwork Experiences" on page 49 for more information.

Special Note on Resume Length

Although the accepted rule is "not more than two pages," sometimes a rule needs to be broken. For senior-level professionals having broad and multidimensional work experiences, this can be particularly true. You may have cut down and prioritized your information by completing the worksheets, and still find that you have too many experiences and accomplishments to fit nicely on two pages. If you find yourself in this situation, think of attaching an addendum commonly used in a curriculum vitiate. This ancillary document is very useful when you want to list a number of items in any of the following categories: training/CEU courses, awards/recognition activities, professional board positions, speaking engagements/presentations, and publications. This approach is one solution if you find it difficult to eliminate any more information or cannot make a more concise statement.

Upon completion of the first draft of your resume, review carefully and slowly all the copy you have written, especially the qualification declaration statement, job descriptions, and achievement listings. These items are usually the most detailed and in-depth sections of your resume document—and the sections where most errors occur.

First, examine the bullets and paragraph sentences, as each one should:

♦ Be clear and concise—contain not more than 20 words.

♦ Be one coherent, smooth, flowing body of information.

♦ Relate to the one before and after, for continuity of story.

♦ Contain only words that contribute to the quality of the sentence and, therefore, to the message of the resume.

♦ Avoid using the same word in a sentence or repeated consistently through the document, particularly those denoting skills and accomplishments.

♦ Begin with a descriptive skill word wherever possible, but specifically, in the overall summary, job descriptions, and achievement-oriented blurbs or bullets.

♦ Not include any specialized professional field- or industry-related jargon unless the reader is from a similar environment.

♦ Form short paragraphs, where applicable, of about five lines or less.

♦ Have a positive and accurate message.

Second, look at the resume as one complete entity, the appearance of which should:

♦ Be set up exactly the way you envisioned and wanted.

♦ Be consistent in style and formatting, with words/phrases capitalized, bolded, italicized, and indented as planned.

♦ Headline pertinent qualifications and results-oriented validations in a targeted way.

♦ Project your ideal professional image by telling your unique story.

When you have completed your first resume draft, look it over and proofread. Then put it away for at least 24 hours to get some distance from the document and attain some objectivity. Continue to read, revise, edit, and above all, proofread. Take a look at the "before and after" resume samples on page 228-233 to see the results of careful and continual redrafting of your resume, so that it truly is targeted and tells your story. The next to final reading is the one in which you have not found any faults or errors in your resume. Have some people who know you do the final reading.

If the comments from your colleagues and peers match the way you want to be positioned then, indeed, your resume is an outstanding marketing document ready to be distributed.

Alternative Resumes and Rebundling Qualifications

Now that you have established a solid basic targeted resume, it is important to give some thought to the idea that having only one version of your resume will not serve all possible targeted market arenas. Depending on the specific opportunity or situation, you most likely will need to have several resumes that are "variations on the same theme" or different presentations of your story, to meet different audiences. As a seasoned professional, you most likely qualify for more than one type of position. On the other hand, you may be interested in making a professional move to a different industry or field. You are able to take the same group of capabilities, achievements, and experiences and, by shifting them around, showcase or emphasize different specific qualifications. The results are that an employer can more easily notice that your background and experience meets their needs.

After completing your basic targeted resume, consider how you would redo this document to have easy access to alternative versions of your resume sections. In this way, depending on the circumstances, different key information can be moved around (cut and pasted) in the following areas: qualifications summary statement, skills listing, job responsibilities description, and achievements. For example, in your primary resume, a skill's priority order is as #5, but because of one specific job requirements, this skill is now in the #2 priority place and more visible. Reasons for having optional versions of your resume on file are:

  • You can never predict when an unexpected opportunity will arise; being prepared and ready may result in the position being offered to you.

  • In response to a position opening that is somewhat out of your normal or expected range of job titles, your qualifications need to be lined up in the same order as are the requirements listed for the hiring position.

  • Having one version reflecting your ideal job position, if nothing else, keeps that vision in front of you as motivation to reach for your dream and see how close to reality you can come. You may be hired for a brand new position that you can shape and form to your interests, strengths, and experience.

One of the easiest and, at the same time, most difficult things to do is to set up different versions of your overall summary statement. Develop a minimum of two statements; it is only by repositioning individual qualifications that you not only retain but can increase your competitive edge in the job market. For example, Mark, a senior-level manager in a technical recruitment department, writes a basic summary statement showcasing his recruitment experience:

> *"A senior-level HR manager with over 10 years IT recruitment experience for a Fortune 500 company with a nationwide IT staff of 3,400. Proven capabilities in expansion of marketing and recruitment arenas, change management, strategic and organizational management. In-depth and diversified background in team facilitation, union relationships and negotiations, and HR staff and budget management."*

Following is an alternate version of the same resume but this time emphasizing his organizational development (OD) expertise:

> *"A senior Human Resources Consultant with approximately 20 years of experience ranging from organizational and strategic management to union relationships and negotiations to IT recruitment. Led team that developed a standardized organizational model for an IT Department of 450 employees of a Fortune 500 company. Proven capabilities in retention and retraining efforts, expansion of marketing and recruitment arenas, and development and implementation of HR policy and regulations."*

Consider the number of different future job possibilities. Create as many appropriate alternative resumes as may be needed. In some instances it may only require some "tweaking," and for other situations you may need to reposition and reprioritize much of the information. Do not forget, you also have the option of taking out some information altogether and replacing it with a professional characteristic or illustrative instance that is a better match to the situation. For example, you might replace a skill set and its related achievement with one that is more pertinent to an unexpected opportunity. If this is a viable option, return to Chapter 2 worksheets and review the items not originally chosen for your basic resume but that now can be used.

One Very Last Check-up

Is your resume ready to be marketed and distributed? Although the resume has been read and proofread several times by you and other readers, it is still a good idea to do one absolute final look at your targeted resume from a marketing perspective, with a comparison to a listing of "perfect resume qualities." The exercise on page 58 provides the means for you to conduct this ultimate final resume review.

Checklist to Determine Marketing Readiness

Instructions: As you do this very last check of your resume, keep this checklist before you and indicate each characteristic that is in place. For a perfect resume or marketing document, all items need to be checked. Are all items checked? If not, you have identified the areas that still need to be improved.

_____ Contact information is accurate, including e-mail address.

_____ Design, layout, and presentation proceeds logically from top to bottom.

_____ Includes all relevant and significant key words and phrases.

_____ Qualification/overview summary is validated by information in the resume body.

_____ Required background, experiences, and accomplishments are easily compared to position specifications.

_____ Overall resume impression projects to the future, with facts from the past as the creditability of your capabilities.

_____ All information is in a priority order reflecting its relationship and significance to presenting your professional image.

_____ All success incidents include hard facts and figures and are linked to specific goals or qualifications.

_____ All employers' names, job titles, and employment dates are easily located and the organizational purposes are clearly understood.

_____ Added values to employer are clearly seen and understood.

_____ Name and page number appears on all pages following the first one, including addendums.

_____ Alternative targeted resumes demonstrate your information, now rebundled, meeting requirements of a position opening outside of your usual job parameters.

_____ Sequence of background and experiences in each alternative resume version have been changed to meet each specific type of opportunity.

_____ All versions of your targeted resume can be used as a guide for informational interviewing and actual job interviewing, as well as in a one-on-one meeting.

_____ You are satisfied and happy that your resumes (basic and alternative versions) tell your individual story that is credible, complete, and that truly reflects your professional self and your story.

Chapter Highlights

To recap Chapter 3, the key concepts that discuss the strategies and guidelines for putting together the elements of your story as an integrated, complete, targeted resume are:

1. When the elements of your story are put together as an integrated complete message with a specific hook (or hooks) to grab the attention of the reviewer, the result is that your entire resume is read.

2. Key words and phrases are the descriptive image words that you want people to think of when they review your resume to match you to their

requirements, and they are also the words you are comfortable using when referring to yourself, your qualifications, and your accomplishments. You believe these key words and phrases truly represent your professional self.

3. To bundle your skills and experience, use key words and phrases as the primary resource. Create a marketing package that clearly defines you for a particular chosen audience to match specific job requirements.

4. Create alternative versions of your resume in which your skills and experiences are rebundled for the qualifying summary statement, skills listing, job descriptions, and achievement statements. It is then possible to exactly match your background and experiences to positions you are interested in but that are outside of the normal range of openings for which you would apply.

5. Job titles alone do not always reflect what was actually involved in your position or role. Therefore, a clear and accurate job description is essential to a reader's understanding of your responsibilities and functions. Make sure that each sentence of the job description includes your key words and phrases and starts with an action verb.

6. Nonwork experiences add another dimension to your story and frequently are what give the individuality to your resume. It is through your nonwork experiences that your personal attributes and strengths are revealed.

7. Include accomplishments that most frequently mention your key words and phrases. As you identify and separate your achievements out, begin to edit and prune the descriptive statements into bullet format for inclusion into your resume.

8. A powerful declaration summary statement is your "wow" statement that acts as the synopsis for your career story. Your professional niche statement serves as the basis for the summary statement. Identify four to five most significant and impressive qualifications and rewrite to form a professional summary statement.

9. When putting your story or resume together, give consideration to name and contact information set-up, resume sections and headings, paragraph vs. bullet layout, and specific accomplishments to illustrate specific qualification(s).

10. When you read your resume and it is a perfect proofing experience, have selected colleagues and peers do a final review to make sure that the resume is on-target and appears as you intended.

Chapter 4 discusses candidates making professional moves and career changes, as well as the special features of their resumes required by their situations.

"I missed all the shots I never took."
—Wayne Gretsky

CHAPTER

4

Resumes for Select Career Transitions

"If you hear a voice within you saying "You are not a painter,"
then by all means paint and that voice will be silenced."
—*Vincent Van Gogh*

Chapter Overview

How do you handle your resume when you are not looking for a similar position as the one you presently have or you have had in the past? If you are planning to make a professional shift or move in a completely different career direction? Changing interests and perception of what constitutes challenging and fulfilling work are a normal part of career mobility, development, and growth processes. Perhaps, you have decided to stay within your profession but shift to a different practice area, for example, remain as an HR specialist, but because of changing professional interests, move from being a learning performance specialist to the role of an executive and leadership coach. Or you may still enjoy the functions of a learning performance specialist within the healthcare industry, but want to change your work environment from a hospital setting to a pharmaceutical company. Maybe you like the organization that you have been with for more than seven years, but now feel you are ready to move up the career ladder and apply for the assistant VP for HR opening. Possibly you are a high school teacher with more than 10 years of experience and have decided to make a career change into training and development.

Any one of these moves presents a challenge regarding the best way to tell your story for the position you are now seeking. Moving into a new part of the work world can be difficult and stressful. Beyond having to prove to an employer your worth to the organization, you also need to convince the hiring agent of your sincere commitment and serious interest in making this professional/career transition. Your usual job search marketing strategies may not work very efficiently and effectively in a career modification situation. For all these scenarios, your task is to identify and emphasize those aspects of your background and experience compatible to your chosen new work arena. Consequently, the reviewer's focus is on how well you match up to the position requirements and away from the fact that you have little or no hands-on experience with the type of employment you are now seeking.

This chapter discusses strategies for those times that call for telling your story from a slightly different angle than the one your basic targeted resume presently does. Before beginning the task of revising your resume in preparation for shifting the direction of your career pathway, ask yourself this fundamental question: "Where and how do I want to work in the next phase of my career?" If you have the answer to this question, you can go ahead with creating an alternative resume targeted for the specific career move situation. Otherwise, we suggest that you take some time for self-reflection and assessment activities, to have a clearer and more precise picture of your future career direction before beginning to look for new employment.

As in any job search, the resume is a vital factor for obtaining a desired position and making a successful transition to a new work arena. Addressed are the three most common career modifications, their special concerns, and the development of resumes to meet these concerns:

- A move from one specialization to another.
- A move within your present organization.
- A career change as an experienced professional.
- Resume tips for select career transitions.
- Targeted resume outline for career modification situations.

A Move From One Specialization to Another

For the experienced professional, this shift in the focal point of your work necessitates a modification in how your resume tells your story. The rebundling of your qualifications is dependent on how you plan to expand your professional experiences and redirect your career. Your decision to make a move from one professional specialization to another is most likely to be one of the following three options:

Move Within Your Profession or Field

To move within your field is to reposition yourself within your professional arena and change practice areas. For example, Amy has decided to shift from instructional design and staff training to strategic and organizational development. For making a move within your professional field, as you identify information to include in your resume, ask yourself these questions:

- What are the reasons for diversifying or expanding my range of subject matter, expertise, or client base?

- What have I done to develop creditability regarding my depth of knowledge or level of skill in the professional or industry arena where I now want to concentrate my efforts and time?

- In moving to a different professional area of practice, do I want to stay with my present employer, start a job search, or do both?

For example, Amy, who would like to change practice areas, answers these questions in the following way:

"I plan to make HR my career and, in order to move up to an executive position, I need experience in other practice areas of the field. I am due to receive my MBA in Organizational Change and Strategic Development this June. My major class project was a study of my present employer's organization culture and succession planning status. My preference is to stay with my present organization, if I can. However, I will initiate a job search, if necessary."

Move Within the Industry

You may wish to remain within the same industry—for instance, consumer products—but change the work setting where you use your HR professional expertise. For example, John, a trainer/facilitator specializing in customer service and sales training workshops, wants to move from working for a toy company chain store to a worldwide entertainment organization.

Move to a Different Industry

In some cases, you may consider changing the industry setting where you use your professional expertise. For example, Sue is looking to change from practicing HR in the banking industry to practicing HR in the hospitality industry.

A Move Within Your Present Organization

When making a move within your organization, it is usually one of two basic options: (1) a move that is a step up (a promotion) or (2) a move that is across the career ladder and/or the organizational structure (a lateral move). Because people are quite familiar with the concept of moving up or advancing a career and what a promotion implies, no further explanation is needed.

However, not everyone may fully understand what a lateral move is and why someone would want to make one. A lateral move involves transferring to a job that is different but equal to the one you presently have. This is a professional shift to consider when you want to remain with your present employer, but want to further develop as a professional and are therefore interested in expanding your skills and experience base. For example, Bill, an HR specialist with some responsibility for writing training materials, develops a growing interest in writing and editing. This results in his request for a lateral move to the in-house publications department, because one future possibility is working for an organization specializing in HR publications.

In either of these moves, one of the challenges that you may have to deal with is how other people see you. If you are seeking a promotion, do they see you as someone on his or her way up in the organizational structure or not? Or if you are making a lateral move to learn new skills, people may think you are not very ambitious, because they are only aware of your desire to make this transfer without knowing the reasons for the change.

Additionally, when attempting to make any type of organizational move, try to be aware of any inside competition you may have and how you can offset their advantages with some of your own. Use the company's informal networking system or your intuitive sense of other colleagues, and be aware of whom else may be applying for this position. On the other hand, if a specific opening does not exist, determine an organizational need/issue, and plan to promote yourself as the person who not only can solve the problem, but is interested, ready, and available to make a move, and you will not have any competition.

For making a move within your present organization, as you identify information to include in your resume, ask yourself these questions:

+ What have I done that demonstrates my leadership potential?
+ What have I done that illustrates my intent to remain and grow with the organization?
+ How will I use my resume (beyond submission to HR for the position opening) to market myself within the organization?

For example, Bill who wants to make the lateral move, answers these questions in the following way:

"Have a growing interest in broadening and increasing my writing and editing skills, to return to the HR division better able to create training manuals and other HR/learning materials for the organization. Presently, manage an HR project focused on future staffing training needs and the development of courses to meet these needs. In four years have moved from being assistant to the recruitment manager to being a learning and performance specialist. I will have my resume available when talking with my supervisor, the in-house publications manager, and some of the editorial staff about my desire for transferring."

A Career Change as an Experienced Professional

Changing careers completely is one of the most difficult transitions to make successfully—that is to change both work tasks and work fields. For example, Charles, a corporate director of training with 20 years of experience, has decided to make a career change from working in private industry to teaching in higher education. One of the concerns he faces, like many senior-level job seekers making this type of transition, is the age factor. Employers tend to focus on salary and benefit package requirements and the possibility of applicants being overqualified, when looking at high-level professionals seeking a job outside of their usual specialized practices or industry.

One good strategy is having the reviewer concentrate on your transferable skills and knowledge, as well as the benefits of hiring a seasoned professional, so that your disadvantages fade into the background. Use your age to your advantage by identifying the chosen market needs, how you can meet those needs, and stressing your solid experience and significant achievements.

In being realistic about making a career change, you need to also consider the possibility that you may actually have to accept a position at a lower level of responsibility and leadership than your present one—and do so with a salary cut. Your resume's fundamental role is to project your professional image in a way that improves the chance of this scenario not happening.

Another defensive strategy is to thoroughly research your new career interest and work environment. By doing your homework, you become aware of the essential required skills and knowledge. Follow up by identifying the proficiencies you possess, in lieu of actual experiences, that can be substitute for education/training. As a selling point, consider taking professional development courses to fill the gaps in your qualifications as proof of your strong commitment to this transition.

For making a career change, as you identify information for inclusion in your resume, ask yourself the following questions:

- What is it, exactly, that I am looking to make a change to—in terms of profession/field, work tasks, people involved, and work environment?
- What is or was the overall focal point of the roles I have played as a project/team manager, resource/information supplier, specialist in a profession/field, and/or organizational/leadership provider? What is my new focal point interest?
- How can I use my proven record of successes as an indicator of future accomplishments?

For example, Charles answers these question in the following way:

"Looking to change from the HRD field to education and teach in a university setting at an undergraduate business school, perhaps in a college town setting. Major functions in my present position have been management and leadership. Would like to return to being an information supplier (classroom teacher) and teach HR basics, such as delivering training and improving human performance. My Ph.D. in Human Resource Management and OD indicates academic proficiencies, while extensive and diverse background in curriculum development and training demonstrates capabilities as an instructor."

Use of a Curriculum Vitae

A new trend appearing on the horizon is use of the curriculum vitae format instead of a traditional resume format by seasoned professionals making a career change. A curriculum vitae or "CV," as it is more commonly known, takes more of a bio sketch approach to present your background and experiences. This is where you can truly tell your story. While a resume is brief and largely focuses on your work history and job responsibilities, a CV is more detailed regarding academics, transferable skills, and professional experiences and activities. Traditionally required for applying for a higher education teaching position, it is being adapted by some people making career transitions and changes that may be nonacademic.

If you are particularly planning to make a career move that takes you abroad, into consulting or research, or into a CEO-level position that is outside of your established professional setting, then strongly consider creating a CV for your job search. The preparation of a CV has greater flexibility in approach, design, and style than a resume. However, following general writing guidelines and standards—or those set by a professional society—is still in order. Additionally, you may need or like to include a portfolio of work samples when using a CV.

A CV, when used in the appropriate situations, has a number of advantages that can be of great assistance for having your qualifications noticed.

- ◆ Although you can list and highlight transferable skills in a resume, in a CV they can really stand out and substantiate your capabilities for a position in a new field or industry. It is acceptable not only to relate the extent of your competencies, but you also are expected to validate your ability to apply the skills/knowledge to a new work arena.

- ◆ In a CV, the introductory statement presents your objectives in seeking a position. Therefore, from the onset the reader knows you are making a career shift or move. It is customary to write a paragraph that includes both short- and long-term goals.

- ◆ If you have an extensive listing of presentations, publications, and/or awards, you are able to attach an addendum.

- ◆ A CV format encourages additional personal information or other relevant background information that is usually kept at a minimum in a traditional resume.

- ◆ Particularly if you are looking to relocate abroad, you are able to fully describe travel or work experiences outside of the United States.

- ◆ In many instances, specifically for consulting and teaching positions, your CV will be read by colleagues who have a professional technical vocabulary and knowledge in common with you. Thus, you can make full use of your specialized key words and phrases (including acronyms) without worrying that the reader does not understand the extent of your experiences and responsibilities or cannot fully appreciate the time and effort that was involved in a specific accomplishment.

- ◆ A CV does not follow strict content, form, and style standards or guidelines that act as a restrictive influence, as a traditional resume format. Consequently, you have more leeway in the design of a CV that reflects your personality and thinking.

Resumes Tips for Select Career Transitions

Whether you are planning a move to shift the focus of your professional expertise, a move up the corporate ladder, or a career change, your resume needs to be revised. The telling of your story will need to emphasize all you have done or accomplished that is in any way related to the work you now want to do. Your edited or new professional profile needs to be easily visible by a quick scan of your resume. This calls for a de-emphasizing of some of the strengths or assets that are part of your old profile and story.

It is not uncommon to find it hard to give up some facts or successes that have been part of your professional identity for a long time. However, you do not have to throw away any materials, just store them on a file in your computer. In this way, you can readily retrieve these bio bytes in the future if your career pathway loops back to a former professional interest. But for now you are free to proceed forward, creating a new professional niche for yourself that will be the focus of your new resume.

Prior to developing this version of your resume, it is important to create a revised professional image with which you are comfortable. The story that your resume delivers should still be direct and clear and, most essentially, not give out mixed messages. The content of your story is the proof that you have what it takes to transition effectively and to perform new and different responsibilities successfully.

The heart of your resume lies with your core transferable skills (review answers for Worksheet #3 on page 31). Think about these skills and select those that can be matched with, applied to, and/or substituted for the skills/knowledge now needed in your new work environment. If necessary, repeat the assessment using Worksheet #7 on page 43. Next, review your accomplishments (review answers for Worksheet #5 on page 36). Select those that illustrate these specific core transferable skills, as well as any successes that give validation to your capabilities.

Although the targeted resume style has been stressed throughout this book, nowhere is it more useful and appropriate than for career modification situations. This is the best format for translating prior experience and knowledge into transferable skills aligned with validating achievements, no matter when, how, or where these successes were gained.

The flexibility of a targeted resume allows for showcasing and documenting your strongest qualifications and savvy that is needed now, and to do it outside the framework of your usual work environments and job titles. Sylvia Gray, a career management and career transition consultant in Washington, D.C., who has worked with candidates in career transitions for more than 10 years, stresses that "the need to emphasize transferable skills can't be overstated. By specifically noting transferable skills, by reemphasizing them in accomplishments most relevant to the new area of specialization or the area you will transition to, you make the information easily obtainable. Frequently, it is the details of the nuances of transition, or 'career modification,' the highlighting of your transferable skills, and the telling of your story in compelling statements, that you present what is important and related to the reader's concept of the position."

In developing a resume or revising one targeted for a career modification situation, there are special or unique characteristics—in addition to the guidelines and strategies presented in the previous chapters—that need to be taken into account. Examine carefully your background and experience:

- See it with a different eye and mindset than if you were seeking a similar job to your present one and/or the positions you have had in the past.

- Think of how you can reduce the reviewer's concern that you may not be successful with this career/professional transition—and therefore that hiring you is a risk of cost and time to the employer.

- Unlike your basic targeted resume, consider having a career or job objective statement as your resume lead section. This can be crucial to the reader immediately understanding that you are not applying for a position similar to your present one.

+ Make sure that the introductory summary or professional overview statement immediately establishes your qualifications, including recently completed degrees/certifications relevant to this transition, and briefly expresses your interest to obtain a position aligned with your present career objectives.

+ Bring to the forefront qualifications from your background and experience that would be of most interest to a potential employer, particularly making note of those gained earlier in your work history.

+ Capitalize on your identified transferable qualifications by highlighting them in your skills/expertise section and evidenced in your achievement descriptions. Employ maximum use of key words and phrases.

+ Similar to a CV, demonstrate your familiarity with the field or industry by use of specific professional terminology and words.

+ Consider how to best present your capabilities and potential when not having actual experience. If you can, include any volunteer work, community work, and/or avocation activities that reflect a long-time interest.

+ If appropriate, illustrate seriousness and intent regarding the professional shift or career change by including professional related activities such as subscribing to the trade publications, and/or joining professional/trade associations.

+ If relevant, provide evidence of your commitment to your new career direction by highlighting volunteer and graduate level internship experiences, course papers, and/or education projects.

+ Reprioritize tasks and responsibilities in job descriptions, emphasizing those that are related to your future career goals—and the employer's— while minimizing the space given to the remaining functions.

+ Given the type of information that can be included as described above, your qualifications sections can be longer than if you were applying for a position similar to the ones held previously.

+ Achievements are proof of your success—no matter what you did—and, therefore, demonstrate your level of ability to meet an employer's needs.

+ Most importantly, a career change (rather than a professional move), calls for the creation of a resume from scratch. Do not try to use a "one size fits all" general resume or your basic one with some minor changes.

Targeted Resume Outline for Career Modification Situations

Although most sections of a resume are set up similar to those of a regular targeted resume, as indicated previously, there are some distinct differences. This outline serves as a guideline for giving high visibility to your core transferable skills and their documented level of ability, your employment history, and work content expertise. Other information, although not relevant to the desired professional move or career change, is required to be included as well.

RESUME OUTLINE FOR PROFESSIONAL MOVES AND CAREER CHANGES

Header
Name and contact information

Career or Job Objective: (optional)

Qualification Summary or Overview Statement: Brief description of qualifications and capabilities. Include a sentence of your refocused professional goal or career direction, because it may not be obvious why you are responding to a position from your opening statement. In a few words, you may want to mention your motivation or reasons for seeking to make a professional shift or career change.

Professional Skills: List, in one or two sentences, core transferable skills (as previously described), showcasing how you can benefit the organization. Organize skills according to focus of the role/function. This is the place to bring—to the top one-third of your resume— qualifications that would most likely attract the attention of a hiring agent, particularly making note of those obtained earlier in your work experiences. In a career modification situation, it is much more appropriate to categorize work by task and function rather than by employer.

Professional Skill Sets (examples)
Administration/Management
Skill #1
Skill #2
Skill #3
Skill #4

Communications
Skill #1
Skill #2
Skill #3

Information Management
Skill #1
Skill #2

Accomplishments: In bullet format, describe as many major accomplishments as are pertinent for documenting core transferable skills.

Major Accomplishments
Accomplishment #1
Accomplishment #2
Accomplishment #3
Accomplishment #4
Accomplishment #5

Professional Work History (with additional relevant accomplishments): Start with your present or most recent experience, with a full description of responsibilities and illustrative examples of success incidents. Next, list past employment background with brief bullets of role/function and accomplishments, if it truly makes an impact statement (go back only 15 years). Present the remaining work history as prior employment in a summary statement.

Professional History

Present or Most Recent Employer
Job Title
Responsibilities and Accomplishments

♦

♦

Next Employer
Job Title
Role/Function and Optional Accomplishments

♦

♦

Next Employer
Job Title
Role/Function and Optional Accomplishments

♦

♦

Prior Work Background: A summary statement of remaining work history, but without dates. Include organizations also, if well-known. For example, "In addition to the above employment listings, worked as an HR assistant for General Foods for three years and also as a Marketing Researcher for two years."

Education: Start with education/training, including dates relevant to the move or change, if any. It is in this section that you would include your thesis and other education projects if the subject matter pertains to your new work direction. Give a short synopsis of topic or research activities and conclusions. All other education/training should be listed without dates. Include licenses and certificates and, if relevant to your present situation, give specifics. Otherwise, just list them.

Other Information: Include if it is relevant or demonstrates capabilities not evident in the preceding information. For example, community or professional board memberships, awards, and military service. **Note:** You may want to set up your volunteer work as a separate subsection if the one or two skills highlighted in the professional skill sets section were gained through these experiences. This allows for the inclusion of more details and visibility for the alignment of capabilities and requirements.

Chapter Highlights

To recap Chapter 4, the key concepts of strategies and tips to develop targeted resumes for professional moves and career changes are:

1. Three of the most common career modifications—moving within a professional field, moving within an organization, and moving to make a career change—each involve special resume concerns.

2. There are three options for moving within a professional field: (1) reposition yourself within your professional arena itself and change practice areas, (2) remain within the same industry but change the setting where you use your professional expertise, and (3) change the industry or field in which you practice.

3. The two options for moving within an organization are (1) moving up the organization structure and (2) moving laterally within the organization.

4. Moving to make a career change consists of completely taking on a new work role and tasks, as well as entering a new work fields.

5. In projecting a revised professional image, each of these moves presents a challenge emphasizing your strengths and qualifications that are more suited for the type of position you are presently interested in seeking.

6. When revising your story, the objective is to have the reviewers focus on your qualifications and capabilities rather than on your lack of the actual work experience required by the job description.

7. Think about what the resume should stress and how to showcase the information in order for your revised or new professional identity to be easily seen when reading your resume.

8. A targeted resume style, stressed through the book, is the best format to use for career modification situations, because its flexibility allows prior experience and knowledge to be translated into transferable skills, with their related achievements, no matter when, how, or where they were gained.

9. Identify those core transferable skills that can be matched with, applied to, and/or substituted for the ones needed in your new work environment and rebundle them for this version of your resume.

10. Review your accomplishments and select those that illustrate these specific core transferable skills as well as any other successes that give creditability to your capabilities.

11. The most important impact of your resume is the demonstration of how you can meet the employer's needs by including anything you have done or accomplished that is at all related to the work you now want to do.

12. Review the tips for developing a targeted resume for a career modification situation before beginning your document.

13. Consider creating a CV that might serve you better in presenting your background, experiences, and qualifications for some career change situations.

Chapter 5 discusses three special groups of professionals and the special features their resumes require in their situations.

> *"If you don't set goals, you can't regret not reaching them."*
> —*Yogi Berra*

CHAPTER

5

Resumes for Select Groups

"If you doubt you can accomplish something, then you can't accomplish it.
You have to have confidence in your ability, and then be tough enough to follow through."
—Rosalynn Carter

Chapter Overview

We recognize that there are certain career transitions that might not be as "cut and dried" as others. Some transitions may require additional information and features that more traditional transitions do not. This chapter addresses three of those "select groups." Because both of us have clients who are involved in the association profession, that was a natural "select group" to choose. We then called upon experts in the military and government sectors to provide us with the necessary tools to develop resumes for candidates in those transitions. The information provided in this chapter is relevant to the individual who is transitioning within one of these sectors, as well as a career changer looking to enter into these fields in a senior-level capacity.

This chapter includes resume development for professionals in:

• Associations and nonprofits.
• Retired military transitioning to civilian.
• Senior-level federal government.

Associations and Nonprofit Professionals

A large number of individuals today seek out opportunities to work for an organization where they are able to fulfill their passion and/or interests. Associations and other nonprofits allow people to meet those needs and to be directly involved with an organization that also aligns with their personal values. Some people, however, work for associations for other reasons than fulfilling a passion or interest. A person who has a background in corporate communications will often move back and forth between a corporate job and an association job. Some people say that associations offer a greater breadth in experiences and topics than working for an individual company. For example, if you work for Verizon you are promoting one company, whereas if you work for a telecommunications association, you are promoting the interests of an entire industry.

Most successful associations today recognize that they function similar to a business. They must be accountable to stakeholders (aka members) vs. stockholders. They will have a different tax status than the corporate world, which affects how members perceive their business operations. Because the organizations are led by volunteers, decision-making in most associations is slower and more diffuse than in the corporate world. They realize that, in order for their association or nonprofit to survive, they must remain competitive with other similar organizations and for-profit firms that provide related services.

Most importantly, association managers need to recognize that volunteer leadership expect and deserve recognition for their service, requiring that much of the work of association staff take place in the background. The association industry is dominated by small staff organizations, with just a handful of groups in which staff size exceeds more than 500 individuals. Working for an organization with a staff of five to 25, with thousands of members is not uncommon, requiring association executives to manage the expectations of diverse populations.

Perhaps you are already an association executive looking to make a job change. In this case, your resume should focus on your successful association career history. For those seeking to be a senior specialist in association management, emphasize your functional knowledge and success in that specialty. For those seeking CEO positions, it is also key to demonstrate your knowledge in a variety of management functions, such as staff leadership, communications, public policy, marketing, and governance. In either case, it is essential that you demonstrate your management ability to create success.

If you are looking to make a career change from another industry into association management, a wide variety of opportunities are available to you. It is important to demonstrate your transferable and marketable skills. You must be able to show how your skills will translate and apply to the position. Don't assume that the hiring individual(s) will understand your skills. You must do the work for them and be able to show how your skills relate to what they are looking for. Do your homework—learn the language of associations and use that language in your resume. Be careful not to use jargon or acronyms from your current industry that may not be familiar to the hiring person at the association. Remember, associations realize today that it is important to operate with sound business principles. So who better to fulfill these needs than someone who already comes to the table with a business mindset?

Here's a story: Matt had a background in marketing and sales. He had worked for numerous retailers across the country. After being laid off from his job, he moved to Washington, D.C., and started hearing about the "whole world of associations." He began to research the association profession, networking with people working in associations, and found that he was drawn to the industry. When he developed his senior-level targeted resume, he emphasized his transferable marketable skills using language that association executives would understand. He showed in his resume how customer service (from his business background) was the same as member services (for associations). He also showed in his resume how he was involved in numerous organizations as a member and board member. Additionally, Matt showed how he had extensive volunteer management experience, which is critical for anyone working in associations and nonprofits. It didn't take Matt long after he put his resume together to land a director-level position in an association. By showing how his skills related and transferred to what an association needed, Matt's resume became an effective marketing tool.

Depending on how you choose to market yourself, you may want to consider a functional resume. If you are marketing yourself strictly on your skill set and you do not have any prior association experience, some human resource professionals may prefer a functional resume. This type of resume lists your skills (or functional areas), such as financial management, staff development, strategic planning, and volunteer management, regardless of where and when you might have done it.

It is also suggested for an association resume to include any professional memberships or affiliations, especially if they are relative to the position. Association executives like to see that you have volunteer experience, because working with members might be a big part of your responsibilities.

So what do human resource professionals in associations look for?

According to Michael Hoagland, CAE, senior director of human resource and development for the American Forest and Paper Association in Washington, D.C., "I look first on a resume for experience and how closely it relates to the open position. Then I look for level of responsibility (size of budget, number of direct reports) and tenure. I also like to see leadership and team-based experience. How have you headed teams within your organization?

"I look to see how well-rounded he or she is as well. Do you speak other languages? If so, list it. We are all global these days and must be diverse in our workplaces. Hobbies, interests, and other involvements are also good to show. Especially in associations, certifications and memberships are very important. Show your affiliations and your certifications in your functional area. It shows a commitment and credibility (hopefully) to your profession."

According to Pamela Kaul, president of Association Strategies, Inc., a metro area D.C.-based executive search and transition firm, "Remember, a single resume does not necessarily fit all occasions. I suggest that job seekers create a couple of resumes,depending on the position they are seeking. Think of your resume as a tool designed to trigger a positive response from a perspective employer—a telephone call expressing interest in you. Use different resumes to test your market. If you're sending out resumes and your telephone is not ringing, there is probably something wrong with your resume. On the other hand, if you are getting the calls but not advancing in the search process, you may want to consider coaching on interview skills.

"I may disagree with some of my colleagues about the ideal length of a resume in that I don't believe your resume should always be limited to just two pages. Longer copy can sell, as long as you adequately tell your story and connect it to the position for which you are applying. As many organizations and search committee members do not know a great deal about other associations outside their own industry or profession, long copy can be an effective way of helping them connect their needs with your specific background."

In some cases, it might also be a good idea to identify the name, size, and scope of the organization. Kaul further states, "Provide a before and after snapshot of how you entered the organization and what you left behind. How was your area of responsibility better as a result of your leadership? Organizations are seeking outcomes and achievement, not just layers of responsibilities."

Just as we have stated earlier, you want to be sure your association resume reflects the results you accomplished. You need to be able to show that you not only accomplished something but what the results were. If you grew membership, say how much. If you developed a strategic plan, what did your efforts result in? Don't assume that the reader will know.

In his book, *Search: Winning Strategies to Get Your Next Job in the Nonprofit World*, Larry Slesinger, founder and CEO of Slesinger Management Services in Bethesda, Maryland, states: "An effective resume is clear, focused on accomplishments, and succinct. It must also be truthful, error-free, and easy on the eye. Take care to avoid anything that gets in the way of presenting information quickly: small fonts, tiny margins, an illogical way of listing items or sections, page breaks at the wrong places, etc."

Whether you are currently in the association profession or making a career change, Larry recommends the use of a chronological resume. "I recommend, in your two- or three-page chronological resume, listing the following items, in this order:

1. Contact information—name, address, home telephone, direct-dial office phone (or wireless), and e-mail address.
2. Employment—most recent employer first, including name of employer, city and state, your title, dates of employment, and a concise description of your accomplishments.
3. Education—starting with your most advanced degree, include the name of the institution and location, degree and major, and the year you obtained your degree.

4. Honors and awards—if relevant and truly impressive.

5. Publications—list articles, chapters, and books that you wrote, if relevant.

6. Memberships—list any professional associations that are relevant to your career."

Larry further states: "Be wary of using commonly used templates to create your resume. Some might not have the categories and sections that make the most sense for you. And if they do, and you use the template, the format might look so much like other resumes using the same template that your resume doesn't help distinguish you from everybody else. Don't use any outlandish font or format, but don't be a slave to a template that many other people are using."

Careers in associations are attractive to people for a variety of reasons. Among the attributes to focus on in your cover letter and resume are such things as:

- Your strong people skills and ability to relate to and work with a wide range of individuals. You will have to relate to members from around the country, committee and board members in leadership positions, and fellow staff members, who all bring different perspectives to the organization.

- Your ability to handle many responsibilities and meet challenging deadlines. Associations are often working with fewer resources than the corporate world has available; show that this is a challenge you are up to.

- Your ability and willingness to travel. Most associations require that you be able to attend meetings and conferences out of the office on a regular basis. Make the employer aware that this won't be an issue for you.

- Your interest in addressing challenging societal and public policy issues. Most associations and nonprofits were created to address a particular interest area. Demonstrate that you are of like mind with the leadership that you will be working with.

Writing a winning resume for an association position requires you to demonstrate that you are a creative, resourceful, and committed individual who will provide executive leadership and strategic thinking for your prospective employer. (Turn to Appendix G on page page 207 for some sample resumes.)

Resources for Targeting Association and Nonprofits

Publications

Search: Winning Strategies to Get Your Next Job in the Nonprofit World, by Larry Slesinger (Piemonte Press, 2004).

Planning Your Career in Association Management, by Paul Belford (American Society of Association Executives, 2002).

National Trade and Professional Associations of the United States (Columbia Books Inc., 2003).

Association Job Search Websites

www.asaenet.org

www.associationtrends.com

www.execsearches.com

www.ceoupdate.com

www.philanthropycareers.com

www.nonprofitcareer.com

www.nonprofitjobs.org

www.wcanonprofits.org

www.mdnonprofit.org

www.pnp-inc.com

Retired Military Professionals

The senior military officer faces a unique challenge in preparing for the nonmilitary world of work. Typically, senior members of the military demonstrate successful leadership in a number of specialties requiring marketing tools consistent with the job requirements outside the military. This is because many potential targets can exist for them. Consequently, it becomes critical to clearly identify targets of interest and choice in order to perform thorough research and develop appropriate marketing and resume strategies for each specific interest. Exceptions here would be when the officer is pursuing a new position within the military, with a military contractor, or with some contractors to some federal organizations. Again, researching the opportunity is most important here as well.

Most of the general conventions for resumes that apply today also apply to documents prepared by senior officers. However, these individuals do need to give serious consideration to the resume format that will give them the most mileage. Frequently, a hybrid document is more effective, which will be discussed later on. Usually the chronological version of the resume is the more effective format when the officer spends most of his or her military career in a series of progressive positions within the same career field. (Writing a resume is a highly personalized process. No sample will meet the requirements of every specific situation, and space limitations preclude a detailed discussion of case histories in crafting these documents.)

A major challenge for the senior officer about to step away from the military is the preparation of the resume. The selection of terminology and examples of achievements in that document frequently represent a significant effort for an individual attempting to demonstrate the value of his or her military service to someone outside the military. The officer needs to present the material in that document in a manner that will be understood *and be most effective* in convincing the reader/decision-maker that the officer has a great deal of relevance to contribute to the organization—and that the accomplishments of the military career have been significant. What is needed here is the clear understanding that one of the key purposes of the resume is the securing of the interview, not the offer. In no case is it recommended that the officer attempt to disguise the fact that much or even most of a career was on active duty. Officers with many years in the reserve components (or with long breaks in service) need to weigh the advantages and disadvantages of various options in tailoring the resume. In no instance should the marketing document use the word "retired" or "retiree," due to the stereotypes associated with such terminology. (There are other military terms and phrases that should be avoided because they may be misunderstood; when in doubt, leave such terminology out.) Research should be done to determine the appropriateness of showing rank in the resume.

Many officers believe that they need to furnish a document that provides a complete history of their military service. This clearly is not the case! The resume is not the same as a military biography. Include in the resume only that which is substantive and relevant to the position being sought. Sometimes it is useful to be creative in formatting the resume to incorporate only what presents the candidate to the best advantage to the targeted decision-maker. It is, of course, always best to craft a unique targeted document for each opportunity sought.

Due to the nature of a diverse military career, the Resume Component Database is a recommended tool to employ in resume development (for details, contact K&D Associates via e-mail at jditt@comcast.net or kaplan@starpower.net). When used properly, it serves many purposes during the job search process. Various elements are stored in the database, in separate folders. The database should include folders for each of the following:

- Objective statements.
- Summary and profile statements.
- Experience, divided by assignments or in some other arrangement that makes sense to the job seeker.
- Listing of accomplishment/ achievement statements, both vocational and avocational, and (when appropriate) education-related.
- Academic education.
- Military and military-sponsored education.
- Professional memberships.
- Security clearances, including date(s) and issuing authority or authorities.
- Biographies.
- Traits brought from the military.
- Life, family, financial, and career goals— as used in the assessment process prior to assembling resumes.

- Publications.
- Presentations, speeches, and panels.
- Civic affiliations and roles (such as chapter president).
- Honors, awards, and special recognitions.
- Cover letter paragraphs used and/or developed.
- Proposals made in response to earlier interviews.
- Special interests and developed hobbies or recognized area(s) of expertise.
- Certifications, licenses, etc.
- Volunteer activities.
- Books and other literature read recently (for interview discussions).
- Key words used and potential use.
- Special folders as appropriate.

Information can and should be added to each of the folders as that information is developed. In this way, the senior military officer can prepare a focused resume, appropriate to the interests and needs of the potential employer, in less than an hour. This includes listing all of the higher security clearances held, where appropriate (see samples in Appendix G). This concept also places the senior military officer in better control of his or her career when the database is maintained.

Employers look for different pieces of information in resumes and few employers look for precisely the same information. With time, employer interests and needs change. Furthermore, interests and needs differ in different parts of the country. The same applies among industries and among employers. Employers write the rules, and the candidate has the responsibility to learn the rules. Research here is key. The military applicants must not assume that they can use the documents and formats that proved successful throughout their military careers.

While the majority of publications stress the chronological resume for military personnel stepping away from active duty and recruiters indicate a preference for the chronological format, experience has shown:

1. Research is essential to establish the preferred format of the receiving organization.

2. Very often the hybrid chronological resume will be found to be most effective.

3. The hybrid chronological resume gives the senior military officer advantages over the straight chronological in that it allows the officer to clearly and succinctly present key achievements.

4. The functional resume is not well-received by many employers for a variety of reasons. Therefore, its use should be considered only when recommended by the organization that will receive the resume.

Another technique that is gaining recognition is the listing of all *key words* used in the resume at the bottom of the first page of the resume. This approach is well-known to recruiters, Web developers, and software developers, but it is not yet commonly discussed in the literature on the subject. The listing of key words increases the "count" for each key word and becomes important when the screening software sets "count minimums" for the key words.

Career military individuals bring to the marketplace a variety of traits not always found in their competition. It is most effective to consider these traits or strengths and incorporate them (as relevant and appropriate) into resumes and the business discussions that the marketplace refers to as interviews. These traits include *leadership* (as distinguished from management), *strategic planning, initiative, self-direction, loyalty, possession of a client/service orientation, specialized advanced training, strong bottom-line orientation,* and *a global orientation.* Additionally, the senior military officer needs to remember that he or she brings demonstrated, effective experience in *leading and building diverse teams* and in *mentoring subordinates.* These and other traits should also be placed in a Resume Component Database folder. In this area, there is a caution in the use of the term "executive," due to the abuse of that term in the private sector. Discussions of leadership, with examples drawn from the "accomplishments/achievements" database folder, will prove more effective in the resume's presentation.

The senior military officer has often held positions where the responsibility and accountability are significantly greater that the role(s) being explored outside of the military. Thus, the officer needs to be sensitive to the role being considered and present the responsibilities and accountabilities to more closely match the position sought. (Example: a project or program of more than $500 million can be broken into component pieces that can more closely reflect the budget and person power considerations of the organization being contacted.)

When the officer holds or held any clearance of Top Secret or above, the level of the clearance or clearances should be shown in the resume's heading, just below the e-mail address(es) when and only when contacting the Department of Defense, Government, or contractors where the clearance is expected or required. This information should not be included in either the resume or the transmittal documents where the role is not involved in security issues. (Do not provide any clearance information that would constitute a security violation in an unclassified document.)

Let's look at this story: John Paul Jones, like most senior military officers, did not have a clear picture of the role or roles he wanted to go after. He knew that he wanted to "contribute back" to his community, but not in a continuation of his work in the military. After working through the assessment process in which he clearly identified his life, family, and financial goals, he was able to begin looking at career fields much more clearly.

He identified those traits he wanted to use, his motivated skills, and then began researching the roles and industries that interested him and that he saw would continue to provide challenge while giving back to the community. In looking at his targets, he understood that geographically he was committed to the local area. This meant that he had to look wider in terms of businesses and industries for his roles of interest. As a senior officer, he quickly understood that the resume is used in the later stages, not the initial stages of his search. He confirmed through his networking what his coaches had shared: the chronological and the hybrid chronological formats were the only acceptable resume formats. The functional format had been passé for some time.

As John Paul became more comfortable in using his networking skills to identify how he could help others, he was able to begin discussions of his interests, which led him to the connections he needed to make in his efforts to secure the type of role he wanted. He also found that by inquiring about and keeping the conversations focused to the organization's needs and issues, he was able to create a resume clearly focused on those needs and to the particular interests of his target individual. This individually targeted and well-focused resume he would take with him for both informational and business (hiring) interviews. His approach, however, was never to offer his resume, but to ask for a critique of the document at the end of the conversation so that he could refine and then return it with even greater focus. This developed even stronger interest on the part of the recipient, as well as any others who viewed John Paul's resume.

Changing career fields was never an issue; the issues and concerns of the business leaders he dealt with were leadership, understanding of the business, customer/client relations, buying into the corporate vision, and specifically, how he could contribute. As a senior military officer, John Paul was quickly able to verbally offer additional specific examples to demonstrate his competencies. These last contributions were not a part of his resume, but came out comfortably as a result of his coaching.

Using his resume in this fashion, John Paul stepped into his new role as executive director of a professional organization after a six-week holiday with his family.

There are several concluding thoughts for the attention of senior military transitioners. These are applicable to the individual's resume and to many other aspects of the job search:

1. Having completed a successful career in the military, learn not to use the term "retire" or "retiring," either verbally or in writing, to indicate that one is looking at opportunities outside the military.

2. Research the organization before including rank (or grade) on the resume or transmittal documents. Some organizations are sensitive to the fact that they do not have that many former military and, regrettably, some organizations are not "military-friendly."

3. Begin developing a personal board of directors, not just for job searching, but for career movement.

4. If friends who have already stepped away from active duty or associates who know that you are departing request a copy of your resume, thank them and ask how the document will be used and to whom it will be sent. Advise those who ask that the need is to have a focused resume to submit—not the generic version that you have available.

5. Submit a generic resume to friends already outside the military and ask for a critique that includes what types of information should be included in the resume for the friend's employer. The same goes for all friends who want to refer a resume.

6. Do not let friends and associates refer resumes that are not focused at least to the specific employer.

Senior-Level Federal Government

If you've ever considered working for the U.S. government, or you are a current federal employee who wants to advance in high-level public service, then this section is for you. Most senior/management jobs in the federal sector are advertised and filled at the GS ("General Schedule") 13 through 15 levels (2004 baseline salary ranges: $62,905 to $87,439). The highest executive and leadership positions (aside from political appointees) are in the Senior Executive Service (SES). Listed in vacancy announcements as "ES-01–06," these positions offered 2004 baseline annual salaries in the range of $113,000 to $138,200. (Salaries are higher in many cities and other designated high cost-of-living areas.)

It should come as no surprise that many, if not most, of the high-level jobs in the federal sector are ultimately filled the same way as many others—through who you know who knows what positions are (or will be) opening. By networking and staying in touch with your current contacts, you position yourself to get that all-important word on when an agency job is going to be announced. Regardless, you will have to complete an application package as part of your process for getting hired into the U. S. government. **Note:** although similar to the job search process in the private sector, there are three key differences to successfully applying for a federal job:

1. A federal-style resume format is created. This provides more detailed personal information, therefore it is longer than your regular resume.

2. In addition, complete and submit one or two supplemental narratives, to respond to each of several key qualification requirements of the position. Known by many names—including "Knowledge, Skills, Abilities, and Other Characteristics" (or "KSAs"), "Technical Qualification Statements," "Executive Core Competencies," etc.—these spell out the specific skills, qualities, and experiences needed for success in each position. Your responses to these KSAs are critical to your success in getting a federal job.

3. It can take a lot longer to fill a federal position than a private sector one.

There are seven application steps for a federal position. The following sections describe these differences in more detail and illustrate some proven strategies for making the process of application for a federal job as easy and effective as possible.

Step 1: Research

As with any of your job opportunity targets, find out as much as possible about the position from your contact(s) and other sources. Research the agency's Website for information on its mission, vision, goals, strategic plan, etc. Who are their key clients or customers, and how are they best served? How can you be the solution to their challenges and needs? (What are the key words the agency uses?)

Step 2: Read the Job Vacancy Announcement

Before beginning your application, read the vacancy announcement *carefully*. (Most federal-sector positions have to be advertised for a certain length of time, on the Office of Personnel Management (OPM)'s official Website, *www.usajobs.opm.gov*, and/or the individual agency's Website. There's a lot of fine print to read and digest, including thorough, detailed instructions you must follow to the letter. You'll also find a lot of information to help you.

A typical job vacancy announcement describes:

* The vacancy announcement number and opening and closing dates.
* The official title of the position, series (the job category system used government-wide), grade ("GS" or "ES" level) and corresponding salary range, duty location, and "who may apply"—that is, some positions are limited to current federal employees or to a certain geographic location.

- Major duties of the position.
- The qualifications required. These are the critically important KSAs needed for success in this position.
- Instructions on how to apply, including any special procedures (for example, completing an online application).
- All of the other information you need to submit.
- Deadline for submitting your application package.
- Other information, including reasonable accommodations for disabilities and EEO statements, whether moving expenses are authorized, and a contact name and phone number.

Step 3: Create a Federal-Style Resume

The good news about applying for a federal job these days is that a cumbersome and lengthy paper form (known as the old SF [Standard Form]-171, or the newer OF [Optional Form]-612) no longer needs to be completed. However, you do have to be sure you provide *all* of the information the vacancy announcement requires. In many cases, you should be able to adapt your current resume to include all the extra information the federal sector needs. Review the segment of a sample federal style resume on page 87. It illustrates one format and many of the details most commonly requested in the vacancy announcements. For additional samples, see Appendix G.

Unlike most other employment sectors, your resume isn't the most important part of your application package. Your resume will basically get a quick initial screening from a human resources specialist (or a computer) just to see whether you meet the minimum requirements of the position—are you a "go" or "no go" for further consideration? The next step is key to successfully completing the application.

Step 4: Address the
Supplemental Qualifications Narratives, or KSAs

This is the single most critical part of your application! Your ability to present your skills and accomplishments in your responses to the KSAs determines whether you're referred for an interview (or even selected outright). In a series of short essays (one to one and a half pages maximum, per KSA), address the stated needs of the particular position and demonstrate how you are the best candidate. Point by point, line up your skills, experience, and those critically important stories—your accomplishments and results—to the specific qualifications required.

Wherever you can in your narratives, repeat the key words from the vacancy announcement and other official descriptions and quantify results with as much detail and specifics as needed, to help the reader understand the scope and impact of what you did. Approach these narratives as written interview questions or an expanded version of a functional or targeted resume format style as discussed in Chapter 1.

Following is a sample KSA from a recent vacancy announcement for a high-level federal position—Director of Public Relations for an agency:

"Marketing and Communication—Expert knowledge of marketing principles and theories and ability to develop internal and external communication strategies that are national in scope. Demonstrated experience in analyzing customer needs and developing products for specific market segments."

How do you create your own clear and compelling responses to KSAs? Some KSAs are written more clearly, specific, and direct than others. When they are written in rather vague or general terms, analyze what the selecting officials are trying to say and answer the question they are *really* asking. In the KSA for "Marketing and Communication" cited above, "Expert knowledge of marketing principles and theories" translates to, "Describe how you applied specific marketing principles and theories." Examples of how it can be completed are:

- To increase purchases of (specified) product or services by $____ over the past _____ (period of time).
- To increase or improve use of XYZ services by ____% over ____ (period of time) to (number and specified) client or customer group(s).
- To add ____ additional clients in the last _____ (period of time), increasing revenues by $___ or ___% over the past year.

In other words, it's not what you know, it's what you did, and the results you got, that matter.

As is emphasized throughout this book, tell your stories! Your accomplishments and results will speak volumes about your skills and what you'll bring to the position. Take your accomplishment bullets from your resume and expand them into full statements by using the same "Problem-Action-Results" (PAR) or "Challenge-Context-Action-Results" (CCAR) approach. Ideally, give three to four examples (stories) for each KSA response. Quantify and give specifics wherever possible. When did you serve as leader or personally perform this activity? How many people/organizations were involved? Who did it help? How? Why does it matter?

Just as you would do in applying for a position in the private sector, highlight your results. Remember and use those all-powerful words: "The outcome was...." Describe in detail the bottom line—how you saved money/time (include amount), improved a process, helped an organization run more effectively, helped develop people (include how many over what period of time), etc.

Your bottom-line results really do count more than how you got to them. For example, in preparing his Executive Core Qualifications (ECQ) statement, a candidate aspiring recently for an SES position followed faithfully the CCAR approach—a little *too* faithfully, however. He lavished so much time and detail describing the "Challenge, Context, and Actions" that his "Results" were almost lost, squeezed into the very end. A hurried reviewer could have easily missed the scope and significance of what he achieved.

Additional tips for your successful qualification statement/KSA response include:

- Keep your response to each KSA to one page, if possible; one and a half pages maximum.

- Don't repeat the same stories in different qualification statements, unless there is a real difference you can showcase via multiple results.
- For additional impact in your summary statements, fold in and relate the "major duties" described in the vacancy announcement wherever you can.

See page 88 at the end of this section for a hypothetical response to the KSA, "marketing and communication," mentioned previously.

If you're applying for an SES position, there are additional requirements that you need to be aware of in order to submit a complete application. First and most essential is addressing each of the five Executive Core Qualifications, or ECQs. Known informally as the "Super KSAs," these require their own individual narrative statements:

1. Leading change.
2. Leading people.
3. Results driven.
4. Business acumen.
5. Building coalitions/communication.

Just as with the other KSA statements, showcase your accomplishments and results that support your success in each of five listed areas. Some vacancy announcements give detailed descriptions for the agency interpretations of each of the five ECQs; other announcements just list them. You can also review OPM's *SES Qualifications Guide* at *www.opm.gov/ses/handbook.html* for some more detailed descriptions of the five ECQs.

Step 5: Gather All Other Requested Information

Submit exactly what they're requesting—no more and no less. If you've served in the military, for example, this will include discharge papers (your "DD-214"). Don't include extraneous materials—copies of degrees or transcripts, references, etc.—unless the vacancy announcement specifically requests them.

Step 6: Rewrite, Revise, and Proofread Your Final Versions

The old saying, "Good writing is RE-writing," is never truer than in your federal application materials. Review the guidelines for a great resume as described in Chapter 1 and make sure you have covered every one in all of your materials. These include:

- Visual: Lots of white space, six lines or less text per paragraph, wide margins, good clean font and type size, etc.
- Style: Strong writing—short, powerful sentences with action verbs. Perfect grammar, spelling, punctuation, and spacing.
- Content: Emphasize your stories—accomplishments with lots of examples, specifics, and results—as measurably as possible.

Assemble your package, and then put it away for a day (or a few days). Only then, look at it again with a fresh and critical eye. Get a trusted friend or colleague to check it. Beyond the basics, double-check to be sure you've addressed all of the selection criteria, answered the KSAs completely, and provided all of the information requested in the agency vacancy announcement.

A growing number of agencies are requesting applicants to complete part or all of their applications online. If you apply online, be especially careful! Save your work and review it again before you hit that final "Submit" key, if at all possible. Unfortunately, it's very easy to hit one wrong key or check the wrong box, and eliminate your application materials from ever being considered, solely on a technicality.

Chapter 6 reviews the basic guidelines for posting resumes online and completing job applications at Websites. The submission of an online federal application has some additional specific procedures. You will need to:

- Create a template (in Microsoft Word format) you can use to cut and paste into your resume, KSAs, and/or ECQ responses.

- Unless you're really constrained by space, your response must be limited to a maximum of 3,000 characters, including spacing and punctuation. Preserve white space for greater readability, even in your online application. Although a computer's database is most likely to be your first reviewer, your materials should be as readable and visually attractive as possible for the subsequent human readers.

Step 7: Submit Your Materials by the Deadline

Then aim for patience. The federal hiring process is designed to be as thorough and fair as possible, and it can take several months to fill a position. You will also want to continue exploring and pursuing your other options. The unexpected can and does happen—a "sure thing" can evaporate just as fast in a federal agency as in other organizations.

But when you get that all-important call or e-mail inviting you to an interview or offering you a federal job, it's worth the wait. You now have the chance to contribute your energy and talents to public service and make a real difference in people's lives as a proud part of the U.S. government.

SAMPLE FEDERAL RESUME (Partial)

Here is a sample beginning for a federal-style resume, illustrating one effective format and the kind of information the agency will usually require:

JANE Q. CITIZEN

1234 Treelined Lane   (202) 555-1234 (Office)
Mytown, MD 20999-5555   (301) 555-5678 (Home)
E-mail: janeqc@xyz.com   (301) 555-9999 (Cell)

U.S. Citizen: Yes
Veteran's Preference: 5 points
Social Security Number: 111-33-5555
Highest Federal Civilian Position: N/A
Security Clearance: N/A

OBJECTIVE: Director of Public Relations, [Agency Name],
   Announcement #Y-04-1234

SKILLS SUMMARY

[Same as your regular resume.]

PROFESSIONAL EXPERIENCE AND ACCOMPLISHMENTS

ABC Company   June 2003–Present
9999 N Street, N. W., Suite 1555   40–45 hrs./week
Washington, DC 20006-1111   Beginning Salary: $78,000
Supervisor: John Q. Public   Current Salary: $87,500
   His Tel. (202) 555-4321
   His E-mail: JohnQ@ABCcomp.com   Supervisor may be contacted.

Director of Marketing (May 2004–Present)
Created and developed fourteen advertising campaigns that resulted in …
(etc.)

Associate Director of Marketing (June 2003–May 2004)
(etc.)

Sample KSA

Marketing and Communication—Expert knowledge of marketing principles and theories and ability to develop internal and external communication strategies that are national in scope. Demonstrated experience in analyzing customer needs and developing products for specific market segments.

Sample Response

As Director of Marketing at ABC Company since 2003, led or coordinated all aspects of public relations. This included 14 successful campaigns to launch eight new XYZ products or increase sales in six existing product lines.

For example, in October 2003, created a seven-person team of specialists that launched an Internet-based survey based on the Gallup Organization methodology. We developed and tested a questionnaire to contact a representative national sampling of 1,800 former and current customers. We then applied their feedback and suggestions to update the QRS product line with more features and ease of use. This increased sales in the first quarter of 2004 by 36.4%, a record-breaking increase of $1,875,000 over the previous quarter.

In February 2004, conceived and implemented a campaign to update our 11,200 employees nationwide on up-to-the-minute happenings in our company via our daily "ABC-O-GRAM" e-mail. Revamped the Employee Suggestion Program to encourage on-the-spot awards for suggestions made and implemented. As a result, our employee suggestions increased by 16% over the previous month and year; 7% of these were adopted, and our company saved approximately $470,000 during the six-month period Jan.–June 2004.

Resources for Federal Job Seekers

Print Resources

Federal Civil Service Jobs, by Michele Lipson and Dawn Mckay (Peterson's, 2003). The reader will find it easy to follow guide to search, select, and apply for Federal jobs. A unique feature is the "Before and After" examples of Federal job applications. Appendixes include listing of jobs that require an examination and a glossary of civil service terms.

Federal Resumes, by Kathryn Troutman (JIST Publishing, 2004). This book is a very through and extensive examination of the procedures and requirements to file a federal application. Includes the steps to writing an effective KSA statement, samples of Federal essays, and OPM's USA JOBS Sites, agency Websites and directory to agencies/departments. Another benefit is the guidelines for sorting through Federal job applications.

Website Resources

www.avuecentral.com. Federal employment service provided absolutely free to the public. It's the fastest and easiest way to find and apply for federal employment. Avue Central offers completely private, safe, and secure access to thousands of federal jobs worldwide.

www.fedjobs.com. The Federal Research Service's Website offers ideas and advice, federal job listing subscriptions, and helpful publications, including "The KSA Handbook" and "The KSA Sampler."

www.firstgov.gov. This "uber-site" for everything related to federal government and services can link you to individual agency Websites.

www.opm.gov/ses/handbook.html. The Office of Personnel Management's (OPM) "SES Qualifications Guide" gives some detailed descriptions of the five Executive Core Qualifications (ECQs).

www.resume-place.com. Kathryn Kraemer Troutman, author of *The Federal Resume Guidebook* and *Ten Steps to Getting a Federal Job*, has great tips and format ideas for your federal resume and KSAs.

www.usajobs.opm.gov. Here's where OPM lists vacancy announcements for federal jobs nationwide. You can also create and store your own federal-style resume online.

Chapter Highlights

Recapping Chapter 5, features of writing your resume for "selected groups" include:

1. For associations, it is essential that you demonstrate your management ability to create success.

2. If you are aiming to be a senior specialist in association management, emphasize your functional knowledge and success in that specialty.

3. If you are seeking CEO positions, it is also key to demonstrate your knowledge in a variety of management functions, such as staff leadership, communications, public policy, marketing, and governance.

4. It is important to demonstrate your transferable and marketable skills. You must be able to show how your skills will translate and apply to the position. Don't assume that the hiring individual(s) will understand your skills.

5. If you are marketing yourself strictly on your skill set and you do not have any prior association experience, some human resource professionals may prefer a functional resume.

6. Include any professional memberships or affiliations, especially if they are relative to the position.

7. If you are a retired military officer transitioning to civilian, the chronological version of the resume is usually the more effective format if you have spent most of your military career in a series of progressive positions within the same career field.

8. As an officer, you need to present the material in that document in a manner that will be understood *and be most effective* in convincing the reader/decision-maker that the officer has a great deal of relevance to contribute to the organization—and that the accomplishments of the military career have been significant.

9. Due to the nature of a diverse military career, the Resume Component Database is a recommended tool to employ in resume development.

10. If you are an officer who holds or held any clearance of top secret or above, the level of the clearance or clearances should be shown in your resume's heading just below the e-mail address(es) when and only when contacting DoD, government, or contractors where the clearance is expected or required.

11. Many of the high-level jobs in the federal sector are ultimately filled the same way as others—through who you know who knows what positions are (or will be) opening. By networking and staying in touch with your current contacts, you position yourself to get that all-important word on when an agency job is going to be announced.

12. There are three key differences to successfully applying for a federal job. More than likely, you will need to create a federal-style resume and one or two supplemental narratives to support key qualifications (KSAs). It also is important to note that it can take a lot longer to fill a federal position than a private sector one.

Chapter 6 presents strategies and guidelines for using and distributing your targeted resume.

"Choose a job you love and you'll never have to work a day in your life."
—*Confucious*

CHAPTER

6

Market Your Story

"You never achieve real success unless you like what you are doing."
—Dale Carnegie

Chapter Overview

Now that your targeted resume and ideal professional image have been created, it is time to plan the marketing campaign of your story. In today's highly competitive job market, you need to take a proactive role in letting potential employers and people who might lead you to job opportunities, know that you are not only available, but actively looking for a new position. Inform them about your qualifications, special expertise, and in-depth experiences. Spread the word and share your resume with as many people as you possibly can. Think of contacting a person you have met only briefly, someone you have been referred to, or an old colleague that you have not been in contact with for a while. Bring them up-to-date regarding your work situation and find out the extent to which they can be of assistance in your job search efforts.

As someone who may have been with the same organization for some time, you may need to review and bring yourself up-to-date regarding promoting yourself as a job candidate. As with resume basics, some fundamental marketing strategies and activities have remained the same, some have changed, and some new ones have recently been put into play. Networking and informational interviewing—two traditional ways of conducting a job search campaign—are still very much practiced, but with some different purposes and goals. A recent trend that is on the fast track to becoming "the way of conducting a job search" is the Internet.

This is the time to review basic ways of marketing yourself and becoming more aware of utilizing the Internet as a job search resource:

* Explore the possibilities of using the Internet, learning how and when it will best work for your situation, qualifications, and interests.
* Assess your networking skills and determining how up-to-date and extensive is your networking circle is.
* Contact specific designated people and set up a schedule of informational interviews to fill in the information gaps that are needed to carry out the best job search campaign you possibly can.

Particular attention is given to the following common ways of marketing your story, other than as a direct response to a job opening:

* Resumes and the Internet.
* Resumes and networking.
* Resumes and informational interviewing.

Resumes and the Internet

If you have not been active in the job market within the last 10 years, you will find that the methodology used by employers to locate and track applicants has undergone a rapid change. Increasingly, more organizations are turning to the Internet to help them find suitable candidates for their job openings by using their own Websites as recruitment portals, as well as turning to independent electronic resume databases. This is true whether the employer is a Fortune 500 company or a medium-sized one. Moreover, most organizations have established computer-based applicant tracking systems. Organizations' increasing reliance on the Internet as their means to receive resumes is reflected by Sam Bresler in his statement, "My organization will generally not accept paper resumes any longer. Only resumes submitted by our Web-enabled system are reviewed. It helps us to search for key words/phrases for specific skill sets and experience when we have openings."

The Internet, if used properly and wisely, can be a very effective and efficient way to market your story. Your resume can be distributed in a matter of minutes, if not seconds, to an unlimited number of recruiters and employers. And therein lies a problem: With a traditional print resume, you can control its distribution and customize your qualifications according to what you believe are the needs of a specific organization.

Consequently, to conduct a targeted marketing campaign on the Internet, a way is needed for selectivity regarding who reads your resume and how to locate the specific audience you want to reach. The use of the Internet for your job search activities requires some caution, because it is also a possibility for your supervisor or a colleague to come across your resume. This is something you do not want to happen, particularly if your current employer is not aware of your plans to seek a new position.

It is assumed that you have familiarity and some experience with basic Internet search engines such as Google or Yahoo. However, prior to using the Internet as a marketing tool in your job search campaign, you can take advantage of the online search engines and Websites as information resources to help focus and narrow your marketing arenas. Think about your marketing and job search needs and utilize Websites to:

- Identify organizations you are interested in working for.
- Research organizations that have job openings for which you intend to apply.
- Review job listings on an organization's Website.
- Locate online job databases specializing in your field and/or industry.
- Become informed about salary range norms and other benefits.
- Learn of local networking events and headhunters' offices.
- Investigate cost of living and other needed community information, if considering relocation.

To help you conduct this information gathering more effectively and efficiently, refer to Appendix E on page 128.

Depending on the circumstances, your resume information can be submitted or distributed electronically through several different options: scanning, as an online document, as an e-mail attachment, and/or transferred to a resume form on an employer's Website.

Upon deciding how, when, and where you want to market your resume via the Internet, some adaptations to the original document are necessary for usability and effectiveness for integration into an electronic database system. The major difference between an online and print resume is the lack of control you have with the electronic one—only one is usually submitted and it can be screened for various job openings. With a paper resume, it is possible to submit more than one version targeted to an employer or headhunter for different position openings for which you qualify.

First and most importantly, for your resume to rise to the top in electronic sort and retrieval activities, it needs to contain key words and phrases. Second, when you upload your resume, it has to be able to be scanned. Third, you will need a copy that has been converted to ASCII or plain text for Web and e-mail readiness and to be stored properly in an applicant database.

Importance of Key Words and Phrases

The role of key words and phrases is important in both print and electronic resumes. However, in electronic resumes, the objective of key words and phrases is to attract the computer's attention, while in a print resume the copy is part of the integral style and layout with its function to showcase qualifications. Because your traditional paper resume is verb-oriented (based on the key word and phrase listing you developed), only a little adjustment or editing should be needed. Review your print

resume and make sure that, for the purposes of an online resume, you have optimized the use of action verbs and their synonyms to ensure chances of an ideal match.

Once your document is entered into a resume database, present or future comparisons are made between the key words and phrases contained in your resume and
the job opening requirements. The more accurate key words and phrases contained
in your resume, the better are your chances for a match. Having the majority of the
required key words and phrases will identify you as a highly qualified candidate to be
called in for further consideration. Libby Sartain reinforces this practice, "We use an
electronic scanning system for a lot of our hiring. Be sure you use key words that are
relevant to the position."

An online resume can be sent or scanned directly into an employer's automated
applicant tracking system or as an attachment to an e-mail. Furthermore, sometimes
an employer does not want your own resume submitted, but asks you to fill out one of
their online applications. Before completing this form, compare your own key word
and phrase listing to the job requirements so that your chances for a match are greatly
improved. It is possible that a different verb is used to describe a skill or expertise
than the one you would normally use. Double check and make sure you are correct in
how you make reference to your qualifications and level of expertise. The difference
between a reviewer scanning your resume and an automatic scanner is that a reviewer
will know that "manage" and "direct" are describing a similar skill; a software program may not.

Ability to Be Scanned

Next, your resume needs to be scanning friendly. Whether you fax or mail your
resume, assume it will be scanned into an applicant tracking system. To have a scannable
version of your resume is a matter of following several specific technical procedures:

- Use a common business, sans serif font—one that the scanner would
  most likely recognized and in which the letters do not touch each other,
  such as Helvetica or Arial.
- If your original resume has a border, omit it, because it is possible that
  the software is an older version and will see it as a single character and
  eliminate the entire section
- If your original resume contains columns, readjust the format, because
  it is possible that in the scanning process the order of words will lose its
  sequential order and lessen the effect of your key words and phrases.
- Do not condense space between letters or use less than a 10-point font;
  a 12-point font is preferred so that the scanner will read the document
  easily.
- Plain white paper or a very lightly tinted one are the best to use.
- Mail rather than fax, use an original crisp copy, and do not fold or staple.
  If it must be faxed (for deadline expediency), use the "fine" fax mode
  and a resume without any staple or crease marks.

+ Follow up with a traditional print resume for two reasons: (1) your resume may not get through due to spam filters and blocks and (2) the transmitted resume may be difficult to read—format may change because it may not be converted in the same exact way as was the original.

+ Do not forget to bring a resume copy to the interview to reference specific information.

ASCII or Plain Text Resume Format

As has been previously mentioned, you need to convert your resume into an ASCII or plain text format for the information to be transferred accurately by e-mail or directly online through electronic storage bases. It is also with this format that you can copy and paste your resume into online resume template forms. In other words, ASCII format has the advantage of being universally recognized and readable by any type of computer. By carrying out the following procedures, you create an electronic version of your resume:

+ Open your resume folder or file and select the "Save As" command from the file menu. Enter a new file name, such as "resumeelect.text," and select "text only," ASCII, or "plain text" as the file type.

+ Reopen the new electronic version, all original formatting should be removed; however, review it carefully, because in the conversion some errors may occur that will need to be corrected.

+ Format all the plain text in a left alignment style, including your name and contact information.

> For example:
> John Doe
> 123 Any Street
> Anywhere, USA
> Phone No. (111) 222-3333
> E-Mail Address jdoe@abc.com

+ Replace bullets with simple ASCII asterisks (*).

+ Eliminate all bolding, underlining, tabs, columns, italics, and centering. "Plain text" means literally plain text. If any line contains more than 65 characters, adjust margins. At the end of each line, insert a hard return so that margins are kept.

+ For some styling, you can block paragraphs for job descriptions, achievements, and education; double space between sections or achievements; and capitalize headings for some eye relief. Also, make use of blank lines or commas for information formerly separated by tabs.

This ASCII version can be used for e-mail attachments or for pasting or embedding into the body of the e-mail message, which is the preference of most employers. This preference is due to virus possibilities associated with attachments. **Note:** if you need to use a third option—pasting your resume into a Web-based form—remove the hard breaks at the end of sentences so that it will automatically wrap to the size of the window.

Other Suggestions for Efficiency and Effectiveness

You may want to consider some other steps to increase your competitiveness when using a resume limited in style and design.

- Do a trial run. Before posting your resume, send it to yourself and to some other people both as an attachment and cut and pasted into the body of an e-mail message. Open both copies to view the results and check with the other recipients to receive their feedback.

- Strategize your e-mail message heading. Use the subject heading of your e-mail message as a marketing tool to promote your expertise and grab the attention of the reader. For example, "RE: HR Executive, over 15 yrs experience" or "HR Professional, health industry expertise—Job # 157A."

- In responding to a specific job listing on an employer's Website, follow instructions exactly. Do not send a cover letter if not asked to do so.

- When posting to a resume database site with no instructions regarding how to send the document, the usual preference is to embed the document directly into the message itself rather than send as an attachment. If there are any database procedures, follow them exactly as stated.

- Do not include your home address or any other confidential information that can be available to anyone once posted on the Internet. You may want to consider renting a mailbox or establishing a code name with a separate e-mail address from your usual one. It is best not to use your work e-mail address for the obvious reasons.

- As a senior professional with specialized expertise, it maybe worth your time and effort to establish a public Web page with your resume. Free services are available or your own ISP may offer free Web page space as part of the fee. Then register your Website with some of the major search engines. This gives employers looking for candidates with your qualifications another way to find you.

Using the Internet as a Broadcast Tool

Although most people think of only using the Internet for the actual submission of resumes or to locate specific employers and positions, the Internet can serve as a very efficient and effective broadcast media. By e-mail, you can inform individual colleagues and colleagues in your professional associations and network groups that you are back in the job market. Think of how quickly you are able to reach dozens of people, all who potentially have a lead or referral for you. However, again be very careful who receives your distribution.

Send out a broadcasting message with your resume attached as a Word document, briefly describing in fewer than five sentences (1) the types of job opportunities you are interested in, (2) the types of organizations you would like to work in, and (3) other information you deem pertinent. Ask to set up a meeting or a phone call to discuss your situation further. In the Reference Section, let people know why you have contacted them by stating, for example: "RE: Job search inquiry."

In summary, it is true that employers and job seekers are more frequently turning to the Internet to conduct their business. However, you should not be looking at electronic resumes and listings as the only way to market your resume and conduct your job search. As an experienced professional, you have several marketing alternatives. After sending out a broadcast e-mailing or using your Rolodex, sitting down with a colleague to discuss your situation is still one of the best ways to learn of opportunities and to inform people that you are in the market.

Some positions are not listed in online resume databases due to their highly specified requirements and needed expertise. Often, the word is spread through certain selected groups or arenas. It is for this reason—and to expand your contact and referral listings—that the roles of networking and informational interview are important in the job search process.

Resumes and Networking

Even in this economy, there are millions of good jobs out there. However, most of the best never make it into the classified ads—especially senior-level ones! They are filled by people who find out about them before they are advertised. How do they find out about these great jobs? By networking, of course. Networking is a critical aspect of any serious job hunter's strategy. Current studies show that about 85 percent of all jobs are filled through networking leads.

Some people might find networking as slimy and manipulative. Not so! We all network even though we don't think of it as networking. How often have you been reading a newspaper or magazine when you remember that that's just what your friend Penny predicted would happen when you were talking to her last week? So you pick up the phone and tell Penny about the article in the paper. Or the time you saw an advertisement for a position that was perfect for your unhappily employed friend, so you call them and tell them about the job announcement. That's networking.

In this section we will review some networking techniques that we (and other career management professionals) have found to be useful with our clients, suggestions for places to network, and how *not* to use your resume when networking. And by the way, a couple of great question to ask as you are networking are, "How did you develop your network?" and "Where did you go to increase your network?"

Here are some recommended tips:

* Be authentic. Be yourself. Don't be concerned about what others might think (we know that is sometimes difficult, but you owe yourself to try). Be real. Don't try to be the "want-to-be" you. Let people see, and get to know *you*.

- Know what you have to offer. Begin conversations with people and tell them what you have to offer. Be bold! Be fearless! Speak intelligently and have interesting things to say (about you, your profession, current events, etc.).

- Have a 30-second elevator speech ready. This is a quick marketing response for the question most often asked (but often not taken advantage of), "What do you do for a living?" Your response to this question needs to clearly describe what you can do for an employer and that you are currently seeking career opportunities. Remember, you are currently in a selling position, and you are the product. Why should someone hire you? What do you offer that others don't? As an executive, what successes have you had?

- Avoid closed-ended questions. Seek to get the other person to talk and then really listen. Instead of asking, "Do you know anyone who...?" ask, "Whom do you know that...?" This will allow for discussion and problem-solving instead of a one-word negative response that stops conversation.

- Use active listening skills. When the other person is talking, do not be considering your response in your head. Instead, just listen! Look into the speaker's eyes and give verbal and nonverbal clues that you are listening and understanding.

- How about calling someone who you do know and inviting them to go with you? That way, at least you will know one person and you won't be alone. Make a plan with them to meet two or three new folks. Make it into a game. "You meet two and I will meet two...that way we can introduce each other's two and know four." Check in with each other. Support each other, and then reward yourself for going to an event and meeting new people!

- If you are not comfortable with large events, try starting off with some smaller networking opportunities. Maybe it means getting involved with an association or group of folks where you can be on a council or committee. They tend to have smaller, more intimate meetings. Get to know some folks that way, so that when you do go to the larger events, you already know people.

- Whatever you do, don't come across as pushy. People sense desperation and neediness. It doesn't work and doesn't engage people. Don't be overly aggressive, follow people around, and just talk incessantly about what you have to offer. And please, *please*, don't just walk around passing your business cards out. This is NOT about how many cards you can pass out. It's about developing relationships with people.

Here is a tip to also keep in mind: Great networkers not only go to events (small or large) to promote themselves; they also go to contribute something to the people they meet. Be sure to know what you can contribute and listen to what they need. Just as you might be going to an event for additional contacts, they might be as well.

Perhaps you have a great contact for them. Maybe you know of someone who can help them solve their problem. Share your information with them as well. Consider how you might help others you meet. The old adage, "what goes around, comes around" has proven to be true. You may not get immediate help, but others will remember that you helped them and will talk well about you. Your reputation will grow and others will seek you out to help make connections and get information. Without a doubt, they will know whom to call when they discover your perfect job.

It's all about building relationships. Relationships are not built overnight. You cannot attend one networking event and say that networking does not work. Networking is a long-term career strategy that will pay huge dividends in your job search and later, in meeting your career goals. It's imperative that once you have a network established and get a job, you keep your networking contacts active. You won't necessarily have to attend all the networking activities. However, you need to find ways to stay in touch with those you have built relationships with. You never know when you'll need them again or become aware of better career opportunities through your network.

It is important that you establish your own personal database of networking contacts. Collect all those business cards of people who you have worked with in the past five years, friends from college and your neighborhood, family members, and others who have an interest in seeing you succeed. Using such contact management software as Outlook, create a list that allows you to communicate with them on a regular basis about your job search. As you meet new people in this process, continue to update your personal database.

Cory Edwards, professional resume writer and career coach, offers these techniques to make your networking more effective:

"First, begin with the end in mind. What is your purpose for networking? If it's to find a job, then we need to begin with an attitude check. The more desperate you are, the more desperate others will perceive you. This makes networking a pressure cooker for both you and those you come into contact with—this is not what you want. So instead, look at networking as an opportunity to not only get information, but also as an opportunity to help others and make connections between people. Take some of the pressure off by not asking direct questions. Don't put others on the spot. Instead of asking, 'Is your company hiring?' Ask, 'Do you know of any companies in your industry that are hiring?' Talk about 'companies like yours,' 'business owners like you,' or 'in your industry.' These phrases offer a more general approach and will not smell of desperation."

Here is a story illustrating successful networking: Chet was seeking an association CEO position. He pulled together a mailing list of more than 500 names, and sent a short cover letter and resume to each person letting them know that he was available for such a job. One of the letters landed on the desk of a hotel salesperson in Florida, where he had recently held a conference. Four days later, the elected president of a national association, who lived in Florida, was talking to his friend the hotel salesman and mentioned that his group was looking for a new CEO for their group based in Washington. The hotel salesperson pulled the letter and resume off his desk and said give this guy a call! Eight weeks later, Chet was CEO of the Passenger Vessel Association.

Having the techniques down is one thing, but where do you go to network? Job fairs and career fairs can be effective networking events. Keep in mind that others you meet there are in the same situation you are and are focused only on getting a job for themselves. However, many others may be willing to share leads and job search ideas. Also, the recruiters may not see you as matched for the job they are filling today, but may think of you in the future.

Every community has numerous opportunities to network. Chambers of Commerce, Toastmasters (learn while you network), clubs, lead share groups, networking groups, industry and trade associations, and community events are just some examples of great networking opportunities. Look in your local community papers and find out who, what, where, and when. Are you a current member of any professional associations or organizations? Do they have meetings in your location? Find out, and begin attending meetings. Get out in your community—finding a job *is* a 9-to-5 job! That's critical, because most job hunters spend only five hours per week searching for a job!

So you have decided to go out and network, and you know of three opportunities and two people to network with this week. What should you do with your resume? Simple: unless someone asks specifically for it, this is NOT the time to be distributing your resume. Remember, you are making contacts, developing your relationships, and giving and getting information. Certainly this is the time to collect business cards and talk with them about follow-up. Later, once you establish a relationship with them and ask them if it is okay to send them your resume, then and only then, send it.

Oh, one last tip: have fun! Look at it as a great way to meet new people, engage in conversations and to be passionate about who you are and what you have to offer. Set a goal and have fun with it. Challenge yourself.

Resumes and Informational Interviewing

Another networking technique, yet quite different, is informational interviewing. Informational interviewing is a screening process. You use this to screen careers, jobs, locations, industries, and employers before you change careers or accept employment with a new company or organization. It is also used to find answers to very specific questions that occur to you during your job hunt.

You conduct informational interviews with people who are in jobs you like, want to have, or think you want to have. You ask them about their job. You are trying to get information to help you make a career decision and at the same time increase your networking contacts. This is not an interview or a request to hire you. You do not conduct these interviews with those who have the power to hire you, you conduct these interviews with those who are doing work that you want to do. Do not take a copy of your resume with you to these interviews. It's not about you; it's about them!

If you have no specific questions to ask, try these:

- How did you get into this particular line of work?
- What educational/training requirements does someone need to succeed in this position?
- What things do you like the most about your job?
- What do you like least about your job?
- What's a typical day like for you?
- Who else is in this same line of work that you recommend I talk to?

Your objective in conducting an informational interview is to get answers and guidance for you to consider your career options. Once you have gathered information, you can process it and begin strategizing. Does this new information reinforce what you already know and the goals you have already set? Or does it cause you to reconsider your present course? Did any new thoughts or ideas come up over the course of your interviews? Are they worth investigating?

Create some next steps or action items as a result of these interviews. Then be persistent! Continue to do what you know to do. Target your resumes for specific jobs and audiences, properly create and submit online resumes, network, and conduct informational interviews. Separately, each technique yields results. All together, as a multipronged aggressive job search, you increase your odds and better your chances of obtaining your ideal job.

Because informational interviews have been so abused in the past, make sure you do not take your resume with you to an informational interview. According to Cory Edwards, "the most positive results are obtained when participants do not have their resumes, but follow up with it as requested." If you are able to produce a resume when asked at an informational interview, then the person you are interviewing knows you weren't serious about the interview, but desperate to get a job. And remember, you don't want to appear desperate! So instead, send your resume as a follow-up if requested.

Chapter Highlights

To recap the features of marketing your story, remember:

1. Take a proactive role in letting employers and people know that you are actively looking for a new position and what are your qualifications, special expertise, and in-depth experience.
2. More organizations are turning to the Internet to help them find suitable candidates for their job openings by using their own Websites as recruitment portals as well as turning to independent electronic resume databases.
3. The Internet, if used properly and wisely, can be a very effective and efficient way to market your story.
4. Depending on the circumstances, your resume information can be submitted or distributed electronically through several different options.

5. For your resume to rise to the top in electronic sorting and retrieval activities, it needs to contain key words and phrases.

6. Use a common business, sans serif font; eliminate all bolding, underlining, tabs, columns, italics, and centering; and do a trial run before posting your resume.

7. Look at electronic resumes and listings as only one of a number of marketing options.

8. Especially at the senior level, networking and informational interviews play important roles in the job search process.

9. Current studies show that about 85 percent of all jobs are filled through networking leads.

10. Networking isn't just about making a sale or getting a job. The main purpose for networking is to get and give useful information.

11. Know what you have to offer. Begin conversations with people and tell them what you have to offer.

12. Have a 30-second elevator speech ready.

Chapter 7 discusses overall standards for assessing and selecting a professional job search service as well as evaluating additional qualities of each individual service.

"Follow your instincts. That's where true wisdom manifests itself."
—Oprah Winfrey

CHAPTER 7

Use of Professional Services

"Our deepest fear is not that we are inadequate. Our deepest fear is that we are powerful beyond measure. It is our light, not our darkness that most frightens us. We ask ourselves, who am I to be brilliant, gorgeous, talented, and fabulous? Actually, who are you not to be?"
—*Nelson Mandela*

Chapter Overview

What if you realize that you cannot begin your resume because you are really not clear about what type of job you are seeking? What if you are having trouble with being concise and succinct in your resume phrasing and sentences? What if your targeted resume is ready to be distributed and you do not really know how to proceed to find your audience or market? These are only some of the reasons that may lead you to seek the help of a professional service provider.

Professional services for job seekers are wide and varied, however, three of the most commonly known groups are career coaches, resume writers, and executive headhunters/recruiters. Each professional service group has many practitioners with very diverse and extensive backgrounds in education/training, approaches/ philosophy, and experience. They can be in business for themselves or as part of a structured national or international job search service agency. How are you able to tell the "good ones" from the "bad ones"—that is, which are honest and capable, which may be just inept and not very helpful, or which are in it for the money and can cause you much grief and harm? Before contacting a practitioner, there are a number of steps you can and need to take to ensure that the service received is the most effective in helping you with your job search concerns or issues.

103

This chapter deals with strategies and guidelines for selecting the agency or individual practitioner that is not only qualified, but who best serves your needs and goals. Using one or more of these services helps you to better know what you want to do and where you want to do it, and to have the perfect targeted resume for conducting a successful job search campaign. Presented are overall standards for assessing a service, as well as any qualities specific to the service:

- Using a professional service.
- Selecting a professional service.
- Assessing additional qualities of a personal service.

Using a Professional Service

It is not unusual to turn to a family member, a close friend, or a colleague when needing help sorting out career and personal issues, help with your resume, and/or job leads or referrals. In many instances, this type of assistance can be very positive and productive because of their knowledge of who you are—including your strengths, weaknesses, interests, values, personal circumstances, and motivations. In many ways, they can provide insights, support, confirmation, and encouragement to keep you on track and progressing forward.

However, the personal relationship can also work as a disadvantage—feelings and biases may be a barrier to telling you the truth and helping you to face reality. In addition, they may lack the knowledge and expertise to guide you properly and effectively. Someone who does not do this type of work professionally may only be willing to advise you on a short-term basis rather than stay with you as long as it takes to resolve the issue or for you to achieve your goals.

The benefits of engaging a professional career/job search practitioner are working with an individual who:

- Is objective and without preconceived ideas of who you are as a person and a professional.
- Brings to the table specialized content knowledge, tools, resources, and the ability to challenge you to complete assignments and achieve your goals.
- Has the credentials to supply, conduct, and interpret needed or desired career and psychological assessment tests (such as MBTI, John Holland's Self Direct Search).
- Is able to make appropriate referrals or direct you to helpful resources (such as a dress consultant and job search directories).
- Has the training and capability to recognize the need for additional or another type of help (for example, if you need a career coach instead of a resume writer or if the concern is more psychological than career-oriented).

- Is able and willing to focus on short- and long-term needs, goals, and solutions.
- Brings a fresh eye to your situation and can make specific recommendations or suggestions based on experience.
- Provides for accountability for action and time management.

You may need a professional resume writer if you become frustrated by knowing your resume is not doing its job (if you are not receiving calls for initial interviews). It is possible, in only one or two sessions, for you to see where you went wrong and suddenly "get it," so that your marketing document projects your ideal professional image. Or you may seek the services of a coach when you know where you want to go but are not sure of how to get there. In this instance, you may need to work with the coach for several months.

Whether you are interested in the services of a coach, resume writer, or headhunter, the services are available either as private sessions (a format used by all three professional groups) or small group sessions (conducted by trained, experienced facilitators).

Private Sessions
- In person—meeting place is mutually agreed upon (not always in an office) with an average length of 45 to 75 minutes per session.
- By phone—with the availability of cell phones, sessions can take place any time of the day or in any time zones, and geography is no longer a factor, with an average time of 30 to 50 minutes per session.
- Through the Internet—an online service that is usually conducted by e-mail (which can result in delayed time between Q&A) and now more frequently via instant messaging, or "IM" (which provides access to real-time dialogue).

Small Group Sessions
- Networking and Support Group—for people in a job search mode whereby participants receive feedback on their job search and career management activities, business leads, and emotional support and encouragement in their efforts to attain their goals.
- Presentations—usually given on a particular aspect of career management or job search activities.

These options give you the choice of working either with a local professional or someone long-distance. Having choices gives you flexibility to set up sessions fitting your personal, family, and work schedules and obligations.

Before turning our attention to how to select a professional service, it may be useful to briefly describe the roles and functions of a career coach, resume writer, and a headhunter/recruiter in relation to your job search campaign. You then can decide how to make the best use of their services.

Although career coaches and resume writers differ in their purposes, specializations, and roles, the practices of these two professions can overlap. A career coach's focus, as you would expect, is to help clients manage their career—that is, making decisions, setting career goals and direction, determining options, developing a plan of action with bench marks, and evaluating progress. If needed, they can assist the client with their job search strategies and activities—that is, resume development, interviewing techniques, and salary negotiations. Some career coaches, even though competent resume writers, are not interested in using this skill and will make recommendations of one or two resume writers to help you at this point of your job search preparation.

A resume writer's primary role is to help clients develop their primary marketing tool for a job search campaign—that is, an individualized resume geared for a specific field or industry. Assistance ranges from starting from scratch and selecting the specific professional and personal bytes to be included to just tweaking or finessing language, format, and/or style a little bit. If needed, a resume writer can offer career advice and help with planning job search strategies and sharpening of job interview skills.

Recruiters and headhunters assist you in finding a job—that is, provide access to the employers looking for candidates with your credentials and experience, act as a third party and arrange for the initial interview, and give feedback on your status as a candidate. If needed, a recruiter can advise you on career matters and assist with the revising and polishing of your resume.

Selecting a Professional Service

How does one locate a reputable career coach, resume writer, or headhunter? To an extent, it is not much different than finding a good tax accountant, financial advisor, or personal trainer. Ask for recommendations from people whose judgment you trust and who have actually used the services of a professional with the expertise and experience you are seeking. Nevertheless, this technique does not always work, and the match may not be a good one. And even with a referral from your most respected colleague or trusted friend, there are steps to take and questions to ask to ensure that you have selected the right one for you. The key question is not "who is the best one?" The key question is, "Who is the best one for me?" And only *you* can answer that question.

Before beginning your search, be aware of exactly why you are willing to make this commitment to pay the required fees. Take some time to outline your objectives, goals, and expectations for seeking help. Are they clearly defined? Do you know the type of assistance you require to address and resolve your concerns and issues?

With the answers to these questions in hand, you can now start the selection process for hiring a professional to assist you in achieving the ultimate goal of a new professional beginning.

Hiring the Right Professional

Selecting a competent and reliable coach, resume writer, and/or headhunter can be an arduous and time-consuming task. This undertaking can be less taxing and more effective by carrying out the following steps:

- Find or receive three or four names. A referral is fine for identifying possible candidates and doing a comparison to others before making a final choice. Another way to locate candidates is through their professional associations, education, and certification programs. (Specifics of this selection method are discussed in the next section.) **Note:** It is not a good idea to speak with too many people; it can lead to confusion and slow down the selection process.

- Arrange for an interview. A good professional is willing to meet with you for an exploratory session and answer all your questions. A free agent may charge you a small fee for this time; ask up front if they do and what the charge would be. However, most professionals will consider the interview as a complimentary consultation. If you are meeting with a member of a firm, there is probably no fee.

- Review marketing and PR information. When arranging for an interview appointment, ask about the availability of marketing or PR information that can be mailed to you. A service firm/agency will have a prepared packet of information. A free agent may have a brochure describing their practice and services. Also, check out any individual or organizational Websites.

- Prepare a list of questions. Ask each candidate the same group of questions so that your comparison is based on the same criteria and standards. Suggestions for questions to include are:

    1. What are your services (free agent) or how does your program work (organization)?

    2. What are your qualifications or those of the members of your organization?

    3. How long have you been doing this type of work or what is the average number of years of experience for your staff?

    4. What is your success rate?

    5. What are your fees and how do you bill (per session or a flat fee paid up-front for a set number of sessions or service)? Are there different fee structures for different services?

    6. Am I required to contract for a minimum number of sessions or can we go session-by-session until closure is brought to the relationship?

    7. How often do you work with clients having similar situations or issues as mine? Can you give me an example of how you and a client worked together to achieve the client's goal? If you are

interviewing a resume writer, ask to see samples of resumes from your field or industry.

8.   Can I get a copy of the contract or agreement statement to read at home?

* Ask for references. Ask for the phone number or e-mail address of two former clients who had, if possible, similar concerns as yours. When in contact with them, ask them about the professional's attitude, consideration, and effectiveness. Find out what it was that they really liked about the individual or the firm/agency.

* Check credentials. Follow up on the qualification responses and get further information about their education, training, and certifications. What do all those initials behind their names stand for? Where were degrees and certifications received and are the institutions accredited or nationally recognized?

* Upon completion of interviews, sit down, review your interview notes, and ask yourself, "Who did I really feel comfortable and at ease with? Whose style, personality, and approach is a good match for me?" Then make your decision.

Assessing Additional Qualities of a Professional Service

In addition to the guidelines and steps previously outlined, each professional service has other specific qualities that should be reviewed before making your final selection. The individual professional associations for members of these service groups have established standards and ethics. They also provide public access to their membership directory to people seeking assistance to attain their career and job goals.

Career Coaching

In recent years, the numbers and areas of specialization in the coaching field have increased rapidly. There are coaches for all areas of your life, both personally and professionally: life, executive, retirement, communications, start-up businesses, and of course, the area addressed here, career coaching. As you begin your quest for a professional, be sure you have been given the names of coaches whose specialization is career management. Again, as with resume writers, it is not that a life or executive coach cannot provide assistance with career issues, but it is not their primary expertise area or interest.

There is a wide variety and diversified range of coaching, training, and certification programs. These preparation programs can range from a three-week course to a two-year commitment and focus on a variety of coaching approaches, philosophies, and techniques. Some certification program options are general, and some are specific for career coaching. An in-depth program will require a specific number of supervised coaching sessions. Although universities award degrees, professional associations or private institutes award the majority of certifications. Check into the creditability of a coach's certification awarded by a private business organization, regarding its reputation and respect in the coaching community.

To locate perspective career coaches or learn more about specific certifications or training programs, go to the following Websites:

Association of Career Professionals International: *www.acpinternational.org*

Career Coach Institute: *www.careercoachinstitute.com*

Career Masters Institute: *www.cminstitute.com*

International Coach Federation: *www.coachfederation.org*

National Board for Certified Counselors: *www.nbcc.org*

Specific career coaching qualities to look for in conducting your selection process include:

- Proposition of a program tailor-made for you in terms of tools, strategies, and/or assessment resources used—not a "one size fits all," generic career approach.

- Individual sessions are emphasized and group sessions serve to enhance or strengthen the one-on-one contact.

- Assessment tools and tests can be used in conjunction with coaching sessions, providing information and data that can be factored into the overall established plan of action, not as replacements to good coaching.

- Although it is not possible to predict the exact number of sessions needed or the length of time required to produce the desired results, a coach, based on the issue/problem and his or her experience, can and should give a general time frame.

- At the end of each session, assignments or homework is clearly understood and copies of exercises/tests are given before the session ends or sent by e-mail within 24 hours.

- Method and frequency of follow-up or feedback should be spelled out, such as e-mail updates, weekly.

Resume Writing

In the mid 1990s, professional resume writers emerged as a separate specialty from career coaching, and resume writing has grown rapidly as a consulting field. It also has its own certification programs. Qualifying for certification, in many instances, requires passing an examination and submission of actual resumes of clients for review by a panel of peers.

In addition to certification, knowing resume software programs, and having a good grasp of the English language and grammar, an effective resume writer needs some employment/business experience. An essential part of having the capability to create a powerful resume is the understanding of how to attract the attention of a recruiter or hiring agent. Also look to engage a practitioner familiar with your profession or industry's requirements and language.

To locate perspective resume writers or learn more about specific certifications or training programs, go to the following Websites:

National Resume Writers' Association: *www.nrwa.org*

Professional Resume Writing and Research Association: *www.prwra.com*

Specific resume writer's qualities to look for in conducting your selection process include:

* In your initial contact with a resume writing firm or agency, meet with the person who will be working directly on your document, not a person who handles the business end of the organization.
* Expect that much of the work on the part of the resume writer be done on the Internet, including loading and downloading of the document.
* Financial arrangements are such that a partial payment is made up front but the final payment is not made until your final approval of the document is given.
* At the conclusion of the working relationship, expect to receive an electronic copy or a CD, enabling you to make your own copies as needed.
* Contractual agreement includes a clause allowing for future changes or updates either included in the original set fee or at a reasonable additional cost.
* Expect to bring a copy of your latest resume, to be quickly reviewed and briefly critiqued for a price quote.
* When asking for resume samples, look to see that they are not template documents, but appear to be tailored to the client's needs and situation.
* Minimally, the process of resume writing involves drafting a resume, returning it to you for further review and revisions, another drafting, again sending it to you for any additional changes, and developing a final copy.
* Specific suggestions and recommendations are made, and if needed, examples of how the problem was resolved for other clients are provided.

Note: The following association has listings of both career coaches and resume writers for you to contact:

Professional Association of Resume Writers & Career Coaches: *www.parwcc.com*

Recruiting/Headhunting

The terms *recruiters* and *headhunters* are used interchangeably. For some people, the term "outplacement" is the same as recruitment and headhunting. However, outplacement specialists are retained by organizations to help their employees manage their careers or prepare them for a job search when a downsizing or layoff has occurred. Unlike the career coaching and resume writing fields, third-party recruitment offers few certification programs for their members.

Many people come into this profession as career changers transitioning from such areas as the military or human resources. Another difference between them is that most recruiters are part of a formal structured business operation, rather than acting as free agents. Many of these firms are large, have branch offices in cities throughout the United States, and serve an international clientele. As a senior-level professional, using this service is most likely your primary means of accessing the organizations looking for candidates with your qualifications and of your caliber.

When registering with a recruiter or headhunter you need to be aware that although they assist candidates in finding new positions, their efforts and actions are really directed towards finding and qualifying new employees for their organization clients. Your resume will only be submitted for a specific opening if you closely match the requirements and appear to be a strong candidate. However, to increase your chances for your resume to be submitted, most recruiters are able to help you improve your job search tools and strategies.

There are two types of executive recruiters or headhunters:

1. **Contingent Recruiters:** These are practitioners who are only paid when their candidate is selected and hired. They usually work on middle-professional or management-level assignments. If a recruiter has a strong and long-term relationship with an employer, they can be given some senior-level openings to fill.

2. **Retained Recruiters:** These are practitioners who usually have an exclusive agreement with their employer clients and are paid for their searches and continue to submit resumes until the position is filled or the client cancels the order. Recruiters work on finding suitable candidates for middle-management to senior-executive levels. They will also help the client to write the job specs and develop the compensation package.

To locate prospective recruiters or headhunters, go to the following Websites:

Association of Executive Search Consultants: *www.aesc.org*
National Association of Executive Recruiters: *www.naer.org*

Specific recruiter's qualities to look for in conducting your selection process include:

♦ A common practice of recruiters is to place blind ads, because the identification of the employer needs to remain confidential. In making a decision to respond, how can you know if it is a legitimate ad or one with a purpose to attract more resumes to a database for possible future use? A legitimate ad lists specific position requirements (for example, "10 years' experience in curriculum development") and includes information on the type of company (such as "an international food and beverage corporation") that it represents, while other ads contains ambiguous, vague, and/or general phrases applicable to many fields and industries (such as, "experience in training" or "a consumer product company").

♦ Resumes are filed according to a set classification system. If possible, find out the heading your resume is filed under and if you are not satisfied, inquire if it can be reclassified.

- Resume databases are maintained and updated. How often do they contact candidates to learn if they are still available and interested?

- Recruiters prefer to work with currently employed candidates, because their employers feel this denotes success and strong self-esteem.

- Upon obtaining your new position, keep the recruiter up-to-date with any promotions you may receive and other accomplishments. They like to remain in touch with people they feel are on the move and track their career progress.

- Recruiters can initiate contact with you, because they were referred to you by someone who knows you or because of your professional reputation. When setting up a time to talk further about the opportunity and your qualifications, try to obtain as much information as possible regarding job description and requirements, and to whom you would report. Revise your targeted resume accordingly before submission.

Chapter Highlights

To recap Chapter 7, the key concepts of strategies and steps for selecting and using professional services are:

1. Professional services for job seekers consist of three basic professional groups: career coaches/consultants, resume writers/coaches, and executive headhunters/recruiters.

2. Be aware of exactly what you want to happen as a result of using the service before making the commitment and paying the required fees.

3. Hiring the right professional involves the following steps: obtaining three or four referrals, setting up screening interviews, preparing a list of questions, asking for references, checking credentials, making comparisons, and choosing your practitioner.

4. Both career coaching and resume writing have a wide variety of education, training, and certification programs, many of which can be checked out by using the Internet.

5. In addition to some shared qualities and characteristics, each group has their own qualities that need to be taken into consideration when conducting your selection process.

6. Practitioners can be located through your network of family, friends, and/or colleagues, as well as by using their professional association's membership directory.

The Conclusion provides our final comments and thoughts regarding our storytelling and marketing approaches, as well as our philosophy regarding resumes for senior-level professionals.

> *"If you limit your choices only to what seems possible or reasonable,*
> *you disconnect yourself from what you truly want, and all that is left is compromise."*
> *—Robert Fritz*

CONCLUSION

"We must become the change we want to see in the world."—Gandhi

Although this book is geared toward developing senior-level resumes, we felt that it was imperative to also address several other issues relevant to your resume and your job search, including:

- The changing world of work.
- Managing your career for increased satisfaction.
- Keeping your resume and career management up-to-date.

The world of work is very different today than it was even five years ago. Major corporations are downsizing every day. Pick up any newspaper in any city and you will hear about another consolidation, no matter what the industry. It's on every newscast and in every magazine. Positions are being eliminated and/or restructured.

Because of this, *you* must take charge of your own career. You cannot wait for your employer to tell you how to enhance your marketability and employment opportunities. If you wait, it might be too late. You must take responsibility and develop a plan with action steps to move yourself forward in your career.

Especially after 9/11, we have found in our career coaching practices that more and more of our clients want to manage their career for enhanced satisfaction. They want to make a difference and want to feel more fulfilled than ever before. Here are some suggested tips to manage your career so you will be more satisfied in whatever you choose to do:

- Find your passion. No matter what it might be, enjoy what you do. Whether you are staying within your career field and looking for a new job or looking to change careers altogether, discover what you find to be meaningful for you. What do you feel passionate about? What creates energy for you and what fits into your "personal mission" statement? Doing what you love for a living will more likely cause less stress and physical illness. Do what you love and you *will* do it well.

- Think of yourself as a "free agent" or self-employed. As stated previously, you cannot expect your employer to manage your career for you. Even if you work for someone else, you must do it. Today you must be able to know what you have to offer and market yourself as a "product." Just as your organization has marketing and strategic plans, so should you. Look at yourself as a consultant, even if within your current company.

- Continue to nurture your network. Develop a strategic plan that allows time for meeting with people you can look to for advice. Continue to expand your involvement in associations, organizations, etc., where you can meet "like-minded" people that will be able to assist you in increasing your network contacts. You want to surround yourself with people who are doing what you want to be doing. The continued growth of your network will also help when you are searching for a job. Don't wait until you are unemployed to develop what can easily be done now.

- Keep yourself current on trends. Whether you are currently searching for a job or not, know the trends that are happening in your industry. Read association publications, business journals, and the like. Keep yourself aware of what is happening. Not only will this help you in your current position, but it will help you feel more confident and knowledgeable when talking with individuals about a new position.

- Become even more valuable in your current organization. Seek out new ways to enhance your skills, take on a new project, or work with other folks who you might not otherwise. This is also a great way to learn what else is happening in your organization, which may lead to performing your current job more effectively.

- Keep a professional development folder to remind yourself of the events you attend, articles you have written, awards received, etc. Maybe keeping a journal of what you have accomplished would work for you. Whatever it takes to remind yourself of the experience and skills you have gained since you updated your resume last time, *just do it*!

- Balance your life outside of work with your personal life. Whether it be volunteer work, working with a religious community, learning a new hobby, traveling, or spending time with supportive significant others, find the time to relax, unwind, and recharge.

These are just a few tips to enhance your career satisfaction. Do whatever works for you. Just do something to enjoy what you do and feel good about it.

One more thought: keep your resume up-to-date. *Now* is the time to do this. Hopefully you have picked up some valuable information in reading this book. Other advice may come from your network, a mentor, or even other career management books. No matter what and where, though, do not procrastinate in preparing your resume. Don't wait until you have to scramble to collect the information and select the right words.

Finally, stories also can be an effective means of communicating your experience and accomplishments during an interview. According to Suzanne Lulewicz, "Stories are vital prior and during the job interview. Sincere, well-thought-out stories can powerfully communicate the direction you want your career to take and instill your vision and goals with the ethics you bring to your endeavors— something that has an intrinsic value, especially in this age of front-page corporate scandals. Stories are a valuable tool that tell the organizational interviewer what you know, what you believe in, and how good a match you will be for the culture of the company. Using what you've learned from *High-Level Resumes*, reflect, write, and connect with the audience that can offer you the job you have a passion and the skill to perform."

Our wish is that this book has inspired you to tell your story in an effective manner so that you achieve your ideal job and lead a fulfilling and meaningful life.

All the best!

—Marshall and Annabelle

"You are the storyteller of your own life, and you can create your own legend or not."
—Isabel Allende

APPENDIX

A

Descriptive
Professional Skills

This list of action verbs for work content skills, professional competencies, and transferable skills is for your reference in identifying the best descriptive word for the skill you want to include in your story. It can also be used to express the same skill with like words. To make it easier to locate the word that best describes your skill or competency, descriptive verbs were grouped according to focus of the action or type of outcome, therefore making the development of your job description and success statements more accurate and precise. In a number of instances, a descriptive verb can illustrate either work content expertise or a transferable skill, depending on the context of its use or if it is considered a primary or secondary skill.

Note: At the beginning of each category are two or three questions to help you start to focus on your most important and essential day-to-day responsibilities and target those for use in your resume.

Administration/Management

Describe the specifics of carrying out this skill:

How did you manage people, data, and/or things?
What type of decisions did you make?

Acted as	Consulted	Met
Administered	Dealt With	Prepared
Approved	Decided	Prioritized
Arranged	Delegated	Recommended
Assigned	Designated	Rewarded
Assisted	Directed	Scheduled
Attended	Downsized	Served as
Authorized	Enforced	Supported
Briefed	Facilitated	Undertook
Carried out	Functioned as	
Conducted	Managed	

Communication

Describe the specifics of carrying out this skill:

What methods of communication did you use?
What was the reason for communicating?
Who was your audience?

Addressed	Delivered	Published
Authored	Disseminated	Quoted
Briefed	Drafted	Recognized
Communicated	Drew up	Reported
Composed	Edited	Summarized
Convened	Gave feedback	Voiced
Corresponded	Met	Wrote
Critiqued	Presented	

Design/Planning

Describe the specifics of carrying out this skill:

What types of design or planning assignments were you involved in?
What were your responsibilities for resolving problems or concerns?

Activated	Designed	Launched
Addressed	Determined	Originated
Approved	Developed	Planned
Authorized	Diagnosed	Presented
Automated	Evaluated	Proposed
Built	Established	Redesigned
Collaborated	Formed	Resolved
Compared	Identified	Scheduled
Conceptualized	Illustrated	Shaped
Conceived	Implemented	Started
Created	Initiated	Structured
Customized	Instituted	
Demonstrated	Introduced	

Human Relations/Interpersonal Skills

Describe the specifics of carrying out this skill:

What has been your involvement in the staffing of the organization?
What responsibilities have you had for staff development and performance improvement activities?
How did you work with people either on a one-on-one basis or in groups/teams?

Addressed	Demonstrated	Hired
Advised	Developed	Instructed
Advocated	Downsized	Interacted
Assigned	Educated	Interfaced
Certified	Employed	Intervened
Coached	Encouraged	Interviewed
Collaborated	Evaluated	Lectured
Contracted	Facilitated	Litigated
Counseled	Guided	Mentored

Oriented	Reported	Taught
Packaged	Scheduled	Transferred
Partnered	Screened	Terminated
Recruited	Staffed	

Information Management

Describe the specifics of carrying out this skill:

What sorts of information did you work with?
What were your responsibilities for managing information?

Activated	Designed	Organized
Adapted	Developed	Produced
Assimilated	Diagnosed	Ran
Built	Handled	Scheduled
Composed	Illustrated	Solved
Computed	Implemented	Transacted
Created	Initiated	Utilized
Customized	Installed	
Demonstrated	Inventoried	

Leadership

Describe the specifics of carrying out this skill:

What was your role in organization development or strategic planning projects/activities?

What were your responsibilities regarding the financial well-being of the organization?

How have you contributed to the achievement of the organization's mission and purpose?

Advocated	Founded	Instilled
Chaired	Led	Instituted
Commanded	Mandated	Officiated
Convened	Monitored business	Presided
Defined expectations	ethics/values	Spearheaded
Envisioned	Influenced	Steered
Executed	Initiated	Took over
Exemplified	Inspired	Transitioned

Negotiations

Describe the specifics of carrying out this skill:

What was the conflict or issue that was the focus of negotiations?
What were your responsibilities in dealing with services goods or products?

Amended	Ensured	Moderated
Arbitrated	Facilitated	Negotiated
Assimilated	Forged	Prevented
Averted	Formalized	Reconciled
Bid	Interceded	Represented
Conciliated	Intervened	Resolved
Contracted	Litigated	Settled
Closed	Mediated	

Operations

Describe the specifics of carrying out this skill:

What day-to-day operations did you perform?
What were your financial responsibilities?
What projects and/or teams did you oversee?

Acquired	Divested	Processed
Appropriated	Estimated	Procured
Automated	Equipped	Programmed
Billed	Expedited	Purchased
Budgeted	Financed	Reconciled
Calculated	Formulated	Regulated
Capitalized on	Generated	Restructured
Carried out	Incorporated	Scheduled
Certified	Insured	Shut down
Charted	Issued	Supplied
Composed	Manufactured	Systematized
Computed	Merged	Teamed
Constructed	Operated	Transacted
Demonstrated	Ordered	Underwrote
Disbursed	Organized	
Diversified	Oversaw	

Persuasion

Describe the specifics of carrying out this skill:

For what type of situations or conditions have you been influential?
Who has been your audience?

Advocated	Lobbied	Promoted
Advertised	Marketed	Publicized
Campaigned	Motivated	Recruited
Closed	Presented	Sold
Convinced	Persuaded	Solicited
Demonstrated	Prevailed on	Targeted
Litigated	or upon	Won over

Research/Analysis

Describe the specifics of carrying out this skill:

What did you discover, improve on, or expand on?
What were the methods, tools, or resources used?

Activated	Customized	Interviewed
Addressed	Defined	Initiated
Analyzed	Demonstrated	Interpreted
Applied	Designed	Investigated
Appraised	Determined	Mapped
Assessed	Developed	Presented
Built	Diagnosed	Predicted
Calculated	Discovered	Reported
Charted	Disseminated	Researched
Collaborated	Estimated	Screened
Compared	Evaluated	Solved
Conceptualized	Examined	Studied
Conducted	Explored	Tested
Controlled	Formulated	Tracked
Constructed	Funded	Validated
Contracted	Identified	

APPENDIX B

Descriptive Personal Attributes

This list of personal attributes is for your reference in developing an introductory statement and describing professional or personal achievements. These descriptive words are helpful for carefully integrating personal characteristics into your resume, giving a multidimensional quality to you as an individual and, thereby, enhancing your story. They can also help clearly present and reflect on your professional summary statement, achievements, volunteerism, and personal attributes, for example.

Achiever	Diligent	Liberal
Adaptable	Discreet	Logical
Adventurous	Disciplined	Loyal
Astute	Driving	Methodical
Artistic	Dynamic	Meticulous
Big-picture focus	Entrepreneurial	Motivational
Candid	Farsighted	Multitalented
Change agent	Genuine	Objective
Conservative	Hands-on style	Open-minded
Competitive	High energy	Open to feedback
Cool under stress	Idea generator	Outgoing
Cost-conscious	Imaginative	Passionate
Creative problem-solver	Influence	Perceptive
Decisive	Intuitive	
Detailed	Level-headed	

Persevering
Persuasive
Practical
Precise
Proactive
Realistic
Resourceful
Resilient

Risk-taker
Self-sufficient
Sense of humor
Service-oriented
Sincere
Solid
Straightforward
Strong sense of conviction

Supportive
Tenacious
Theoretician
Think on my feet
Thorough
Versatile
Visionary
Warm

APPENDIX

C

Descriptive Achievement Results

This list of descriptive words is for your reference, to give more strength and power to telling the accomplishments part of your story. In the write-up of each achievement, these descriptive words can help you to quantify the results and/or explain your role in the resulting change. Some of these words are different forms of verbs listed in Appendix A. The use of a variety of words referring to the same intent or outcome has a greater impact on the reader.

Accelerated	Contributed	Forecasted
Accounted for	Converted	Formed
Acquired	Decreased	Formalized
Advanced	Devised	Furthered
Attained	Disposed	Generated
Awarded	Diversified	Improved
Benefited	Divested	Improvised
Boosted	Economized	Increased
Broadened	Effected	Inspired
Capitalized on	Eliminated	Instilled
Centralized	Enabled	Integrated
Completed	Enhanced	Learned
Condensed	Enlarged	Leveraged
Conserved	Expanded	Liquidated
Consolidated	Finalized	Lowered

Maintained

Mastered

Maximized

Merged

Minimized

Mobilized

Modified

Motivated

Mounted

Multiplied

Netted

Optimized

Originated

Overhauled

Partnered

Performed

Pioneered

Positioned

Predicted

Prevented

Produced

Projected

Raised

Reclaimed

Reduced

Rehabilitated

Rejuvenated

Remedied

Restructured

Resulted in

Retained

Revamped

Reversed

Revitalized

Saved

Secured

Simplified

Solidified

Spearheaded

Specialized

Stabilized

Standardized

Stimulated

Streamlined

Strengthened

Structured

Substantiated

Surpassed

Synthesized

Synergized

Systemized

Targeted

Trimmed

Tripled

Troubleshot

Turned around

Uncovered

Undertook

Unified

Upheld

United

Updated

Upgraded

Validated

Volunteered

APPENDIX

D

Headings for Resume Sections

A number of options exist for organizing information and data, depending on the professional image you want to project and the facts you want to emphasize. Some key headings can have subheadings. Information is placed and grouped in a way that you are comfortable with and that makes most sense to you. These are only suggested titles for your headings. If you have other thoughts regarding the heading for a section, then by all means use it. A good guideline is not more than five key headings.

Key heading options are grouped in one of two ways: by subject matter (such as "Introductory Statement" and "Skills/Competency") or for more than one similar qualification (for example, "Education and Training").

1. Introduction/Opening Summary Statement Headings

Professional Summary * Summary of Qualifications
Selected Career Highlights Profile * Qualifications Highlights
Career Overview * Background Statement * Professional Services

2. Skills/Competencies Headings

Skills * Relevant Skills and Experience * Core Competencies or Proficiencies
Qualifications * Capabilities * Specialized Abilities * Language Proficiencies
Proven Professional Strengths * Knowledge of * Areas of Expertise
Key Assets * Knowledge Encompasses * Core Professional Strengths
Special Strengths * Additional Skills or Knowledge

3. Work/Employment Experience Headings

Work Experience * Employment History * Employment Background
Professional History * Client Listing * Professional Experience Summary
Contract Assignments * Project Assignments * Additional Work Experience
Prior Experience * Prior Career Summary

4. Achievements/Accomplishment Headings

Achievements * Accomplishments * Key Achievements
Significant Accomplishments * Research Projects * Awards
Community Honors * Professional Recognition

5. Education/Training Headings

Education * Education and Training * Additional Courses and Training
Specialized Training * Certification * Licensures * Professional Licenses
Continued Professional Development * CEUs * Workshops and Conferences

6. Membership/Affiliation Headings

Professional Memberships * Professional Activities * Trade Associations
Professional or Membership Affiliations * Volunteerism * Community Involvement
Community Service * Civic Affiliations * Board Positions

7. Technical/Computer Skills Headings

(Use when these skills are not primary-level proficiencies, but germane to position.)

Technical Skills * Computer Skills * Software Programs Expertise
Internet/Web Savvy * Database Knowledge * Technical Qualifications

8. Additional Background/Experience Headings

Publications * Professional Writings * Presentations * Military
Foreign Languages * Patents * Security Clearances

Note: If your personal background contains information that would add an interesting dimension to you as an individual, include it as a biographical statement at the end of the resume, for example, "participation in long-distance races, come from a military family and lived and went to school in seven different countries." Suggested headings include:

Bio Summary * Personal Highlights * Personal Background

APPENDIX

E

Job Search Resources

In planning and conducting your job search, the availability of both print and Website resources—to help locate needed and/or desired information—is critical to a successful job search. The following resource listings will make it easier to locate the appropriate and related materials that meet your specific needs and help you find your ideal work situation.

Print Resources

Allen, Jeffrey. *The Resume Makeover*. **New York: John Wiley & Sons, 2001.**

This book includes 50 before and after examples from a wide range of fields illustrating what to do and not to do in creating a successful resume.

Bermont, Todd. *10 Insider's Secrets to a Winning Job Search*. **Franklin Lakes, N.J.: Career Press, 2004.**

Step-by-step guide to getting a job—fast. Gives the perspective from both sides of the hiring desk featuring a complete job hunting road map with directions that are logical and easy-to-follow.

Bolles, Richard N. *What Color Is Your Parachute?* **Berkley, Calif.: Ten Speed Press, 2004.**

One of the most widely known classic career management publications published annually. A practical manual containing a number of helpful exercises and worksheet that job hunters and career changers can use to facilitate their job search.

Critchley, Robert K. *Rewired, Rehired, or Retired.* **San Francisco: John Wiley & Sons, 2003.**

This is a global guide for the Baby Boomer generation's experienced workers who are now ready to explore other employment options rather than just retire completely from the work world. A combination of personal experiences, client experiences, and practical guidelines presented for people ready to plan their next phase of life.

The Directory of Executive Recruiters Annual Publication. **Peterbourgh, N.H.: Kennedy Information, 2003.**

The directory readers should turn to when searching for appropriate recruiters, because information is organized by job function, industry, geographical location, and individual specialties. Also included are guidelines for working with recruiters—both retainer and contingency firms.

Fry, Ron. *101 Great Answers to the Toughest Interview Questions.* **Franklin Lakes, N.J.: Career Press, 2000.**

Presents an overview of the interviewing process. One unique feature is that questions are grouped by chapter so as to cover a broad spectrum of topics with good and inappropriate replies. Reviews how to prepare for a job interview.

Fry, Ron. *101 Great Resumes.* **Franklin Lakes, N.J.: Career Press, 2002.**

Comprehensive sample of resumes covering all types of occupational, job, and career situations and categories including: out of work for many months, recently laid off, an erratic work history, and women in male occupations.

Isaacs, Kim and Karen Hofferber. *The Career Change Resume.* **New York: McGraw Hill, 2003.**

Written by the official resume writers for Monster.com and one if its career advisors, the book focuses on the need for career changers to reinvent themselves—create a new persona. More than 100 resume samples. Particularly useful is the discussion on how to leverage your success to transition from one career/industry to another.

Jackson, Acy and C. Kathleen Geckeis. *How To Prepare Your Curriculum Vitae.* **New York: The McGraw Hill Companies, 2003.**

Jackson and Geckeis give a detailed explanation of curriculum vitae components, as well as instructions for condensing your career into a concise bio sketch that is not only appropriate for academia positions but also for the professional in a career transition.

Kaplan, Robbie Miller. *How to Say It In Your Job Search.* **Paramus, N.J.: Prentice Hall Press, 2002.**

Provides the job seeker with the needed materials to write resumes and cover letters and to conduct a job interview. The reader is taken step-by-step through the process of choosing words, phrases, sentences, and paragraphs applicable for all job search activities.

Kleiman, Carol. *Wining the Job Game.* **New York: John Wiley & Sons, 2002.**

Kleiman sets out the rules for dealing with a changing economic and job markets as well as using headhunters and temp work to your advantage. One unique feature are the three chapters focused on what to do when out of work.

Krannich, Ronald L. *Change Your Job, Change Your Life*. **Manassas Park, Va.: Impact Publications, 2004.**

Featured in *U.S. News & World Report* as one of the top career books, this latest edition for leading readers through process of a successful career transition. Discusses and offers practical advise for recareering in today's "boom/bust" economy. Includes features such as the 100 best companies to work for, the 50 best cities with good job opportunities, relocation concerns, and job situations that will require new skills.

Krannich, Ronald L. and Caryl Krannich. *America's Top Internet Job Sites*. **Manassas Park, Va.: Impact Publications, 2003.**

Provides an overall view of doing an online job search, including both the pros and cons of using this approach to finding a job.

Marcus, John J. *The Resume Makeover*. **New York: McGraw Hill, 2003.**

Discusses 50 common problems with actual samples resumes and cover letters for each problem and presents suggestions and ways to fix them. Some of the common and frequent situations addressed are gaps in employment history, being fired, the age issue, job-hopping, and other resume weaknesses.

Montag, William E. *CareerJournal.com Resume Guide for $100,000+ Executive Jobs*. **Hoboken, N.J.: John Wiley & Sons, 2002.**

Montag presents an updated and expanded edition of his classic job search publication. Partnering with CareerJournal.com, he presents a three-step marketing strategy used successfully with his clients, including a 24/7 online job search plan. Throughout the book, case studies based on clients are integrated in the text.

Moses, Barbara. *What Next? The Complete Guide to Taking Control of Your Working Life*. **New York: DK Publishing, 2003.**

This manual shows you how to understand your career needs, face any challenge, and find work you'll love. It will help you discover your unique talents through assessment tools that identify your motivational type and show you how to make the right career decisions. Written by the world's leading career activist, *What Next?* is essential for anyone seeking career advice, direction, and work satisfaction.

Pontow, Regina. *Proven Resumes*. **Berkeley, Calif.: Ten Speed Press, 1999.**

Although an older book, the outstanding feature of this book is its listings of approximately 2,000 skills, by profession and field, with sample sentences for their use. For people who are doing professional shifts and changing careers, this book is very helpful.

Rafal, Marvin. *To Find A Job...Start A New Career*. **Kansas City, Miss.: Andrew McMeel Publishing, 2003.**

This is a practical guide to discovering and building a new career providing new challenges and new opportunities and allows one to have a more balanced life. Contains individual personality and other self-assessment inventories.

Satterthwaite, Frank and Gary D'orsi. *The Career Portfolio Workbook*. **New York: McGraw Hill, 2003.**

The authors explain how to create a career portfolio and the benefits of using one as a tool for a job search. They introduce a strategy for portfolio development: *PEAKS—* Personal Characteristics, Experience, Accomplishments, Knowledge, and Skills.

Taylor, Jeff. *Monster Careers: How To Land The Job of Your Life*. **London: Penguin Books, 2004.**

Readers are introduced to the Monster's *FAME* approach to career management and learn to: Think Like a Free Agent, Train Like an Athlete, Prepare Like a Marketeer, and Work Like an Entrepreneur. The book is based on the resources and data from Monster.com's Website.

Usheroff, Roz. *Customize Your Career*. **New York: McGraw Hill, 2004.**

Strategies are presented for taking responsibility for yourself and your future by being in charge of your career—to move up, move ahead, or move on. The author stresses a customized career development approach building on your authenticity.

***Weedle's Job Search: Guide to Employment Web Sites*. Stamford, Conn.: Weedle's, 2004.**

This book contains 250 employment-related Websites.

Whitcomb, Susan Britton. *Resume Magic*. **Indianapolis, Ind.: JIST Publishing, 2003.**

With almost 600 pages, *Resume Magic* is the most comprehensive and in-depth coverage for nuts and bolts of resume development, strategies, and usage. The reader is taken through a detailed resume writing process with "before and after" examples regarding the blending of marketing and business formats for a resume. Unique features include: applicant tracking software, a survey of what HR professionals want in a resume, and application of a copywriter's approach and formula to resume development.

Wilson, Robert F. *Executive Job Search Handbook*. **Franklin Lakes, N.J.: Career Press, 2003.**

Written for executives who are at a career crossroad and need to make some decisions about their next career move and job search. Includes strategies for coping with career change and transition as well as a number of interactive exercises to help with the process.

Wood, Lamont. *Your 24/7 Online Job Search Guide*. **New York: John Wiley & Sons, 2002.**

Provides a good introduction to the Internet job search resources, mechanics of conducting online job search, and building your online resume. Geared for people who have not had much experience using the Web for a job search campaign.

Standard Job Search Website Resources

4Work: *www.4work.com*

Low-cost online job posting service devoted to matching talent with opportunity.

A+Online Resumes: *www.ol-resume.com/*

Service provider for converting resumes to HTML and posting on their site, giving direct access to HR specialists and headhunters. Resume can be located either by job category or geographical locations. Efficient way of distributing resume as fee includes registration with many of the large search engines.

All Job Search: *www.alljobsearch.com*

A powerful and comprehensive job search engine. Searches leading job search sites, sorting by industry, keyword, and geographic locations.

America's Job Bank: *www.ajb.dni.us*

Job seekers can post their resume where thousands of employers search every day, search for job openings automatically, and find their dream job fast.

Career Builder: *www.careerbuilder.com*

The nation's leading recruitment resource, with presence in more than 130 local newspapers and more than 26 million unique visitors to its newspaper sites each month.

CareerJournal: *www.careerjournal.com*

Content comes from the powerful editorial resources of *The Wall Street Journal* and CareerJournal's editorial team. You'll find daily updates and thousands of archived articles detailing the news and trends that are critical to your job search and career advancement.

Career Magazine: *www.careermag.com*

Combines job postings from Usenet newsgroups into a searchable database. Career Magazine is a comprehensive online career resource with daily job updates, employer profiles, discussion groups, and news articles.

Career Resource Center: *www.careers.org*

Provides a comprehensive site for job information. It includes links to more than 1,300 career-related Websites including employers, news groups, colleges, and government job sources.

Direct Employers: *www.DirectEmployers.com*

Provides access to job and resume banks.

DiversityLink: *www.diversitylink.com*

Maintains both job and resume banks used by major corporations and headhunters.

Flipdog: *www.flipdog.com*

A multiuse job search site including articles, more than 300,000 listings, resume banks, resume critiquing, and a resource center.

Global Careers: *www.globalcareers.com*

An international job bank for finance, business, management, and transportation professionals and bilingual specialists.

Hoovers Online: *www.hooversonline.com*

A valuable search engine to identify potential employers.

Job Bank USA: *www.jobbankusa.com*

This site features U.S. and international job listings. A special feature lets users search any of the 12 largest job Websites.

Jobs.com: *www.jobs.com*

Conducts global job searches.

JobStar: *www.jobstar.org*

JobStar continues to enjoy support from **CareerJournal.com**, the career site of the *Wall Street Journal*. CareerJournal has joined with JobStar to offer users access to their excellent collection of career and job search information.

Metacrawler: *www.metacrawler.com*

Conducts searches through key words either single words or phrases to identify relevant sites.

Monster Jobs: *www.monster.com*

Search over 800,000 jobs, build and post your resume, and access thousands of pages of career info and advice.

NationJob: *www.nationjob.com*

This integrated network of Internet sites and services is consistently ranked among the top employment sites on the Web.

Recruiters Online Network: *www.ipa.com*

This site gives you the opportunity to give visibility to your resume in front of approximately 8,000 headhunters globally.

ResumeAgent: *www.resumeagent.com*

Posts resumes to 30 leading job sites. Will do a targeted e-mail broadcast.

ResumeZapper: *www.resumezapper.com*

Distributes resumes for job seekers only to recruiters in their industry and targeted geographic locations.

Vault: *www.vault.com*

Site's main feature is its comprehensive major topic or subject matter headings and subheadings. Publications created by this group are available for purchase.

Wetfeet: *www.wetfeet.com*

One of the easiest sites to conduct research on, because linkage sites are grouped by subject, for example, Careers and Industries, Salary and Perks, Companies, International. You can also purchase their job search and career publications at the site.

Work Tree: *www.worktree.com*

The largest job search portal in the world. The most complete and up-to-date research tool for the online job seeker.

Yahoo! Hot Jobs: *www.hotjobs.com*

HotJobs' tools and advice put job seekers in control of their careers and make it easier and more cost-effective for recruiters and employers to find qualified candidates.

Executive Job Search Website Resources

6FigureJobs.com: *www.6figurejobs.com*

Leading online resource for connecting senior managers with motivated employers and recruiters. View thousands of prescreened $100K+ opportunities from top-tier firms.

Boyden Global Executive Search: *www.boyden.com*

Recruits senior executives for permanent and interim assignments in all fields and industries.

CEOExpress: *ceoexpress.com/html/careerframed.asp*

CEOExpress Company has been featured in many of the world's most influential business magazines including *Fortune, Bloomberg, Business Week, Fast Company, Wired* and most recently, *Forbes*, where it was named among the "Best of the Web."

CEO Update: *www.associationjobs.com*

CEO Update reports on senior-level job opportunities in nonprofit organizations.

Christian & Timbers: *www.ctnet.com*

Tenth largest recruitment organization in the United States, specializing in technology and life sciences.

Dahl-Morrow International: *www.dhinte.com*

Specializes in recruitment for high-tech, financial services, education, and telecommunications.

Dinte Resources: *www.dinte.com*

Focuses on intelligence, defense, security, and high-tech employers.

ExecuNet: *www.execunet.com*

Celebrating 16 years of service, ExecuNet has helped more than 150,000 executives succeed and 15,000 recruiters connect with top quality candidates.

Executive Advisors: *www.executive-advisors.com*

Executive advisors provides a complete and confidential marketing service for senior executives planning to make a career change.

Executive Jobs: *www.jobsreport.net*

A subscription site focused on sales and marketing jobs up to $300K, Executive Jobs also offers a free resume evaluation service.

Executives Only: *www.executivesonly.com*

North America's most powerful executive employment network.

ExecutiveRegistry: *www.executiveregistry.com*

Provides free electronic newsletter for executive-level job seekers. Allied with **CareerJournal** of *The Wall Street Journal*.

Futurestep.com: *www.futurestep.com*

Futurestep is a global leader in middle-management recruitment. It provides customized recruitment solutions to employers, and offers candidates access to exclusive job opportunities around the world.

Headhunter.net: *www.headhunter.net*

One of the largest Websites devoted to headhunting firms, specializing in middle- to top-level positions.

HotJobs2000: *www.hotjobs2000.com*

Technology executive search engine.

Interim Executives: *www.imcor.com*

Offers contract positions for executives starting at $75K. Some opportunities for conversion to a permanent position.

JDG Associates: *www.jdgsearch.com*

Focuses on associations, information technology, healthcare, accounting, and finance organizations.

JobHuntersBible.com: *www.jobhuntersbible.com*

This site is designed as a supplement to the 2004 edition of *What Color Is Your Parachute? A Practical Manual for Job-Hunters and Career-Changers*, published by and available from Ten Speed Press. It is particularly helpful ias a supplement, as there is much that is covered there that cannot be covered on the site.

JobseekersNetwork: *www.jobseekersnetwork.com*

Resume distributor/manager for 100K+ search engines, free job search toolbar, and weekly job notifications.

Korn/Ferry International: *www.kornferry.com*

One of the four largest headhunting companies with global opportunities in public and private companies, government, and nonprofits. Job seekers can videotape interviews.

MBA Management: *www.mbamanagement.com*

Specializes in construction, real estate, and land development companies.

McCormick Group: *www.mccormickgroup.com*

Particularly focuses on government and professional services job opportunities.

Monster Jobs: *www.monster.com*

Search more than 800,000 jobs, build and post your resume and access thousands of pages of career info and advice. To search executive jobs, click on "Job Search" and choose "Executive Management" from the "Choose Job Category" list.

Personnel Decisions International: *www.pdi.com*

Provides career management services for executives including, executive assessment, job search support, and coaching.

Quintessential Careers: *www.quintcareers.com/executive_jobs.html*

Find career and job sites that specialize in assisting executives and top managers.

Ritesite.com: *www.ritesite.com*

RiteSite's purpose is to provide the strongest and most comprehensive possible help to job-hunting and career-building executives.

Russell Reynolds Associates: *www.russellreynolds.com*

One of the four largest headhunter agencies globally, working with executive job seekers across all fields and industries.

SearchFirm: *www.searchfirm.com*

Publishes free online executive recruiter's directory.

Spencer Stuart: *www.spencerstuart.com*

One of the four largest headhunter agencies globally. Publishes directories of executive recruiters.

The Ladders: *www.theladders.com*

The Ladders is a group of industry-focused job newsletters providing hundreds of $100K+ jobs weekly.

USAJOBS Senior Executive Search: *jobsearch.usajobs.opm.gov/ses.asp*

USAJOBS provides worldwide job vacancy information that is updated each day from a database of more than 17,000 worldwide job opportunities.

WEDDLES.com: *www.weddles.com/jobcatalog.htm*

WEDDLE's has conducted groundbreaking surveys of recruiters, job seekers, and Websites providing employment-related services on the Internet. Its findings and other research have been cited in such publications as *The Wall Street Journal, Money, Fortune,* and *Inc.* magazines and on national television and radio shows, including *CBS This Morning, The Today Show,* and *Bloomberg Financial News*.

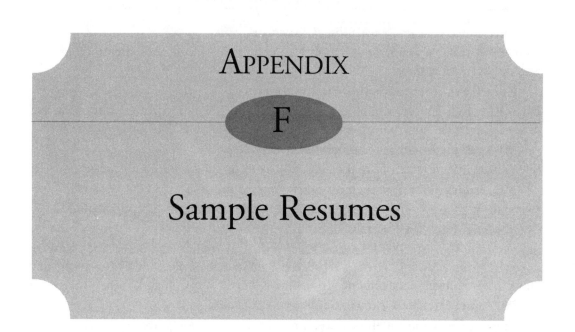

APPENDIX

F

Sample Resumes

RICHARD BOESCH

2001 Rockwood Terrace ~ Vienna, VA 22182 ~ rmboesch@aol.com ~ 703-281-7043

PROFESSIONAL PROFILE

Experienced and proven Human Resource Professional with record of significant accomplishments and contributions. Demonstrated ability to galvanize teams to achieve ambitious results. Expertise in labor and employee relations, negotiations, performance management, and training and development. Especially strong in developing policy, procedures and programs, which support, enhance and strengthen business initiatives.

EDUCATION

MBA, California State University, San Francisco, CA
Juris Doctor, George Mason University, Fairfax, VA

CORE COMPETENCIES

Labor Relations	Performance Management	Policy Development
Employee Relations	Employee Training & Development	Subject Matter Expert

SELECTED ACCOMPLISHMENTS

❑ Collaborated in 2002 National negotiations successfully achieving strategic, operational and tactical bargaining objectives for the Internal Revenue Service.

❑ Deployed web-based National Agreement Resource Center, providing immediate, up-to-date information to all IRS managers.

❑ Reviewed and revised 9 comprehensive internal labor and employee relations manuals.

❑ Developed and published 2 guides; ethics and conduct for employees, and good conduct and disciplinary measures for managers.

❑ Key architect for Vice-President's National Performance Review, making significant contributions on the National Partnership Council Planning Group.

❑ Designed and spearheaded implementation of DoD's Administrative Grievance System, Performance Appraisal System, and Awards Program and published all appropriate guidelines.

❑ Conceived, initiated and implemented first-ever information sharing system for all DoD agencies, providing current, up-to-date information and policy changes for human resource professionals.

❑ Managed DoD Labor Relations program, providing DoD-wide program advice and guidance governing a workforce initially numbering over 1 million employees.

WORK HISTORY

Internal Revenue Service, Washington, DC   2001 – 2004
Chief, Workforce Relations

- Design, develop, coordinate, implement, monitor and administer employee and labor relations policies, programs and procedures serving a workforce of 120,000 union and non-union employees.
- Direct, coordinate and manage work of 16 employees and 2 managers, ensuring compatibility and consistency with current guidelines and programs and adherence to all applicable laws and regulations.
- Conduct comprehensive operational and program reviews, recommend necessary actions, revisions, and changes.
- Oversee and review all local and national negotiations and agreements.
- Manage and allocate $1.2 Million office budget.
- Advise senior management on labor relations issues, goals, and status.
- Designed, developed and delivered various training sessions for diverse employee populations.
- Collaborated to effectively train over 300 HR professionals who subsequently trained 10,000 managers.

- Benchmarked Employee Relations Program by researching and examining best practices of other agencies. Compiled and analyzed information in comprehensive report.
- Significantly streamlined several operational processes, which resulted in cost savings.
- Managed a comprehensive, automated labor and employee relations tracking system, providing real-time case status.

Department of Defense, Washington, DC   1980 – 2000
Deputy Director, Workforce Relations
- Developed policies and procedures in labor relations, performance management, awards, employee relations, and grievance procedures that were implemented nationwide.
- Developed and/or collaborated in the development of government-wide legislation, executive orders, regulations, and demonstration projects making recommendations for approval, disapproval and revisions.
- Initiated legislative and regulatory reforms regarding performance management and award systems.
- Consulted with unions and provided advice and guidance to managers on labor relations issues.
- Conducted comprehensive research on unusually difficult and unusual labor relations issues, analyzing all sides and developing policy and recommendations for effective resolutions.

Department of Treasury, Washington, DC   1978 – 1980
U.S. Air Force, Washington, DC   1973 – 1978
Labor Relations Specialist
- Performed full range of labor relations duties, including developing and implementing policies and programs, reviewing labor agreements and proposed policy changes, advised and counseled regarding labor and employee relations issues, and conducted training initiatives.
- Collaborated to develop and institute labor relations reforms and legislation.
- Prepared Agency position papers on major policy issues.
- Advised management on short- and long-term implications of proposed regulations and policy changes and revisions.
- Reviewed unfair labor practice charges and complaints, providing guidance and resolutions.

U.S. Air Force, Dugway Proving Grounds, Dugway, UT   1970 – 1973
Employee Relations Specialist
- Served over 3,000 employees, providing guidance and expertise in labor relations, employee discipline and grievances, performance management and awards, equal employment opportunity, and employee motivation and counseling.
- Processed employee grievances and appeals, ensuring timeliness and completeness.
- Assisted in designing creative resolutions and recommended appropriate actions.
- Designed and aided implementation of creative work environment to improve morale and increase productivity and effectiveness.
- Advised employees and managers of rights and responsibilities.
- Served as negotiation team member.

PROFESSIONAL DEVELOPMENT

Distinguished Graduate, US Air Force Officers Training School
Basic Placement and Employee Relations
Management Development Seminar
Leadership for a Democratic Society, Federal Executive Institute

MAJOR AWARDS

Defense Medal for Exceptional Service, Office of the Secretary of Defense
Civilian Career Service Award, Office of the Secretary of Defense
Honor Award, Office of the Secretary of the Treasury

Christine S. Sunnis

50201 Bluemont Square • Broomfield, CO 80038 • (303) 712-3975 • csunnis@juno.com

PROFESSIONAL SUMMARY

Dynamic IT executive with demonstrated expertise in analysis, design, development, test and support of complex software systems. Twenty years' proven excellence in IT environments, providing management and leadership for troubleshooting and resolutions, technical requirement interpretations, life cycle project management and technical guidance. Strong project management skills and visionary team leader. Proficiency in building strategic alliances and providing customer service that exceeds expectations.

EDUCATION

OCP8i™ DBA Certification, Aurora, CO (Anticipated 3/2005)

Master of Science, Management Information Systems, 1993, American University

Bachelor of Science, Computer Science, 1988, American University

TECHNICAL EXPERTISE

Hardware:	HP 9000series, Sun, StarServer FT 3000, Sequoia, IBM 3090/4381, IBM PCs and compatibles.
OS:	UNIX (TOPIX, SVR4/5, HP-UX Solaris) Windows 95, 98, NT, 2000, CICS CMS, MVS/ESA, MS-DOS
Networks:	TCP/IP, X.25
Languages:	FOCUS 4GL, OS/JCL, PASCAL, HTML, SQL
Software Tools:	Veritas Vista REPLAY, XRunner, Exceed, all CLEAR, ABC FlowCharter, Sablime, Compas, PVCS Tracker, DDTS, XWindows, Norton Ghost, ImageCast, PCAnywhere, MS Office 2000

RELEVANT PROFESSIONAL WORK HISTORY

Avant Grey, Bluster, CO   **Director, Information Systems**   2000 – 2001
- Tested multimedia-messaging products as director of Applications Group.
- Significantly reduced time to market and verified products to specifications.
- Modified existing testing procedures and ensured product enhancements did not impact functionality.
- Performed quality and consistency tests throughout phased development cycles.
- Successfully provided project management driving projects from inception to on time and within budget guidelines and requirements.
- Wrote and executed test plans and test cases and wrote defect reports.
- Conceived and implemented improved testing procedures significantly streamlining processes.
- Proactively contributed to all team efforts, ensuring project completions and quality products and results.

Qusar Diamond, Denver, CO   **Test Engineer**   1999 – 2000
- Tested intranet applications running in a clustered environment consisting of NT and UNIX servers.
- Performed system and interoperability testing, completing all processes, procedures designed to achieve Capability Maturity Model (CMM) Level 2 certification.
- Successfully implemented the use of DDTS tool for tracking software anomalies.

Christine S. Sunnis

BlueGlobe Technologies, Westminster, CO   **Test Engineer**   1999 – 2000
- Member of self-directed team tested stand-alone PC-based configuration tools used by international sales force to order Business Communication System products.
- Defined customer profiles and test strategies.
- Successfully implemented test plans and produced summary reports.
- Used source control software, bug-tracking software and test-tool development.
- Performed Quality Factor Assessment process verifying, measuring, and assessing quality.
- Executed test cases, diagnosed and resolved problems and generated problem reports.

Deere International, Columbus, OH   **System Test Coordinator**   1996 – 1999
- Tested customized network traffic management products for global customers in Europe, Asia and Latin America.
- Coordinated testing efforts of team for multimillion-dollar project in India involving installation of real-time traffic management software; provided and ensured smooth deployment.
- Planned system tests interval, established environment and executed test cases to ensure product compliance with Y2K efforts and ISO 9001 requirements.
- Utilized SQL to validate user screen output against database.

Summit Group, Somerset, NJ   **Test Engineer**   1995 – 1996
- Developed, coordinated and implemented automated testing procedures on performance analysis and surveillance products running AT&T / NCR 3000 series platforms.
  Telephone Network Traffic Management Project (NetMinder)
  - Introduced fully automated testing process using XRunner significantly reduced life cycle testing time requirements.
  - Served as Project Manager, coordinated all phases of testing, verification and documentation in collaboration with AT&T test team.
  - Developed independent system test plan for software porting from AT&T / StarServer FT R3000 platform to AT&T / NCR 3500 series platform.
  Telecommunication Multi-Functional Operations System Project (MFOS)
  - Performed automated system and regression testing on surveillance and operations system for international network switches.
  - Developed regression-testing baseline that facilitated the implementation of automated testing using Veritas Vista REPLAY.
  - Successfully completed final phase of project porting software from HP-UX 9000 platform to AT&T / NCR platform.

Research Analysis, Potomac, VA   **Quality Assurance**   1993 – 1995
- Coordinated testing of enhancements to database application monitoring worldwide transportation and logistics programs.
- Developed system test plan and coordinated test efforts, ensuring operability and quality within customer specifications.

American University, Washington, D.C.   **Senior Programmer**   1983 – 1993
- Designed, coded, tested and documented alumni, financial, and decision support programs.
- Analyzed customer requests, designed and developed software solutions that supported and enhanced fundraising efforts and results.
- Collaborated in the conversion of systems from Wang MV 2200 to IBM 3090 mainframe without loss or corruption of data.
- Converted programs from BASIC to FOCUS 4GL.

STEVEN A. LANSING, C.P.M.

778 Hill Drive • Boston, MA 55555 • 555-555-5555 • salansing@aol.com

SENIOR MANAGEMENT - PROCUREMENT

Supply Chain & Materials Management in ISO-9001 Manufacturing Environment

Certified Purchasing Executive with expertise that contributes long-term value to the purchasing/procurement process. Five-year career distinguished by consistent track record of adding to bottom-line profitability through cost and cycle time reductions, long-term supplier agreements and streamlined sourcing functions. Well versed in quality issues related to oil and gas equipment manufacturing with strong qualifications in planning/scheduling manufacturing software, BOM creation/maintenance and computerized inventory management. Recognized for leadership and team-building strengths. Technical competencies: Job Boss (ERP), Alliance Manufacturing for Windows (MRP), Cincom Manage for Manufacturing and Crystal Report Writer.

- *Just-in-Time (JIT) Purchasing*
- *Inventory Management/Forecasting*
- *Contract Negotiations/Management*
- *Cycle Time Reduction*
- *ERP & MRP Systems*

- *Materials Replenishment Ordering*
- *Vendor Sourcing*
- *Cost Analysis/Cost Reduction*
- *Specification Compliance*
- *Supplier Consolidation/Standardization*

PROFESSIONAL EXPERIENCE

Morgan Industries, Boston, MA   **1985 to Present**

Vice President – Supply Chain & Quality

Transformed purchasing function into value-added, strategic department by driving a 7% increase in bottom-line profitability at a multibillion-dollar global manufacturing leader in the environmental technology industry. Manage procurement of industrial commodities, services, MRO supplies and equipment critical to production and projects; annual purchasing volume exceeds $4 million.

Team with engineers, project managers and finance staff to plan and coordinate equipment design, specifications, project cost analyses and material lead times; build and lead cross-functional teams for strategic purchases.

Key Achievements:

Cost / Cycle Time Reductions

- Led successful initiative to lower costs and cycle times in the acquisition of materials and equipment without compromising quality. Exceeded goals by reducing inventory nearly $200,000, decreasing material lead time 50-70%, cutting core supplier list 75% and reducing hard costs 25%.
- Facilitated 41% reduction in machining expenses by developing subcontract partnership that slashed lead time 35% and resulted in a significant increase in quality.
- Cut lead time 50% and saved 26% on standardized equipment purchases by streamlining management of annual contracts and supplier partnerships.

Vendor / Supplier Selection & Negotiation

- Challenged to deliver a 50% increase in subcontractor capacity, introduced more than $300,000 in anticipated savings, reduced lead time by 14 days.

STEVEN A. LANSING, C.P.M.
PAGE 2

Vice President – Supply Chain & Quality continued...

- Streamlined ordering processing through parts standards, BOM templates, product classes and approved vendors; implemented Supplier Qualification and Performance Tracking System to meet ISO-9001 requirements for quality/manufacturing standards.

- Established mechanical and electrical MRO supplier contracts that upgraded order-processing cycle for production staff and reduced material costs 25% while enhancing order accuracy and eliminating purchase order issues.

Sourcing

- Created and manage Preferred Supplier and Equipment systems to reinforce ISO-9001 standards throughout organization and to provide a comprehensive cross-reference database of parts, suppliers and costs. Positive results include a 10-25% cost reduction in valve, electrical and instrumentation materials.

- Achieved outstanding results after outsourcing time-consuming machining and component processing projects that detracted from production and wasted labor time.

Inventory Management / Planning

- Developed automated tracking and forecasting analysis tool, using spreadsheet query analysis and Crystal Reports, to provide immediate access to inventory values, usage and material cost variances.

- Cross-functional team member in the on-time implementation of Job Boss ERP manufacturing software. Led team to install, train users, populate database and set up standard Bill of Materials.

Quality Management

- Selected to function concurrently as Quality Manager, ensuring that ISO-9001 standards are met and maintained by monitoring quality, operations and documentation processes.

- Accountable for supplier qualification and performance/quality audits, equipment source inspection to applicable design codes, creation of quality/inspection documentation for project and design code requirements and material/equipment compliance to purchasing/outsourcing specifications.

EDUCATION / CERTIFICATION

M.B.A.
B.S., Business & Finance Management
BOSTON UNIVERSITY, BOSTON, MA

Certified Purchasing Manager
American Production and Inventory Control Society

AFFILIATIONS

National Association of Purchasing Management (NASPM)
American Production and Inventory Control Society (APICS)
American Society for Quality (ASQ)

ALEXIS BROWN

589 Fernleaf Street
Croton, NY 10520

(555) 555-5555   sjaa4@aol.com

CAREER PROFILE

Strategic **Human Resources Executive** and proactive business partner to senior operating management to guide in the development of performance-driven, customer-driven and market-driven organizations. Demonstrated effectiveness in providing vision and counsel in steering organizations through accelerated growth as well as in turning around under-performing businesses. Diverse background includes multinational organizations in the medical equipment and manufacturing industries.

Expertise in all generalist HR initiatives:

Recruitment & Employment Management ... Leadership Training & Development ... Benefits & Compensation Design ... Reorganization & Culture Change ... Merger & Acquisition Integration ... Union & Nonunion Employee Relations ... Succession Planning ... Expatriate Programs ... Long-Range Business Planning ... HR Policies & Procedures.

PROFESSIONAL EXPERIENCE

MARCON MANUFACTURING COMPANY, Peekskill, NY
Vice President, Human Resources (1996–Present)

Challenge:	Recruited to create HR infrastructure to support business growth at a $30-million global manufacturing company with underachieving sales, exceedingly high turnover, and lack of cohesive management processes in U.S. and Asia.
Actions:	Partnered with the President and Board of Directors to reorganize company, reduce overhead expenses, rebuild sales and management infrastructure.

Results:
- Established HR staff of 5, including development of policies and procedures; renegotiated cost-effective benefit programs saving $1.5 million annually.
- Reorganized operations and facilitated seamless integration of 150 employees from 2 new acquisitions within parent company.
- Reduced sales force turnover to nearly nonexistent, upgraded quality of candidates hired by implementing interview skills training and management development programs. Results led to improved sales performance.
- Recruited all management personnel, developed HR policies and procedures, and fostered team culture at newly built Malaysian plant with 125 employees.
- Initiated business reorganization plan, resulting in consolidation of New York and Virginia operations and $6.5 million in cost reductions.

BINGHAMTON COMPANY, New York, NY
Director, Human Resources & Administration (1993–1996)

Challenge:	Lead HR and Administration function supporting 1,600 employees at $500-million manufacturer of medical equipment. Support company's turnaround efforts, business unit consolidations, and transition to consumer products focus.
Actions:	Established cross-functional teams from each site and provided training in team building to coordinate product development efforts, implement new manufacturing processes, and speed products to market. Identified cost reduction opportunities; instrumental in reorganization initiatives that included closing union plant in Texas and building new plant in North Carolina. Managed HR staff of 12.

ALEXIS BROWN • PAGE 2

Director, Human Resources & Administration continued...

Results:
- Instituted worldwide cross-functional team culture that provided the foundation for successful new product launches and recapture of company's leading edge despite intense competition.
- Led flawless integration of 2 operations into single, cohesive European business unit, resulting in profitable business turnaround.
- Restructured and positioned HR organization in the German business unit as customer-focused partner to support European sales and marketing units.
- Initiated major benefit cost reductions of $3 million in year one and $1 million annually while gaining employee acceptance through concerted education and communications efforts.

ARCADIA CORPORATION, New York, NY
Director, Human Resources (1989–1993)

Challenge: HR support to corporate office and field units of an $800-million organization with 150 global operations employing 4,500 people.

Actions: Promoted from Assistant Director of HR to lead staff of 10 in all HR and labor relations functions. Established separate international recruitment function and designed staffing plan to accommodate rapid business growth. Negotiated cost-effective benefits contracts for union and non-union employees.

Results:
- Oversaw successful UAW, Teamsters, and labor contract negotiations.
- Established and staffed HR function for major contract award with U.S. government agency.
- Introduced incentive plans for field unit managers and an expatriate program that attracted both internal and external candidates for international assignments in the Middle East.
- Managed HR issues associated with 2 business acquisitions while accomplishing a smooth transition and retention of all key personnel.
- Restructured HR function with no service disruption to the business while saving $500,000 annually.

EDUCATION

M.B.A., Cornell University, New York, NY
B.A., Business Administration, Amherst College, Amherst, MA

AFFILIATIONS

Society for Human Resource Management
Human Resource Council of Albany

Jacob F. Hornburger

7715 South Terrace • Beltsville, MD 20705 • (301) 306-7200 • (410) 378-9123 • jhornburger@juno.net

EXECUTIVE SUMMARY

Dynamic executive IT professional with track record of successes in team development, leadership, customer relationship management, negotiations, project management, and development and implementation of large, complex global IT projects. Expertise in application development life cycle and architecture, data resource management, and information technology infrastructures. Excelled in several high profile project advisor roles for global corporations involving IT systems implementations. Clients have included, Aetna, Travelers, Bank of New York, First Union, Bank of America, Credit Suisse First Boston, Chase Manhattan Bank, JP Morgan Chase, Office Depot, and AT&T. Proficient public speaking skills, dynamic coaching and mentoring, and superior team and individual development. Record of averting IT crises and leading project teams to success with on time and within budget completions.

"He is in high demand for the combination of overall skills he brings to any client. Somehow, he has the unique ability of performing at extremely high levels without compromising on the quality of his deliverables even though he is stretched thin across multiple projects. He is a great technologist as well as a leader with multi-faceted skills." – Credit Suisse First Boston Partner

PROFESSIONAL WORK SUMMARY

Chase Manhattan Bank   Feb. 1995 to Present
Principal Consultant / Senior Manager

PROJECT RESULTS

"Jacob's oversight and direction of this team in a complex environment that is technically and politically challenged is essential and his professional competence in handling this has not only tremendously helped the overall progress of these projects, but has also significantly contributed toward anchoring our engagement of this client for the long-term." – JPMC Project Partner

- Project Manager of numerous successful large-scale and complex projects, including integration and consolidation of enterprise systems of 2 large investment banks, Global PeopleSoft ERP HR and Financials implementation, data warehouse for HR, benefits and payroll, workforce analytics, and employee/manager self-service.
- Directed, led, and coordinated multiple project teams implementing technology strategy and PeopleSoft ERP implementation through life cycle of project.
- Led successful implementation of large, complex infrastructure supporting over 375,000 employees, including migration of payroll systems supporting 60,000 US employees from biweekly to semimonthly system; rolled-out application to over 1,500 users in 25 countries; converted over 27 million records.
- Strategically aligned IT solutions with business objectives; led selection of appropriate technology and vendor products; evaluated ERP products SAP, PeopleSoft, and Oracle.

CLIENT RELATIONSHIPS

"Jacob's sound thought leadership has been influential such that his ideas are more than welcome and his recommendations are highly considered by the senior management." –America Financial Services Partner

- Project Advisor for B2E web strategy for Fortune 500 insurance company. Advised project team on methodology and approach to develop e-HR vision and portal strategy.

Jacob F. Hornburger

- Conducted high-level assessment study, including overview of HR Internet solution, HR portal vision, current environmental assessment, target environmental assessment, and approach for implementation.
- Provided outsourcing evaluation for Fortune 500 global bank. Analyzed and evaluated benefits and risks of outsourcing bank's HR and payroll functions.
- Developed effective rapport and strategic client relationships with many senior executives by providing technology advice and consultation in solo high-profile roles; recognized by client senior management as valued advisor.

INNOVATION

"Jacob can be counted on coming up with creative solutions and alternative approaches." – Aetna Project Partner

- Masterminded an innovative solution for PeopleSoft process optimization involving HR, payroll, and benefits. Solution identified as best practice for process area and consequently leveraged by multiple clients.
- Architected state-of-the-art system that is stable, robust, highly versatile, high performance, enterprise-wide, and global with 24/7 capabilities.
- Analyzed and evaluated several system architecture paradigms and platform-specific options involving Enterprise Servers and Enterprise Storage systems.
- Proposed and achieved significant cost-saving strategy for PeopleSoft ERP system by performing capacity analysis and generating archiving solution.
- Originated and drove revamp and upgrade of systems architecture, providing advanced robust platform and innovative enterprise architecture for corporate systems.

FINANCIAL MANAGEMENT

"Jacob was key toward influencing additional revenue generation opportunities. He effectively leveraged his relationship with the Technology VP of the bank to secure the portal opportunity." – Travelers Project Partner

- Successfully managed and rolled out strong portfolio of several multimillion-dollar projects.
- Identified new opportunities for revenue generation and proactively proposed and obtained additional revenues achieving significant sales record.
- Recognized as the Top Performer for revenue generation and business development.

LEADERSHIP

"Jacob's leadership of his team is exemplary. He inspires, motivates, and generates loyalty from his team members." – AT&T IT Lead Partner

- Spearheaded design, development, and implementation of complex systems infrastructure for large Fortune 500 bank, involving the first "big bang" implementation of PeopleSoft payroll, benefits administration, HR, and pension modules.
- Provided direction, advice, and critical review of team activities involving 100+ members through all phases of project.
- Served as primary contact and project liaison with business owners and steering committee, including periodic face-to-face debriefings with senior management.
- Identified, assessed, and developed target individuals building high performance teams for successful project completions.
- Spearheaded custom implementation and design of billing systems for large telecommunications company.
- Recognized as effective and admired coach/mentor by staff.

Jacob F. Hornburger

KNOWLEDGE MANAGEMENT

"He is always in demand for his skill, and the knowledge he possesses has been leveraged at multiple projects and yet achieves maximum effectiveness." – Office Depot Project Partner

- Served as quality assurance reviewer on most challenging projects.
- Provided subject matter expertise and thought leadership for multi-national technical team implementing PeopleSoft v8.0 Financials.
- Successfully completed conversion from NT-based systems to Unix-based platform and migration of RDBMS from Sybase to Oracle.
- Systems Architect consulting with Fortune 500 insurance company, providing analysis, and quality assurance reviews for "big bang" implementation of PeopleSoft HRMS.
- Subject Matter Expert (SME) in project planning, design, architecture and integration of systems, network administration, server and database management, performance and stress testing, and reporting warehouse implementation.
- Designed and architectured setup and configuration of HP Enterprise servers, operating system platform layout, directory structures, and application setup design.
- Led development efforts involving logical and physical database design, software design and development, application and database tuning on various hardware/software platforms.
- Leveraged technical knowledge across the firm as formally acknowledged by practice unit IT leadership.

AT&T   Jun. 1993 to Jan. 1995
Systems Architect

Exxon Corporation   Jan. 1990 to Jun. 1993
Systems Analyst

EDUCATION
Bachelor of Science Degree, Electrical Engineering
University of Virginia, 1990

PUBLICATIONS & PRESENTATIONS
White Paper, "Tuning Oracle for PeopleSoft Application"
Speaker, Oracle Users Group Conference
SME Speaker, PwC Learning Center
Experienced Project Manager, Seminar Speaker
Executive Speaker Series, University Initiative

WILLIAM T. PARKERSON

35 Sunderland Drive   *E-mail: parkersonw@compuserv.com*   *Home: (555) 555–5555*
Cedar Grove, NJ 55555   *Fax: (555) 555–5555*

PLANT / OPERATIONS / GENERAL MANAGEMENT EXECUTIVE

Multi-site manufacturing plant/general management career building and leading high-growth, transition and start-up operations in domestic and international environments with annual revenues of up to $680 million.

Expertise: Organizational Development • Productivity & Cost Reduction Improvements • Supply Chain Management • Acquisitions & Divestitures • IPOs • Plant Rationalizations • Safety Performance • Customer Relations • Change Agent.

CORE COMPETENCIES

Manufacturing Leadership—Strong P&L track record with functional management experience in all discipline of manufacturing operations • Developing and managing operating budgets • Spearheading restructuring and rationalization of plants and contracted distribution facilities • Initiating lean manufacturing processes, utilizing SMED principles • Establishing performance metrics and supply chain management teams.

Continuous Improvement & Training—Designing and instituting leadership enhancement training program for all key plant management • Instituting Total Quality System (TQS) process in domestic plants to promote the business culture of continuous improvement and leading ISO 9001 certification process.

New Product Development—Initiating plant-based "New Product Development Think Tank" that developed 130 new products for marketing review, resulting in the successful launch of 5 new products in 2000.

Engineering Management—Oversight of corporate machine design and development teams • Developing 3-year operating plan • Directing the design, fabrication and installation of several proprietary machines • Creating project cost tracking systems and introducing ROI accountability.

PROFESSIONAL EXPERIENCE

BEACON INDUSTRIES, INC., Maspeth, NY (1994–Present)
Record of continuous promotions to executive-level position in manufacturing and operations management despite periods of transition/acquisition at a $680-million Fortune 500 international manufacturing company. Career highlights include:

Vice President of Manufacturing (1997–Present)

Senior Operating Executive responsible for the performance of 7 manufacturing/distribution facilities for company that experienced rapid growth from 4 plants generating $350 million in annual revenues to 14 manufacturing facilities with revenues of $680 million. Charged with driving the organization to becoming a low-cost producer. Established performance indicators, operating goals, realignment initiatives, productivity improvements and cost reduction programs that consistently improved product output, product quality and customer satisfaction.

Achievements:

- Selected to lead corporate team in developing and driving forward cost reduction initiatives that will result in $21 million saved over the next 3 years through capital infusion, process automation and additional rationalizations.
- Saved $13 million annually by reducing fixed spending 11% and variable overhead spending 18% through effective utilization of operating resources and cost improvement initiatives.
- Cut workers' compensation costs 40% ($750,000 annually) by implementing effective health and safety plans, employee training, management accountability and equipment safeguarding. Led company to achieve recognition as "Best in Industry" regarding OSHA frequency and Loss Workday Incident rates.
- Reduced waste generation 31%, saving $1 million in material usage by optimizing manufacturing processes as well as instituting controls and accountability.
- Enhanced customer service satisfaction 3% annually during past year (measured by order fill and on-time delivery percentage) through supply chain management initiatives, inventory control and flexible manufacturing practices.
- Trimmed manufacturing and shipping related credits to customers from 1.04% to .5% of total sales in 1999, representing annual $1.8 million reduction.

WILLIAM T. PARKERSON • (555) 555-5555 • Page 2

General Manager, Northeast (1994–1997)

Assumed full P&L responsibility of 2 manufacturing facilities and a $20-million annual operating budget. Directly supervised facility managers and, indirectly, 250 employees in a multi-line, multicultural manufacturing environment. Planned and realigned organizational structure and operations to position company for high growth as a result of acquiring a major account, 2 new product lines and 800 additional SKUs.

Achievements:

- Reduced operating costs by $4.5 million through consolidation of 2 distribution locations without adverse impact on customer service.

- Accomplished the start-up of 2 new manufacturing operations, which encompassed a plant closing and the integration acquired equipment into existing production lines for 2 new product lines without interruption to customer service; achieved 2 months ahead of target and $400,000 below budget.

- Increased operating performance by 15% while reducing labor costs by $540,000.

- Reduced frequency and severity of accidents by 50% in 3 years, contributing to a workers' compensation and cost avoidance reduction of $1 million.

- Decreased operating waste by 2% for an annual cost savings of $800,000 in 2 manufacturing facilities.

- Negotiated turnkey contracts for 2 distribution warehouses to meet expanded volume requirements.

- Maintained general management and administrative cost (GMA) at a flat rate as sales grew by 25% annually over 3 years.

ROMELARD CORPORATION, Detroit, MI (1980–1994)
Division Manufacturing Director (1989–1994)

Fast-track advancement in engineering, manufacturing and operations management to division-level position. Retained by new corporate owners and promoted in 1994 based upon consistent contributions to revenue growth, profit improvements and cost reductions. Scope of responsibility encompassed P&L for 3 manufacturing facilities and a distribution center with 500 employees in production, quality, distribution, inventory control and maintenance.

Achievements:

- Delivered strong and sustainable operating gains: increased customer fill rate by 18%; improved operating performanc by 20%; reduced operating waste by 15% and reduced inventory by $6 million.

- Justified, sourced and directed the installation of $10 million of automated plant equipment.

- Implemented and managed a centralized master scheduling for all manufacturing facilities.

- Reduced annual workers' compensation costs by $600,000.

- Created Customer Satisfaction Initiative program to identify areas of concern and implemented recommendations, significantly improving customer satisfaction.

Prior Positions: Manufacturing Manager (1987–1989); Plant Manager (1986–1987); Engineering Manager (1984–1986); Plant Industrial Engineer (1980–1984).

EDUCATION & PROFESSIONAL DEVELOPMENT

Bachelor of Science in Manufacturing Engineering
Syracuse University, Syracuse, NY

Continuing professional development programs in
Executive Management, Leadership and Finance

LISA DiBLASIO

6 Park Avenue • New York, NY 20019
(212) 777-7777 • ldiblasio@aol.net

SENIOR HUMAN RESOURCES EXECUTIVE
Fortune 500, High Growth Company, Department Start-ups, Restructuring HR Services

Business partner with senior management team in building environment with high performance standards and high value on human capital. Provided leadership to total human resources function at the field and corporate levels. Catalyst for a series of HR innovative initiatives impacting 2000 employees at the largest revenue-generating hotel for premier hospitality company. A creative thinker, problem solver and decision maker. Strong written communications, presentation and interpersonal skills. Focused and energetic.

Professional Experience

MARRIOTT INTERNATIONAL, Washington, DC   1982 – 2003

Marriott International is a leading worldwide hospitality company known for its leadership and progressive business management. Received subsequent promotions and cross training throughout a 20-year tenure with this world class company. Progressive Human Resources growth from a Director of a $40M, 600-employee property to a Director of a $260M, 2000-employee property.

New York Manhattan Marriott, New York, NY
Resident Manager (*2001 – 2003*)
Cross training opportunity to lead a hotel's Rooms and Loss Prevention operations. Responsible for Front Office, Business Center, Retail, Fitness Center, Housekeeping, $22M budget, staff of 100. Kept Operational team focused on the critical components of operations to drive guest satisfaction and the desired financial results.

- Achieved second highest Customer Service Survey rating for "Intent to Return" in the country.
- Increased productivity to 1.26 vs. a 1.33, saved over $100,000 in salary and wages.
- Built supportive relationships with outlet owners of auxiliary property services to reduce expenses and increase customer satisfaction.

New York Marriott Marquis, New York, NY
Director of Human Resources (*1993 – 2001*)
Developed and led Human Resources strategies and activities for recruitment, total compensation, training and development and employee relations with a staff of 15, for the company's most successful and largest revenue generating hotel, with 2000 employees, over $260M revenue. Member of the Executive Committee.

- Spearheaded the start up of a training & development department that grew to offer 255 management and employee development classes.
- Facilitated the restructuring of our Performance Management process to include quarterly presentations by department heads and 360-degree reviews for 250 managers.
- Led the talent inventory and succession planning for 8 New York City hotels; quarterly assessment of 94 key positions.
- Designed and implemented a Mentor Program in which 74 line managers and department heads participated.
- Received 1999 Innovative Recruitment Award for the Northeast Region. Reduced time to fill open positions from 6-8 weeks to 2-4 weeks.
- Achieved the highest employee satisfaction rating for like hotels in the country.

LISA DiBLASIO   **Page 2**

Crystal Gateway Marriott, Arlington, VA
Director of Human Resources *(1990 – 1993)*
Successfully directed all Human Resources functions of a $40M, 600-employee hotel with a staff of 6.

- Led strategic business planning process for hotel executive committee.
- Facilitated large-scale service enhancement training for 250 people a session.

Director and Human Resources, **Key Bridge Marriott**
Human Resources Manager, **Orlando World Center**
Division Human Resources Manager, **Corporate Headquarters**
1985 –1990

- Responsible for recruitment, selection and placement of management personnel for 12 states.
- Developed Human Resources services for Travel Plazas during three major acquisitions.

Marriott's Roy Rogers Restaurant Division

General Manager *(1982 – 1985)*

Overall business responsibility for stand-alone restaurant.

- Developed period cleaning and sanitation chart used Division-wide.

Education

- Pennsylvania State University, State College, PA.
- BA in Industrial/Organizational Psychology.
- Successfully completed Columbia University Graduate School of Business, Finance and Accounting and Negotiating Skills Executive Programs 1999.

Other

- Certified New York City Fire Safety Director, 2002.
- Certified trainer of Diversity Awareness and Diversity Skills.
- Certified instructor of Navigating Through Change.
- Certified administrator of Myers-Briggs Type Indicator.
- Certified instructor of Covey's; Seven Habits of Highly Effective People.
- Member of 1999 North American Lodging Organization Advisory Council.
- Board member of the Penn State Industrial Psychology Advisory Council 1993-96.
- Received two awards at the 1996 HR International Conference for Best Associate Satisfaction and Best Retention.

WILLIAM McCAFFREY

954.612.9564　•　2500 NE 28th Terrace　•　Ft Lauderdale, FL 33026　•　mmccaffrey@aol.com

OPERATIONS / GENERAL MANAGEMENT EXECUTIVE
Startup, Turnaround, High-Growth Organizations

Decisive customer- and results-driven Executive with track record of driving revenue and profit improvements in challenging environments. Forward-thinking leader and enterprising problem solver with strategic vision and keen bottom-line focus. Strong team builder and communicator who gains consensus and creates/executes plans to deliver measurable results. Expert in building and energizing a company's organizational infrastructure, products/services, processes, and sales/marketing strategies to optimize results

Executive Leadership Competencies

Strategic/Tactical Planning	Value-Added Products & Services
Revenue/Market Growth & Profit Improvement	Customer & Vendor Relationships
Organizational Leadership and Development	Competitive Product & Service Positioning
Business & Multi-Site Operations	Business Process Reengineering
Executive Sales, Marketing & Business Development	Strategic Partnerships & Vendor Negotiations
Regional Sales & Customer Service Operations	Cross-Functional Matrix Team Building & Leadership

MBA in Technology Management and Information & Decision Support Systems

---

PROFESSIONAL EXPERIENCE

MOLLY, INC., Ft. Lauderdale, FL
Founder/President, 2002-2004

Personally founded and invested in Molly, a privately held wireless high-speed Internet services company focused on providing Internet access and location-driven content solutions to business and residential consumers.

- Developed business plan and negotiated vendor financing & strategic partnerships.
- Codeveloped service design/delivery systems.

NATIONAL URBAN TELECOMMUNICATIONS, Miami, FL
Managing Director, Internet Services Division, 2001-2002

Recruited to turnaround four-year-old $5.25M Internet services business line as Managing Director with full P&L responsibility. Business provided Internet services to member companies and their subscribers. Division plagued by dwindling business customers & high end-user subscriber churn, cost overruns, inadequate outsourcing contracts, and poor service design/delivery.

- Rapidly assessed business state. Identified requirements and formulated action plans. Stabilized customer base through direct meetings, realigned resources, and troubleshot vendor, customer, and technical issues.
- Developed new vision and business plan, repositioning business from dial-up Internet access support only to complete Internet solutions provider with greater emphasis on solutions development/support, operations, and retention. Launched three additional product/service lines.
- Negotiated revenue generating partnerships with industry leading Internetworking equipment and service providers.
- Negotiated new vendor contract for outsourced subscriber customer care.
- Increased revenue by 25% and delivered division's first profits.
- Implemented comprehensive technical audit program that included monthly customer technical health reviews to ensure properly managed technical growth and reduced subscriber churn. Resulted in residential subscriber growth of 46%. Delivered new & improved Web-based customer-managed account tools.

William McCaffrey **page 2**

APICS GLOBAL, INC., Fairfax, VA
Executive Director of Business Operations, 1999-2000

Recruited to define, establish, and direct the Business Operations Department responsible for customer focused post-sales operations including customer installations, contract administration, customer care, order management, and business information systems.

- Created and established a Project Management team to coordinate customer installations and ensure timely delivery of services through a defined implementation process; improved customer installation delivery by 65% to within 30-45 day industry standard.
- Led design and implementation of customer care processes to proactively manage customer issues and ensure immediate attention to troubleshooting technical issues and personally introduced the organization and processes to customers.
- Took charge of key account relationship management. Retained company's largest customer after customer had requested immediate contract termination. Highly impressed with new organization and processes, customer doubled its order within 30 days, increasing annual revenue to $7.25M.
- Identified requirements, established resources, and directed internal audits between actual customer service contract and billing invoices.
- Directed customer account audits that uncovered $195K in previously unbilled monthly recurring revenue, $345K in uncollected revenue, and over 50% of customer base in arrears totaling over $1M. Instituted core business processes with the Finance Department and Project Management team to ensure accurate customer invoicing and monthly recurring revenues.
- Developed core business processes to maintain updated customer information in all functional areas.

ABCCOMM, Herndon, VA
General Manager/Director of Operations, 1998-1999

Promoted to lead division turnaround with full operating and P&L responsibility following management restructuring.

- Within three months: created new vision and business plan for division that repositioned business unit with narrower market focus; reduced annual operating expenses by nearly $5M; and reengineered sales processes.
- Negotiated joint marketing agreement with Fortune 100 Company; product designed to reduce client operating costs by 35%.
- Initiated pilot project with world's largest petroleum corporation with account potential in excess of $25M.
- Merged business unit with another division to produce additional efficiencies and create global distribution channel for the solution.
- Led design, development, and implementation of corporate extranet with inherent corporate and vendor workflow collaboration and management capabilities.
- Negotiated and developed strategic vendor partner relationships for manufacturing, logistics, and product installation.
- Drove product design and manufacturing improvements incorporating just-in-time manufacturing, e-commerce and supply chain management techniques.
- Directed full life-cycle management of product from design into production.
- Orchestrated corporate facilities relocation.

U.S. MARINE CORPS, Various U.S. and International Locations, 1992-1998
Commissioned Officer. Career highlighted by rapid advancement and multiple commendations.

Plans, Policy, and Operations Officer

Staff officer responsible for research, analysis, and presentation of Marine Corps critical long-range planning and policy-development issues in support of the intelligence community.

- Provided oversight and guidance on development of evolving telecommunications technologies.
- Led extensive cross-agency process improvement study in response to customer requirements.
- Organized and chaired conference on technical skills development/career path progression for senior technical officers. Codeveloped recommended courses of action, authored conference report, and designed & led presentation to senior executives.

William McCaffrey   **page 3**

Operations Control and Analysis Manager

Challenged with turnaround of critical 35-person group responsible for on-site technical analysis and support of global operations. Unit beleaguered with low morale, poor training, and dissatisfied customers. Directed daily operations and multi-site operations support. Led tactical planning in support of global operations. Served as technical issues liaison to external and international organizations.

- Introduced and instituted performance-driven mobile support teams.
- Developed/implemented aggressive training and qualification program for technical personnel.
- Spearheaded acquisition and deployment of specialized information systems to support ad hoc customer requirements.
- Initiated, designed, and implemented organization's remote access capabilities to select national-level communications systems.
- Honored by Chief Executive for leadership, conceptual acumen, and numerous technical and organizational initiatives determined to have lasting impact.

Division Manager, Training Manager, Section Supervisor, and Career Counselor

Led 130-person multinational technical division. Directed operations, personnel, resources, staff training. Served as technical issues representative to external national organizations. Additionally, managed a 50-person group and provided career development services for 115-person organization.

- Awarded **Chief Executive in Europe's annual Leadership Award** from a field of 14,000 candidates.
- Delivered performance and efficiency improvements of 40% through process reengineering.
- Developed/implemented comprehensive training program benchmarked as the model training program. Resulted in 60% improvement in number of certified personnel.

Operations Staff Officer/Analyst, Security Manager, and Public Affairs Officer

Signals Intelligence Analyst/Electronic Warfare Systems Operator

---

EDUCATION

- **MBA (Technology Management and Information & Decision Support Systems)**,
  The Ohio State University, Columbus, Ohio, 1998.
- **U.S. Marine Corps Communications Officers School**, Quantico, Virginia, 1993.
- **Post Graduate Intelligence Program (Masters Degree Equivalent)**, Joint Military Intelligence College, Washington, DC, 1991.
- **B.S. Liberal Studies (Computer Systems Analysis concentration)**, The University of the State of California, Berkley, California, 1987.

TEACHING and TRAINING EXPERIENCE

- **Adjunct Faculty,** National Technical School, 1991-1996.
  Taught analysis and reporting techniques for highly technical communications-related information.

DOUGLAS S. BARNHAM

1214 Kingsmill Drive
Mitchellville, Maryland 20721

(301) 555-9457
dbarnham12@aol.com

EXECUTIVE PROFILE

Accomplished senior-level manager with extensive corporate and nonprofit experience. Effective combination of leadership, communication, interpersonal, and analytical skills. Highly successful at developing and establishing subtenant and joint venture partnerships. Consistently successful in building consensus and driving cooperative relationships with staffs, Board of Directors, government agencies, and business partners. Keen administrative, organizational, and business-development skills. M.B.A. Degree.

CORPORATE EXPERIENCE

JANSEN CORPORATION, Bethesda, Maryland
(Formerly Delmarva Services Corporation)
Vice President-Government Affairs *(1988-2001)*

Provided strategic planning, financial, and administrative management in the acquisition of airport contracts and all leasing arrangements for the Disadvantage Business Enterprise Program (DBE) for women and minorities. Assumed role of business developer in addition to managing all subcontracting activity.

- Instrumental in establishing the largest and most comprehensive subtenant program, including Women and Minority Disadvantaged Enterprises, in the hospitality industry.
- Designed, coordinated, and executed requests for proposals and requests for qualifications and personally negotiated agreements at many airports including, Anchorage, Baltimore, Birmingham, Charlotte, Detroit, JFK, LaGuardia, Seattle, Tampa, Raleigh-Durham, Indianapolis, Memphis, Minneapolis, San Diego, and St. Louis.
- Increased the accounts in the subtenant program from 50 to 260, resulting in growth of the annual sales volume from less than $100 million to over $230 million.
- Assisted operations, legal, finance, and development in the implementation and management of over 260 women/minority business enterprise contracts in more than 50 airports.
- In addition to regular duties, assumed role of Director of Development for the Greensboro, NC and Milwaukee, WI airports food, beverage, and merchandise lease agreements. Successfully maintained those accounts by building relationships with the landlord, airport staff, and branch operations.
- Assisted in the design and implementation of a process to identify appropriate development costs, expended by Host, to be reimbursed by the women and minority subtenants. Resulted in saving the corporation hundreds of thousands of dollars.
- Provided technical assistance to corporate and branch staff regarding interpretation and implementation of the Code of Federal Regulations #49, Parts 23 and 26.
- Mediated disputes between local branch staff and subtenants, which minimized potential litigation and resulted in a positive company image.

KENTUCKY FRIED CHICKEN CORPORATION, Hanover, Maryland
Real Estate Director *(1983-1988)*

Scope of responsibility included identifying, evaluating, and recommending sites for KFC restaurants. Supervised and directed work activities of 15-member staff.

- Acquired demographic data, sought rezoning, prepared proposals, negotiated contracts, and made presentations to regulatory bodies/agencies and community groups.
- Gained approval for over 20 restaurants.

ALLIED INSURANCE COMPANY, Washington, DC
Associate Investment Manager *(1980-1983)*

- Managed office buildings, shopping centers and industrial warehouses. Directed budgeting, leasing, and maintenance for a $10-million-plus portfolio through on-site managers.

DOUGLAS S. BARNHAM   PAGE 2

NONPROFIT EXPERIENCE
SUMMITHILL CARES, INC. (SCI), Annapolis, MD
Chair, Board of Directors *(1996-present)*

Provide executive leadership to this 11-member Board of Directors with Board oversight to this fully accredited Early Childhood, Before/After Care and Summer Enrichment Programs with a student population of over 600. Work in cooperation with Executive Director and Board Members to drive strategic planning and annual budgeting processes.

- As a founding member, established board guidelines and policies and set expectations for prospective board members.
- Ensure that all sponsored or supported activities are consistent with the organization's mission to promote quality education.
- Instrumental in helping the organization to receive National Early Childhood Accreditation, one of the few centers in the state of Maryland achieving this status.
- Conceived and launched a banking program with major bank, resulting in $2 million in assets.
- Developed and implemented a formal documented evaluation process for Executive Director position that meets standards of fairness and practicality.
- Take appropriate actions to maintain nonprofit status under the Federal income tax law.
- Served as 2nd Vice Chairperson to umbrella organization that provides administrative oversight and support in identifying and securing financial resources for four corporations, including Summithill Cares, Inc.

EDUCATION

Master of Business Administration
University of Wisconsin-Madison, WI

Bachelor of Science in Commerce
North Carolina Central University, Durham, NC

AWARDS

Recipient of Consortium for Graduate Study in Management Fellowship
Recipient of American Institute of Certified Public Accountants Scholarship

PROFESSIONAL AFFILIATIONS

- American Association of Airport Executives (AAAE)
- Airports Council International/North America (ACI/NA)
- Airport Minority Advisory Council (AMAC)
- National Forum for Black Public Administrators (NFBPA)
    (Former member-Corporate Advisory Council Executive Committee)
- Embry-Riddle Aeronautical University

BRADLEY SULLIVAN

669 Gillvrey Road
Croton, New York 08890

(555) 555-5555
bradsull@aol.com

PRIVATE BANKING ... RELATIONSHIP MANAGEMENT ... COMMERCIAL LENDING

Consistent achievements as a top producer, increasing revenues, portfolios and profits through expertise in business development, relationship building, exceptional customer service and attentive follow-up. Recognized for managing the highest quality portfolios and providing creative leadership.

Strategic planning, sales and marketing experience combine with qualifications in training, developing, coaching and managing staff to achieve performance objectives.

PROFESSIONAL EXPERIENCE & ACCOMPLISHMENTS

FIRSTBANK, New York, New York (1999–present)
Vice President, Business Development Officer – Private Clients Group (2000–present)
Private Banker (1999–2000)

Cultivate and manage new and existing client relationships of high-net-worth individuals and their related businesses. Develop sales plan for each relationship to provide an array of services: investment management, estate planning, credit and personal banking products. Continually expand referral network through contact with various internal business partners and external financial intermediaries. Coordinate events/seminars for new business development.

Results

♦ Successful track record of fee generation (through sale of investment management accounts), surpassing industry benchmark for the market: $2 million in 2000 and $5.5 million in 2001.

♦ Selected based on product expertise and sales results to train business development officers of newly acquired organization in private equity investment products.

♦ Recognized for top sales performance, generating over $1 million in fees from 2000 to 2001.

BANK OF NEW YORK, New York, New York (1989–1996)
Fast-track advancement through progressively responsible positions in Private Banking. FirstBank acquired Bank of New York in 1995.

Vice President and Unit Manager – Private Banking Group *(1993–1996)*

Promoted to provide management direction to 2 business units with combined portfolios of $425 million in deposits, loans and assets under management. Designed and executed successful relationship banking marketing plan for the sale of credit, trust (investment management and estate planning) and transaction products/services. Developed, coached and supervised team of 8 relationship managers and administrative assistants.

Results

♦ Evaluated and improved quality of the portfolios at both offices; credited for consistently maintaining the highest quality portfolios, which included managing highly sensitive corporate relationships.

♦ Achieved revenue and customer retention goals while increasing client profitability through relationship building, outstanding service delivery, cross-selling and referral development.

♦ Contributed $550,000 annually in fees through referral business to various banking divisions within the company.

BRADLEY SULLIVAN - PAGE 2

Vice President – Private Banking Group (1990–1993)

Managed the Greenwood private banking office and staff. Managed $53-million portfolio (loans and deposits). Aggressively marketed and cross-sold all bank services. Reviewed and strengthened asset quality, including performing workouts, restructures and transfers of problem credits.

Results:

♦ Consistently exceeded production goals for new loans, deposits and fee income. Recognized as an effective negotiator, generating highest level of fee income ($350,000 annually) division-wide.

♦ Turned around an adversarial relationship between consumer lending and private banking and forged a cohesive team.

Assistant Vice President – Private Banking Group (1989–1990)

Recruited to establish, build and manage Westchester office private banking operations. Designed marketing plan and originated new business by nurturing existing relationships and referral sources.

♦ Built book of clients from zero base and managed top quality loan, investment and deposit portfolio ($7.1+ million) with no loan losses. Generated over $50,000 in annual fees.

WEBBER BANK, New York, New York (1984–1989)
   Banking Officer – Private Banking and Trust Division (1984–1989)
   Banking Representative II – Community Banking (1983–1984)

Developed and executed an effective business development plan through intermediaries, colleagues and existing client base. Built and managed solid client relationships; communicated with other bank division personnel to effectively resolve any client issues.

♦ Grew and managed $12-million deposit portfolio and $6-million loan portfolio.

EDUCATION / LICENSURE

Columbia University, New York, New York
M.B.A. in Finance, 1994
B.A. in Finance, 1983

Hold NASD Series 7 and 63 licenses.

PROFESSIONAL DEVELOPMENT / TRAINING

Credit Development Program
Fiduciary Banking
Management Information Systems
Asset Allocation Service and Estate Planning

Penny Webb

19 Pacific View Road
San Diego, CA 94563

Pwebb94563@yahoo.com

Home: 925 284-8304
Cellular: 925 284-8305

IT EXECUTIVE

IT Executive possessing superior skill in defining technical/program vision, communicating direction, and leading successful execution of IT initiatives in Fortune 100 environments. Successful record of delivering insightful IT solutions that take into account financial and human resources concerns. Established business and technology expertise to support enterprise growth and create clear milestones and objectives and resolve business issues in a cost effective manner. Possess demonstrated ability to move fluidly between executive, professional, and support staff.

Areas of Expertise

- IT Business / Strategic Planning
- Fiscal Management
- Project Management
- Hardware / Network Implementation
- Quality Assurance
- Data Center and Ops Management

- Enterprise Applications
- System Architecture / Integration
- 24/7 Call Center Operations
- Contingency and Disaster Planning
- Corporate Acquisition Due Diligence
- Staff Development / Mentoring

CAREER HIGHLIGHTS

CENTURYCOMM, INC. — San Diego, CA
CONSULTANT, 1998 to present
Key Engagements:

Engaged to manage the planning and execution for the rapid deployment of an Enterprise Resource Planning (ERP) project across multiple divisions in 27 countries. ERP systems were used to manage the supply chain, or flow of materials through a company from its suppliers to its final destination, its customers. Managed client IT and business cross functional (Finance, Manufacturing, Sales/Marketing) teams comprised of 150+ staff. Provided IT subject matter leadership and managed Quality Control/Quality Assurance (QA/QC) for all groups within IS and across business functions (at Director, Sr. Staff, and administrative levels). Results enabled annual IT support savings of $10 million by consolidating applications and reducing maintenance and support costs.

- Project oversight resulted in teams moving more rapidly than industry norm for ERP implementations (9-12 months) and achieving same results in only 7 months.

- Initiated system reduced time to close books from 10 days to 3 days. Increased efficiencies allowed for staff reduction (and subsequent additional savings) of $5 million per year.

- Successful completion of project enabled the reduction of staff from 6500 to 4500 across all operating units. Financial savings resulting from staff reductions, facilities closures, and consolidation of operating units reduced quarterly burn rate by $200 million.

Managed the IT related divestiture activities (1998-2001). Organized and directed IT and staff separation activities for three divisions (MIPS, Craft Research, Media/Clark) with a total combined value of $1.6 billion. Monitored and assessed all (intellectual property and physical) asset activities, and IT investment management aspects associated with the divestitures. Participated, as parent company IT representative, in due diligence process for sale of all three divisions.

Penny Webb
Page Two

CAREER HIGHLIGHTS

- Developed the IT strategic plan for MIPS divestiture. Plan outlined growth scenarios, costs, staffing, and presented completed plan to Board of Directors. Plan successfully supported the IPO of the $500-million spin-off and allowed the managed growth of the company's IT capabilities from 100 staff in 1998 to 575 staff in 2000.

Managed IT customer service delivery team as a Interim Director for Aspect Communications. Engagement involved guiding a significant downsizing of IT operations support by reorganizing team. The reduction of delivery staffing worldwide from 130 to 65 staff in less than 90 days was accomplished while maintaining existing support and delivery service agreements.

- Managed operational support for 24/7 customer service line of business, including development and operations support for three instances of Clarify, one in EMEA and two in North America.

SMITH, JONES AND COOPER, LLP — San Francisco, CA
PRINCIPAL CONSULTANT / LEAD, NETWORK ARCHITECTURE COE, 1996 to 1998
Key Engagements:

- Developed and guided network redesign project, presenting concept and business case to Board of Directors of parent company. Total cost of implementation $37 million. Smith, Jones and Cooper's consulting revenue from network project exceeded $6.5 million.

- Created Infrastructure COE (Center of Excellence) for firm. Group formed to deliver network infrastructure design, project management, and technical troubleshooting expertise to clients across all consulting industry areas. Implemented staffing and recruiting model, budget and revenue targets, and exceeded quotas in first year by 30% ($7.3 million in revenue).

- Presented to Board of Directors of client firm for highly visible projects with large budgets and short implementation time horizons. Reported to parent company CIO and CFO on spin-off progress, issues, and budget on a weekly basis. Created summary reports and presented them to Board of Directors of client firm and subsidiary outlining success criteria for both parties in divestiture.

- Performed acting CIO role for client firm's divestiture of a $700-million chip manufacturing subsidiary. Ability to rapidly divest operating unit from parent firm by target deadline allowed successful IPO to take place. IPO resulted in profit of $500 million for parent firm in value of stock retained after split.

- Formulated, and concurrently managed, 6 technical initiatives while also playing key cross-functional coordination role in organizational transformation/reengineering project. Initiative areas included: Data Center Consolidation, Standards Creation and Rollout, Messaging Standardization, Server consolidation and migration, Internet/Extranet development, chargeback methodology, and staff reductions and redeployments. Total costs of projects in excess of $50 million.

- Supervised teams as large as 150 employees at Universal Pictures and Sony Pictures. Participated in 360 review process on both projects. Received one of the highest ratings of 96.5% on a scale of 1 to 100.

ANNE HULL
12 Main Street
New York, New York 10014
(555) 555-5555

FINANCE EXECUTIVE

**Finance/Accounting Management … Cash Management … Information Systems … Budgeting
Insurance & Risk Management … Tax & Regulatory Compliance … Banking Relations**

Finance, public accounting and administration executive with diverse industry experience in retail/wholesale distribution, financial services and manufacturing. Proven ability to improve operations, impact business growth and maximize profits through achievements in finance management, cost reductions, internal controls and productivity/efficiency improvements. Strong qualifications in general management, business planning, systems technology design and implementation, and staff development/leadership.

PROFESSIONAL EXPERIENCE

SOUTHINGTON COMPANY • New York, New York • 1991-2003
Treasurer/Senior Controller • 1996-2003
Corporate Controller • 1991-1996

Member of the Senior Leadership Team. Functioned as Chief Financial Officer and Treasurer, directing $500M international consumer products company. Accountable for strategic planning, development and leadership of entire finance function as well as day-to-day operations management of company's largest domestic division. Recruited, developed and managed team of finance professionals, managers and support staff.

Operations Achievements

♦ **Instrumental in improving operating profits from less than $400K to over $4M, equity from $8.6M to $13.6M and assets from $29.7M to $44.4M.**

♦ **Boosted market penetration by 27%, which increased gross sales 32%, through acquisition of 25 operating units as key member of due diligence team.**

♦ **Initiated strategies to redeploy company resources, resulting in 54% increase in gross margin by partial withdrawal from high-risk/low-margin product lines.**

♦ **Directed annual plan review process and strengthened accountability by partnering with senior-level department and district managers in all business units.**

Financial Achievements

♦ **Cut receivable write-offs $440K by developing credit policies, instituting aggressive collection strategies and establishing constructive dialogue with delinquent accounts.**

♦ **Negotiated and structured financing agreements, resulting in basis point reductions, easing/more favorable covenant restrictions and simplification of borrowing process.**

♦ **Saved over $2M through self-insurance strategy and an estimated $200K annually by positioning company to qualify to self-insure future workers' compensation claims.**

♦ **Designed executive and management reporting systems and tailored financial and operating reporting system to meet requirements of 100+ business units.**

ANNE HULL • **(555) 555-5555** • **Page 2**

Southington Company continued...

Technology Achievements

♦ Turned around organization-wide resistance toward automation and streamlined procedures that significantly improved efficiency while reducing costs.

♦ Championed installation of leading-edge systems technology resolving long-standing profit measurement problems and created infrastructure to support corporate growth.

♦ Implemented automated cash management system in over 100 business unit locations and reduced daily idle cash by 50% ($750K).

♦ Recognized critical need and upgraded automated systems to track long-term assets which had increased from $28M to $48.8M in 5 years.

HAMDEN COMPANY • New York, New York • 1987-1991
Chief Financial Officer

Recruited for 3-year executive assignment to assume key role in building solid management infrastructure and positioning $15M company for its profitable sale in 1991. Directed general accounting, cash management, financial and tax reporting, banking relations, credit and collections, data processing, employee benefits, and administration. Managed and developed staff.

♦ Converted company to small business corporation saving $450K in taxes over 3-year period.

♦ Realized $195K in accumulated tax savings through strategies adopting LIFO inventory method, minimizing taxes on a continual basis.

♦ Secured 25% of company's major client base (50% of total sales volume) by leading design, installation and administration of computer-based EDI program.

♦ Reduced collection period from 3 weeks to 5 days by initiating new policies and procedures.

MADISON COMPANY • New York, New York • 1981-1987
Partner

Jointly acquired and managed public accounting firm serving privately held companies (up to $200M in revenues) in wholesale distribution, financial services and manufacturing industries. Concurrent responsibility for practice administration and providing accounting, business and MIS consulting services to corporate clients.

EDUCATION

B.S. in Accounting
New York University • New York, New York

Certified Public Accountant - New York

Gary Mochety

3705 Southwestern Blvd., Dallas, Texas 75225 (214) 457-0044 / gmochety@gte.net

VP Marketing
Business Development / Brand Building / CRM Programs / P&L
Strategic Alliances / Membership Expansion / Health Care Marketing / Data Mining

Executive leadership spans both the for-profit and not-for-profit arenas. Currently a paid consultant to the American Heart Association, and the International Trachoma Initiative, an organization dedicated to ending blindness caused by bacteria. Fifteen years as volunteer for the Juvenile Diabetes Research Foundation, at the national and local levels. For JDRF, pioneered innovative fund raising initiatives aided new branding activities, analyzed research-funding alternatives.

Proven track record of expanding business and building consumer/patient affinity relationships. Successfully increased revenue and enhanced brand image for Kimberly Clark, UniLever, GlaxoSmithKlein, Hasbro, NBC and GTE brands.

Earned an **MBA** from **Northwestern University** and a **BBA** from the **University of Wisconsin**.

Professional Achievements

Led online branding and affinity marketing for GlaxoSmithKlein prescription drugs. Led strategy development of online marketing, online media planning and content intensive, community building Web sites for Flonase, Imitrex, and Conbivir.

Successfully launched CNBC in the international market. Engineered innovative distribution deals to increase exposure of CNBC broadcast among International viewers. Used strategic alliances to uncover low-cost, non-traditional ways to transmit CNBC to the UK, Europe, Japan, Canada, and Asia.

Saved GTE $80 million in start up costs by joining a cable company strategic alliance. Led GTE's analysis and negotiations to join the Americast cable consortium (Bell South, SBC, Ameritech, Disney, SNET). Participation in the consortium saved development costs and built a substantial brand quickly.

Evaluated diabetes prevention research protocols for potential funding. Supported JDRF lay review committee in evaluating research alternatives for potential funding. Selected Stanford University (Dr. Mickee) "islet cell protection" project.

Created "Transformers" toy line marketing concept for Hasbro resulting in annual sales of $600 million and 300+ licensees. Led branding campaign to reposition a Hasbro toy line. Renamed the toys Transformers, devised a TV series and comic book communication programs to market the toy.

Led new subscriber acquisition for GTE.net. Led database marketing initiative to secure new subscribers for GTE's ISP service. Grew user base to 3 million+ subs and initiated affinity content.

Led Luminant's Midwest business expansion increasing revenue 25% within 9 months. Landed new assignments from Kimberly Clark, Container Store and Dr. Pepper.

Conceived a formula-based marketing campaign that built Dove into a $300-million brand. Restaged Dove with a "1/4 moisturizing cream" ingredient strategy. The repositioning changed Dove from a cleansing agent to an integral part of a woman's beauty regimen.

Pioneered interactive television and advertising on GTE's digital cable network. Led marketing of Mainstreet, GTE's interactive television subscription service. Achieved 14% market penetration. Also developed CRM program that dramatically increased subscriber revenue.

Introduced Aim Toothpaste and built it into the #3 best-selling brand. Using an advertising strategy of cavity efficacy plus good taste cultivated trial and loyal usage among both children and adults.

Career Highlights

Partner, Waldo Digital, 2001 to present. Clients include the International Trachoma Initiative (ITI), American Heart Association (AHA), and Just for the Kids. For ITI, developing a long-term strategic plan. For AHA, working to enhance the ROI of database marketing, enhance the ROI of direct mail programs recruiting new donors, use CRM to enhance current donor loyalty. Also leading strategy and tactical development of new programs targeting the Hispanic market, e-mail marketing, e-fund raising.

Partner, Luminant Worldwide, 1999 to 2001. Recruited to lead business development and consulting services for the marketing strategy and e-marketing arm of this $130 million professional services firm. Clients included Kimberly Clark, Container Store, Dr. Pepper/7Up.

Vice-President, Business Development, GTE Media Ventures, 1995 to 1999. Grew subscribers and revenue for GTE's start up cable TV and ISP divisions. Generated new sources of revenue from interactive TV and personalized Internet via the TV. Introduced new e-commerce and ad revenue opportunities to other GTE business units including GTE Airfone and GTE's Public Communications.

Principal, Waldo Communications, 1993 to 1995. Entrepreneurial consulting group provided marketing strategy and new media expertise. Worked with clients in refining business models, adding new revenue streams and expanding distribution. Clients included Pics Previews, Cafe USA.

Vice President & Managing Director, NBC International, 1988 to 1993. Recruited to increase revenue and expand international customer base for NBC programs and services. Grew customer base 23% and increased annual revenue by 70%+ while creating business relationships with broadcasters worldwide. Secured $10 million P&G corporate sponsorship for new TV series concept.

Senior Vice President, Sales and Marketing, Sunbow Productions, 1985 to 1988. Launched a new animation company into world television and home video markets. Managed staff of 17 creative, sales and operations people. Increased revenue 140%. Directed the distribution and marketing of four top-rated children's syndicated TV programs—Transformers, GI Joe, Jem and My Little Pony.

Early Career, Ogilvy & Mather, Grey Advertising and Griffin Bacal, 1979 to 1985. Began career with premier advertising agencies. Progressed to Senior Vice President. Led advertising and media strategy for major accounts Hasbro, 3M, Unilever, Sports Illustrated, Revlon, and Nabisco.
- Directed Hasbro's $65-million Boy's Toy Business: Transformers, GI Joe.
- Repositioned 3M's Scotch videocassettes increasing market share from 7% to 21% in a rapidly expanding VCR market.
- Initiated award-winning advertising for Revlon's Flex Hair Care products.
- Developed the campaign redefining Dove Soap as "1/4 moisturizing cream."
- Launched Aim Toothpaste and built into the #3 market share brand.

Organizations / Affiliations

Member of the Association of Interactive Media. Active volunteer for the Juvenile Diabetes Research Foundation at both the national and local (Dallas) level. Member of the JDRF National Public Affairs Committee. Volunteer soccer coach for the YMCA. Volunteer fund raiser for Leukemia Society. All Conference (Big Ten) baseball player.

JONAH GELLER

7095 Guarino Road
Pittsburgh, PA 15217
(412) 777-9889

CHIEF INFORMATION OFFICER
VICE PRESIDENT OF PROFESSIONAL SERVICES
PRESIDENT / CHIEF OPERATIONS OFFICER

Seasoned IT and operations executive offering a proven track record of success leading all facets of technology integration, project management, product development/launch, and tactical and strategic business planning. Contribute expertise in revenue enhancement, cost reduction, resource allocation, budget administration, and team building. Innate talent for melding technology between corporate and customer concerns, effectively translating needs, issues, and information between all levels of management and technology specialists. Dynamic, intense leadership style, highly results-driven, thrive on change, and never satisfied with the status quo.

PROFESSIONAL EXPERIENCE

AMERICA ONLINE / I-PLANET E-COMMERCE SOLUTIONS, Santa Clara, California (1998-Present)

VICE PRESIDENT / CHIEF OPERATIONS OFFICER
Direct sales, marketing, P&L, and general operations for the Professional Services department of an international e-commerce software firm, with full accountability for business development, client relationship development, and management of projects valued at $70 million. Lead meetings with customers, internal departments, and project/consulting teams, presenting executive value propositions, building customer confidence, and creating organizational loyalty. Define new business opportunities, innovate customer solutions, and establish business strategy for 7 regions within the Americas, laying the groundwork for each region to function as small business operators. Recruit, train, and supervise a multi-location senior management team of 9 executives and a support staff of 10+. Collaborate with external vendors to acquire supplemental staffing to meet requisite project needs. Key liaison and decision-maker to company legal counsel in determining acceptable risk and intellectual property positions.

Key Results (Since June 2002):

- Boosted profitability 100% by creating packaged product/service offerings.
- Grew business 10% quarter-over-quarter with a 15%-20% margin contribution.
- Contained expense overruns of $6 million quarterly, brought organization to profitability in just 4 months.
- Slashed overhead 25% by streamlining and automating routine operations.
- Devised a solution methodology that established the standard for follow-on sales of a key technology.
- Enabled company to move core business into higher value service offerings by creating a services marketplace to segment the customer engagement model.
- Sponsored over 10 projects critical to long-term success of the services business.
- Cut external labor costs by creating leveraged buying strategies and standardization of skill sets.

Key Results (1998-2001):

- Developed and managed 75% of company revenue in 1998, serving as the anchor for the region.
- Structured more than $2 million in large services engagements, minimizing business and technical risk.
- Established a business plan for a remote development center with lower cost development capabilities.
- Created the organization's first outsourcing and monitoring strategy as well as a global account initiative to more effectively manage Fortune 50 clients.

Jonah Geller • Page Two

CHRYSLER CORPORATION, Auburn Hills, Michigan (1993-1997)

PROGRAM MANAGER – SPECIAL PROJECTS

Recruited to direct special projects in support of a variety of corporate growth initiatives and serve as a change agent with regard to introduction, integration, and management of computing technology advances to enhance and expand business processes. Managed infrastructure and applications development projects on multiple technology platforms in effecting vital changes in the business process. Organized multi-functional teams and support staff of up to 25 personnel.

Key Results:

- Conceptualized, piloted, and produced Chrysler's systems management vision using Tivoli's TME/10, establishing the architecture and infrastructure of the management environment.
- Led implementation of the first technology-based project management system, which used a Lotus Notes platform and included process definition and system development.
- Engineered conceptualization, process mapping, technology selection, and implementation of the inventory management and equipment deployment application, the first project to use a "System Thinker" approach to organizational arrangement.
- Directed audit of a business partner's Internet firewall, including intrusion and audit verification.
- Oversaw development and management of SCAAP, a critical supercomputing partnership with Ford and General Motors.
- Directed construction of two data centers and the associated communications infrastructure, delivering the project on time and under budget.
- Managed the evaluation and introduction of an alternative supercomputing platform, overseeing all aspects of the project including hardware/software evaluation, management presentations, facilities management, purchasing, and time line.
- Led project that determined an emerging technology utilizing parallel software (CFD and Stress/Strain) on a MPP platform.
- Spearheaded creation of electronic mail and Internet use policies.
- Developed the first-ever Web application; tracked hardware installation from warehouse to desktop.
- Rescued company historical assets and artifacts from further demulsification and other damages by developing internal image capture and multi-terabyte storage systems and outsourcing scanning solutions.
- Served as Technical Computing spokesperson in developing the Engineering Computing position on infrastructure and application topics and presenting to Chrysler's executive management team.

EDUCATION

BS in Management, University of Michigan
BS in Computer Science, University of Wisconsin

TRAINING AND PROFESSIONAL DEVELOPMENT

High Performance Web Applications Development • Open Standards-Based System Development
Messaging and Collaboration • Conflict Resolution and Management
Project Management • Time Management • Meeting Leadership

ELIZABETH S. MATHUS

135 Bluemont Street, Suite 102, Cambridge MA 02142
Phone: 617-741-0786 • Cell phone: 617-721-3381

PROFILE

Senior health policy executive with extensive experience in coalition building, policy development, strategic planning, program implementation and evaluation, and clinical practice in public, private, and not-for-profit sectors and at international, federal, state, and local levels. Skillfully organized and led national healthcare coalition through development and enactment of Health Insurance Portability and Accountability Act (HIPAA), mandating practices to streamline payment of healthcare claims electronically. Extensive knowledge of healthcare—delivery, policy, strategic planning, and practices. Effective record as expert during congressional deliberations, in diplomacy and interpersonal relations, and with coalition building and lobbying.

CAREER ACCOMPLISHMENTS

- Developed and directed effective industry coalition providing public education and policy guidance on HIPAA provisions governing exchanges of healthcare information and privacy protection. Gained multi-industry consensus on common electronic information exchange standard and secured adoption of that standard in law.

- Nearly 11 years of federal service, including policy team leadership at the National Institute of Alcohol Abuse and Alcoholism, including detail to Congress (implementing very successful, historic food safety hearings and development of legislation).

- Directed international relief operation team in West Africa during time of famine and extreme malnutrition. As clinician, provided diagnostic services in clinics. As Director, represented team and negotiated contracts at all levels of civilian and military government. Served as chief liaison with other international non-government organizations (NGOs).

PROFESSIONAL EXPERIENCE

Director of Public Policy, National Programs, and Public Relations, Boston, MA   1997 - Present
ALLIANCE FOR THE PRUDENT USE OF ANTIBIOTICS (APUA)
Director for international organization, dedicated to education, research, and advocacy of the prudent use of antibiotics. Successful collaboration with government organizations, legislative and regulatory branches, and promotion and presentation of education for health professionals, and trade-shows. Manage press inquires and arrange press conferences, including management of PR contracts.
➤ Direct international surveillance study, The Global Advisory on Antibiotic Resistance Data, comprised of major pharmaceutical companies with CDC and WHO as advisors.
➤ Provide profitable fundraising and development activities.

Executive Director, Boston, MA   1995 - 1996
WORKGROUP FOR ELECTRONIC DATA INTERCHANGE (WEDI)
Directed establishment and operations of nonprofit association to conduct research and public education regarding key provisions of the Health Insurance Portability and Accountability Act (HIPAA). Developed strategic and operating plans, including long- and short-term goals, membership criteria, budget planning and execution, recruitment and development of human and information resources to support intensive operation. Developed 25-member board of directors broadly reflecting divergent concerns about electronic standards and privacy provisions governing transmission of financial data in healthcare. Conducted effective liaison with House and Senate Committees, providing frequent technical briefings on issues and ensuring presentation of coalition witnesses at key hearings and meetings.

ELIZABETH S. MATHUS (continued)

➢ Sustained coalition through enactment of law, successfully doubling membership during leadership.

Division Vice President and Counsel to the President, Hartford, CT   1992 - 1995
THE TRAVELERS INSURANCE COMPANY

Served as Travelers' key strategist on administrative simplification and formulation and execution of Workgroup for Electronic Data Interchange (WEDI) mission, and on public policy affecting healthcare information technology and healthcare reform for the five largest insurers. Determined company positions and negotiated with other insurers prior to work with many outside coalitions in the policy and legislative arenas. Proposed and drafted legislation at federal and state levels to maintain private sector flexibility and role. Developed and conducted briefings for president and board of directors to enable corporate leadership in national policy deliberations.

➢ Developed and published coalition blueprint for reform in healthcare information exchanges.

➢ Successfully presented completed concept report to the Secretary of Health and Human Services within six months of project kickoff.

➢ Developed and published 400-page report to the Secretary of Health and Human Services providing foundation for policies governing electronic exchange of information in healthcare. Incorporated effective privacy protections while facilitating effective implementation of emergent technologies.

OTHER WORK

Director of Health Issues, Hartford, CT   1989 - 1992
TRAVELERS INSURANCE COMPANIES

Deputy Director, OFFICE OF POLICY ANALYSIS, Rockville, MD   1985 - 1989
NATIONAL INSTITUTE ON ALCOHOL ABUSE AND ALCOHOLISM

Acting Director, OFFICE OF POLICY ANALYSIS, Rockville, MD   1983 - 1985
NATIONAL INSTITUTE ON ALCOHOL ABUSE AND ALCOHOLISM

Public Health Advisor, BUREAU OF HEALTH PLANNING, Rockville and Hyattsville, MD 1973 - 1983
DEPARTMENT OF HEALTH, EDUCATION, AND WELFARE

International Relief Team Director, Nigeria, West Africa   1968 - 1971

EDUCATION

Ph.D.   *Brandeis University*, Health and Social Welfare   1989
                       Heller Graduate School for Advanced Studies in Social Welfare
M.P.H.   *Johns Hopkins University,* Public Health Planning and Administration   1973
                       School of Hygiene and Public Health

B.S.N.   *Goshen College,* Nursing   1968

William Schwartz
161 Beakman Street
Washington, DC 20008
bpcs@yahoo.com
202-232-4343

Profile   Visionary eBusiness executive with proven ability to integrate sound strategies and technologies to produce measurable business results. Combines dedicated team leadership, business savvy and solid technical background to develop eBusiness portfolios that increase top and bottom line performance.

Uses effective communication to set clear expectations and smoothly resolve issues among customers, partners, subordinates, peers and supervisors. Leads teams by establishing a shared vision, valuing individual strengths, maintaining open communication, and mentoring. Especially adept at leading teams to be successful in rapidly changing business environments.

Experience **VP, Supply Chain Practice Business Manager**   1999–Present
Digital Trends - Reston, VA

Establishing and growing a new eBusiness services practice. Close engagements with prospective clients. Hire, manage, and mentor software developers and project managers. Estimate fixed price engagements, write proposals and lead business development teams. Ultimately responsible for exceeding clients' expectations and growing long-term relationships.

- **Managing five eBusiness programs encompassing 18 eBusiness solutions** that have generated over $8M in services revenue. **Increased revenue by 153%** in 2000. During the 2001 recession, maintained revenue at 80% of 2000.
- Grew relationship with Fortune 40 pharmaceutical distributor from $225K to $5.7M. This relationship is now a **cornerstone customer account** for Digital Trends.
- Designed and led development of a **B2B eProcurement portal** for a $45B pharmaceutical distributor. This mission critical system is being rolled out to 8,000 customers who place $100M in orders daily. Resulting cost savings are directly improving this client's profitability.
- Maintaining exceedingly high levels of **employee loyalty** through mentoring, leveraging personal aptitudes, and insightful career guidance. Resulted in a secure 16-person staff that rapidly adapts to change and does whatever it takes to exceed client expectations.

Consulting Manager   1998–1999
Kingstar Systems, Inc. - Alexandria, VA

Led technical consulting teams and business development teams. Lead CORBA consulting expert. Established and grew new client relationships.

- Managed the **object-oriented analysis and design (OOA&D)** and development of the flight reservation and crew scheduling system for an executive aircraft company. Trained internal IT staff in technical and management skills for developing this core system.
- Led a team to complete the design and then implement a distributed mortgage pricing system. The CORBA based architecture supports 8,000 concurrent users.
- Taught a 40-hour "VisiBroker for Java" course monthly, under a contract with the Systems Corporation. Consistently received excellent reviews as a certified **CORBA Instructor**.

- Led the design and development of a pharmaceutical Intranet. This NetDynamics Java application caches documents in memory resulting in an extremely responsive user interface.

Software Management Director, USAF Officer, Captain   1996–1998
National Reconnaissance Office – Quantico, VA

Managed a **$10-million budget** to select, buy, and install commercial software to meet the needs of an 8,500-person organization. Led an 8-person team responsible for assessing internal customer business requirements and providing software to increase productivity and efficiency.

- Established software development standards to improve quality. Topics included**: N-tier architectures, Intranet standards, component development**, development environments, workflow, query/reporting, coding conventions, and testing. Lowered costs and increased productivity by increasing technical architecture and user interface consistency across contractor developed applications.
- Managed the development of a web-based application that enabled a **geographically dispersed team** to orchestrate satellite launches.

Satellite Mission Control System Project Officer, USAF Officer   1993–1996
San Diego Air Force Base, MILSATCOM Program Office – San Diego, CA

Managed contracts and delivered satellite control subsystems to the USAF Space Command which ensured command and control of US Forces under any combat conditions.

- Led 15-person advisory group to target exorbitant software maintenance costs. Initiated and led an **object-oriented analysis and redesign** of the Ground Control System software.
- Led the design of a $20 million telecommunications satellite component that included custom firmware. Resolved environmental testing issues. **Delivered 25% ahead of schedule**.
- Managed a $24-million contract for a Satellite Mobile Control system. By improving the relationship between the government and the contractor, **reduced negotiating time** for contract changes from 6 months to 6 weeks.

Staff Scientist   1992–1993
Science International Corporation (SIC) – Los Angeles, CA

- Used FORTRAN models to assess the ability of different sensor satellite configurations to detect and track targets. Analysis results used to plan a multibillion-dollar USAF program.

Education   **Master of Business Administration**
San Diego University – San Diego, CA

Bachelor of Science in Electrical Engineering
Northeastern University – Boston, MA

Professional   • Supply Chain Management in the Internet Age - *MIT Sloan School of Mgmt.*
Development   • Seven Habits of Highly Effective People, Certified Instructor
and   • Sun Certified Java Programmer
Certifications   • VisiBroker for Java (CORBA ORB), Inprise Certified Instructor

Technical   • Enterprise Java Architect and Programmer
Experience   • Designed numerous systems using the Unified Modeling Language (UML)
       • Established eXtreme Programming as a methodology within Digital Focus
       • Extensive use of Design Patterns
       • RDBMS design and experience includes Oracle, SQL Server, and MySQL
       • Fluent in Windows, Solaris and Linux

JACK GOLD, CPA

7890 Flower Drive
Arlington, Virginia 22015

703-555-8655
gold123@msn.com

SENIOR FINANCE MANAGER
Accounting/Audit/Controllership/Banking & Investor Relations

Senior financial executive with over 20 years experience in Financial/Accounting. Strengths include supporting growth in loan production from $200 million to $3 billion, servicing portfolio from $1 billion to $7 billion and assets from $100 million to $600 million. Strategic business leader with strong management, human resource, communication, team-building, problem-solving and decision-making skills. Success in optimizing efficiency and profitability through delivery of value-added systems, programs and procedures. Committed to protecting integrity of the corporation.

PROFESSIONAL EXPERIENCE

GREENPOINT MORTGAGE SERVICES, INC., Fairfax, Virginia   1995-2002
Chief Financial Officer

Recruited to spearhead the development and management of investor relationship for Wholesale and Retail Lending. Reported directly to President with direct leadership for 10 staff members. Managed all secondary functions and indirectly supervised an additional 10 employees.

- Directly responsible for managing loan and accounting functions, $75 million to $150 million in loan pipeline, including the development of lock policies and servicing of the portfolio.
- Managed Quality Control staff producing satisfactory audit results while doubling loan production.
- Created pricing modules for pricing and locking portfolio on a flow basis.
- Directly involved in creating and implementing policies for seven new retail branches.
- Developed reporting and analytical financial data on branch level for review by senior management.
- Liaison for Corporate Human Resources providing all incentive disbursement and other payroll related duties for 75 employees.
- Created and trained staff for Accounting, secondary, quality controls, and post closing functions.

MORTGAGE EDGE CORPORATION, *McLean, Virginia*   1994-1995
Controller (Part-Time)

- Played a key role in the start-up of the company, including licensing, investor recruitment, acquisition of warehouse line, development of payroll system, selection of health and dental insurance plan and day-to-day troubleshooting.
- Created and implemented policies and procedures for newly established retail, wholesale and B/C credit accounting division.

MORTGAGE SERVICE AMERICAN COMPANY, *Fairfax, Virginia*   1993-1994
Controller

Responsibilities included the operation function of accounting for a regional banking firm operating in 14 states. Managed and directly accountable for accounts payable, incentive and commission tracking and payment, loan origination fee accounting, financial accounting and reporting, and cost containment.

- Coordinated and produced annual budgets, which included maintaining the corporate financial forecast.
- Development and formatted financial reporting for the Eastern Region.
- Hired and trained and accounting staff of 11 with a $750,000 budget for a newly developed department.
- Instituted new Accounting system, which resulted in a dramatic improvement in the accuracy and timeliness of financial data as well as strengthening relationships with investors, bankers and clients.
- Assisted in merger by providing a dual controllership role for MSA and Dominion.

DOMINION BANKSHARES MORTGAGE CORPORATION, *McLean, Virginia*   1991-1993
Controller

Managed accounting staff of 18 with a $1-million budget. Responsibilities included financial accounting, cash management, management reporting, forecasting, analyzing servicing portfolio to maximize returns, and valuation of Mortgage Held for Sale.

- Analyzed the largest deal creating $4.5 million in deferred income and reducing intangible assets by $11 million.
- Automated financial reporting reducing staff by two employees.
- Participated in revision Uniform Single Audit Program for Mortgage Banker.
- Formatted financial reports for expansion of the Retail Banking Production.
- Analyzed the feasibility of a Limited Partnership for the investment in servicing rights.
- Eliminated manual effort related to commission tracking by enhancing use of CPI reports.
- Continual review of discretionary expenditures for cost containment.

DOMINION BANKSHARES MORTGAGE CORPORATION, *McLean, Virginia*   1984-1990
Accounting Manager

Responsible for analysis of prospective acquisitions, presented information and pricing recommendation to Senior Management and assisted in Controllers function.

- Instituted new procedures to obtain control over credit reports and appraisal fees.
- Developed management reporting for reconciliations.
- Documented historical information of variable for valuation and pricing schedules.
- Acted as coordinator for transfer to Accounts Payable function.
- Maintained integrity and accuracy of general ledger, producing satisfactory audits during downsizing, absence of four senior employees and double loan production.
- Detected and resolved problems with FHLMC investor reconciliations.
- Wrote accounting policies and procedures for capitalization of servicing rights and excess servicing.
- Received Administrative Award in 1987 for improvement of financial reporting.

DOMINION BANKSHARES MORTGAGE CORPORATION, *McLean, Virginia*   1980-1983
Staff Accountant

Responsible for maintenance of an automated fixed asset accounting system and reconciliation of general ledger and trust accounts. Supervised two employees accountable for data entry and maintenance of new loan accounting system. Provided backup to Accounting Manager, assisted Accounts Payable and recorded Cash Receipts.

EDUCATION

BS Administration, Concentration in Accounting
George Washington University, Washington, DC

Completed Mortgage Banking School I and II
Certified Public Accountant, State of Virginia 1995

Computer literate in spreadsheets and various word processing software

BRAM LEVY
833 Martel Avenue
Hollywood, CA 90046
Home 213-651-1900
Cell 213-208-6822

SUMMARY

Senior level general manager with a record of redirecting business strategy, managing start-up situations and negotiating favorable business agreements. Extensive experience in international operations, strategic management and marketing. Skilled in labor negotiations, community relations and public affairs. Record of applying business strategies and managing cultural diversity in challenging markets to achieve profits. Have worked and lived outside of the USA for over 10 years.

PROFESSIONAL EXPERIENCE

ML ROBINSON INVESTMENTS, New York, NY (2001-2004)
Chief Executive Officer – Karachi, Pakistan

CEO and Managing Board Director for a full service Investment Company formed in 2000. Shares are publicly held. Shareholders include: Alphacom, Betacom, and Deltacom. Full management and P&L responsibility for a $40-million business reporting to the Chairman and Board of Directors.

- Fulfilled assignment to deliver strong 2002 financial results, analyze current business plan and future prospects, and work with the Chairman and the Board to identify a CEO from the local market.
- Raised 2002 profits to $1.4 million versus $150,000 in 2001. Stock price increased by 72%, from 18 to 31 per share. Local CEO installed after smooth transfer and management.

EURAM INTERNATIONAL INC., New York, NY (1999-2001)
Senior Director – Country General Manager – Amsterdam, Netherlands

Recruited to manage the Amsterdam Division and lead a major restructuring program to strengthen the balance sheet and improve efficiency and profitability.

- Full profit and loss responsibility for $70-million business.
- Conducted complete business review and prepared detailed strategic plan setting out options and future growth potential for the business.
- Restructured branch, eliminating one business line and sharpening focus on another. Resulted in doubling of net income.

INTERNATIONAL BANK, New York, NY (1992-1999)
Senior Director-Special Transactions Group – New York (1998-1999)

Formed Transactional Business Unit to provide specialist expertise to international private banking clients. Created a customer driven proactive management group designed to meet customer needs.

- From a starting point of zero, generated unit fee income of $1 million in its first year.
- Successfully established strong relationships with over 15 major clients and investment companies.

First Vice President & General Manager – Germany, Holland, Greece – Frankfurt, Germany (1996-1998)

Managed European division in preparation for transfer of operating contract. The division is a retail branch business under contract with the United States Department of Defense consisting of 135 branches in three countries, 1,700 employees, with full profit and loss responsibility for $75 million division.

- Coordinated interaction with European Military Command and the Pentagon.
- Handled complex negotiations with German Labor Union. Negotiations involved continuity of employment terms and conditions, transfer of pension's benefits and resolution of outstanding labor cases.
- Led management team of eight direct reports in day-to-day operations and in planning, documenting and executing a detailer.

First Vice President & General Manager – Far East Region – Honolulu, Hawaii (1992-1996)

Managed Far East Region with full profit center responsibility for Hawaii Headquarters and Operations Center plus retail branches in Korea, the Philippines, Japan, Okinawa, and Panama, with total revenues of $18 million. The region consisted of 40 branches, 600 employees, 70,000 accounts and total assets of $100 million. Key management challenges: run a multicultural business with diverse labor features and business practices; set strategy or collective bargaining and labor relations in four countries; establish targets for requirements and budget goals while developing new services, sites, and income opportunities.

- Recognized for reducing Hawaii Headquarters Office overall costs by $900,000 from $3.7 million to $2.8 million. This was accomplished by reducing management layers and streamlining existing operations and systems areas.
- Improved bottom line financial results for the Region in 1995 by 43% over contract/budget.
- Handled and completed lengthy and difficult collective bargaining negotiations with the Japanese Labor Union on the termination of 106 local national employees required by the Department of Defense as a result of a change of contractor in Japan/Okinawa.
- Opened two "new concept" low staff, low cost branches in Panama, and introduced mobile "business units" in Korea.

OVERSEAS FINANCE CORPORATION - Washington, DC (1989-1992)
Vice President/Director – Syndicate Dept./Project Finance – London, England (1991-1992)

Structured and syndicated project financing transactions for sovereign nations and private companies, usually in support of major international projects or capital equipment exports. Negotiated pricing, terms and conditions with Borrowers, Export Credit Agencies, and other financing institutions.

Worked closely with outside legal and tax advisors on legal, structural and tax matters in the following countries: Spain, Portugal, Germany, France, Switzerland, United Kingdom, Denmark, Italy, Malaysia, Turkey, Greece, Pakistan, Algeria, Bahrain, Egypt and then U.S.S.R.

- Teamed with Project Finance Specialist and Sources of Capital to complete and syndicate transactions with a total value of $1.8 billion.

Assistant Treasurer, Multinational Banking Group, New York, NY (1990-1991)

Asia Region – Military Banking Division (1989)

- District Manager – Japan
- Manager of Operations – Saigon (Defense Attaché Office)
- Management Training – Philippines

EDUCATION

George Washington University, M.B.A. 1988
Harvard University B.S. 1986

Merry Korn

7 Kentwood Road, Morristown, New Jersey 07876 (201)123-4567 sjk@col.com

SUMMARY: Over 19 years of progressive, diverse and extensive experience in the pharmaceutical industry. Broad background and accomplishments in manufacturing, packaging, engineering and facilities management. Outstanding track record turning around and building strong organizations through leadership and organizational abilities. Recognized skilled problem solver.

PROFESSIONAL EXPERIENCE:

SJK, Inc., Morristown, NJ (1985-present)
Vice-President, Facilities Administration (2000-present)
Responsible for all facilities operations and services, engineering and environment / safety for 14 sites in NJ. Staff of over 300 BJB employees, and over 250 contract employees. Operating budget of $81M and capital budget of $39M.

- Managed the 65% growth of the headquarters site from 735,000 to 1.2M square feet, mostly in new laboratories.

- Supervised the accelerated construction and flawless start-up of a new site – 78,000 square feet, 3 buildings, 2000 employees.

- Restructured the organization improving customer service, operating efficiency and personnel development.

- Consolidated and closed down smaller sites attaining operating efficiencies and cost reductions.

- Implemented commitment accounting in all operating and engineering departments resulting in no variances to budgets.

Senior Director, Pharmaceutical Operations (1995-2000)
Responsible for all pharmaceutical dosage forms manufacturing in NJ, IN, NC, and Puerto Rico. Staff of over 8000 employees. Manufactured products supported sales of over $1.2 billion.

- Integrated the multi-site manufacturing operations in the four locations by product transfers, restructuring, team-building and information sharing, raising efficiency by 22%.

- Initiated employee involvement groups including union employees resulting in productivity gains.

- Reduced rejections by 75% and brought inventory levels within plan.

Established staff training leading to improved working relationship between Puerto Rico and US sites through team-building, communication, teamwork, and doing what is "right."

Merry Korn
Page 2

Senior Director, Engineering and Maintenance (1989-1995)
Responsible for engineering, construction, utilities, maintenance and technology group on site – 2400 employees and 1.6M square feet. Operating budget of $40M and a capital budget of $20M.

- Installed highly computerized high speed lines for high volume Lyophilized products, resulting in savings of over $2M.

- Led a three-member team in the successful negotiation of the co-union contract.

- Decentralized selected groups to provide improved services.

- Facilitated cogeneration project resulting in over $2M in production cost savings.

- Initiated benchmarking of services, resulting in downsizing of construction and maintenance groups by 12%. Increased outsourcing of engineering support functions by 5%.

Director, Parenteral Operations (1985-1989)
Responsible for the sterile manufacturing of powdered, lyophilized and liquid injectable products. Staff of over 200 employees. Manufactured products supported sales of over $300M.

- Member of a three-member team that constructed and validated a new highly computerized 135k-square-foot parenteral facility.

- Successfully validated and started the parenteral facility without a 483 observation.

- Installed highly computerized manufacturing system eliminating rejections and improving yields by 2%.

- Developed excellent relationship with FDA National Inspector.

Additional experience with SJK, Inc:
Manager, Parenteral Manufacturing
Section Head, Parenteral Manufacturing
Section Head, Dosage Manufacturing
Supervisor, Tablet Manufacturing

EDUCATION: MBA, Pharmaceutical Marketing, Fairleigh Dickenson Universtiy

BS, Chemical Engineering, Newark College of Engineering

CHARLES JACKSON

1211 Liberty Lane, Apt. 508 Rockville, MD 20852
Home: 301-984-4444 • Cellular: 301-423-5064 • charlesjackson35@aol.com

EXPERIENCE

AMERITRADE HOLDING CORPORATION / *Annapolis Junction, Maryland*   November 1999 – Present
Senior Technology Negotiator

- Draft, revise and negotiate technology licensing and purchase contracts to maximize protection and minimize risk and total cost of ownership. Utilize requirements-based, cross-functional team approach to technology acquisition. Contracts negotiated include Software License Agreements, Software Development Agreements, Non-Disclosure Agreements, Evaluation Agreements, Professional Services Agreements, Master Purchase Agreements and others. Negotiate with counsel of corporations including IBM, Rational Software, Money.net, Reuters, Lipper, Tidal Software, Equifax, Cisco Systems, Hewlett Packard and others. Prepare requests for proposals and evaluation of vendor proposals.
- Research and develop the technology leasing initiative for the parent company and all affiliates and subsidiaries. Draft, revise and negotiate technology leasing contracts to maximize favorable lease terms and conditions. Technology leasing contracts negotiated include Master Lease Agreements, Certificates of Incumbency, Acceptance including GE Capital, Forsythe McArthur, IBM Credit Corporation, Cisco Capital, CIT/Newcourt Financial, and CSI Leasing. Interact with members of the finance, risk management, legal, tax, and regulatory departments to facilitate the execution and implementation of lease contracts.
- Develop and negotiate complex technology agreements, including, among others: software licenses, content development/license agreements, Website agreements, privacy policies, hardware/software maintenance agreements, hosting agreements, linking agreements, trademark license agreements, subscriptions services agreements, and others. Counsel business and technology units on intellectual property issues/protection, website legal issues and compliance, e-commerce issues and general corporate matters.

UNITED STATES DEPARTMENT OF JUSTICE / *Washington, D.C.*   May 1999 – November 1999
Consultant / Litigation Management

Contracted to work on the Winstar Litigation with the Commercial Litigation Division of the Department of Justice; gather, prepare, and summarize relevant materials for use by trial team attorney in preparation of opinions, briefs and other legal documents; summarize depositions and other transcripts; index, track and control exhibits and other materials at depositions.

SUDER & SUDER, P.A. / *Baltimore, Maryland*   September 1998 – May 1999
Law Clerk

Prepare pleadings, motions, discovery, correspondence; conduct client interviews; manage case files; perform legal and medical research; schedule and assists during depositions; prepare cases for, and assist during jury trials.

A.E.G. & ASSOCIATES, INC. / *Washington, D.C.*   June 1997 – August 1998
Technology Negotiator

Facilitated the technology acquisition process for a high-technology media company; drafted and filed all incorporation documents, including articles of incorporation, articles or organization, bylaws, minutes, amendments and other business documents; negotiated procurement orders with vendors; drafted the business terms and conditions for technology agreements, memorandum of understanding, maintenance agreements, and non-disclosure agreements.

UNITED STATES PATENT & TRADEMARK OFFICE / *Arlington, Virginia*   January 1997 – May 1997
Trademark Intern

Gathered relevant primary and secondary evidence to substantiate trademark registration refusals; conducted on-line research utilizing various trademark database services; summarized recent Trademark Trial and Appeal Board (TTAB) case decisions for in-house case digest.

TSI TELSYS, INC. / *Columbia, Maryland*   May 1996 – October 1996
Intellectual Property Specialist

Research, developed, synthesized and compiled intellectual property protection manual for a high-technology satellite communications company; performed on-line research using various intellectual property databases; utilized software design programs extensively on finished product; organized a non-disclosure agreement database with participating vendor clients.

CHARLES JACKSON   **Page Two**

HUGHES NETWORK SYSTEMS, INC. / *Germantown, Maryland*   May 1994 – August 1994
Consultant / Contracts Specialist

Coordinated the management of requirement and supply contracts for *Alcatel Sel*, an in-house subsidiary; contracted client sites to verify scheduling progress and updates.

JUDICAL EXPERIENCE

HONORABLE DAVID B. MITCHELL, CIRCUIT COURT FOR BALTIMORE CITY / *Baltimore, Maryland*
Judicial Clerk   May 1995 – August 1994

Researched and wrote Post-Conviction Memorandum and Orders; coordinated protocol procedures in the judge's chambers; answered letters from inmates requesting information on pending appeals; filed motions and memoranda with court clerk; observed both civil and criminal proceedings.

EDUCATION

UNIVERSITY OF BALTIMORE SCHOOL OF LAW / *Baltimore, Maryland*   August 1994 – May 1997
JURIS DOCTORATE with concentration in Intellectual Property

      Academic: *Member, National Trademark Moot Court Team, 1995-1996
                *Staff Member, University of Baltimore Intellectual Property Law Journal, 1996-1997
                *Member, Sigma Delta Kappa Law Fraternity, 1995-1997

      Specialized Curriculum:
                **Merrick School of Business*; Lab-to-Market Program; Opportunity Analysis
                *School of Law; Intellectual Property (Patents, Trademark and Copyright);
                        Technology Transfer; Copyright & the Arts; Contracts; Corporate Law

FRANKLIN AND MARSHALL COLLEGE / *Lancaster, Pennsylvania*   August 1990 – May 1994
BACHELOR OF ARTS in Government with a minor in History

      Academic: *Recipient, Dean's List, 1991 – 1994

PROFESSIONAL TRAINING

- Business Method Patents, "Protecting Your Intellectual Property in the Digital Age"
- Managed Acquisition Process (MAP) Workshop
- Burning Issues in Technology Leasing "How to Do Better Technology Lease Deals"
- Leasing Negotiation Workshop
- Commerce Service Providers, "A Brave New World In The 21st Century"
- Society of Information Managers (SIM) Information Technology Working Group covering Revenue Recognition, Reseller vs. Direct Model, e-commerce Strategy, Commerce Linking Agreements
- Revenue Recognition, "How Revenue Recognition Issues Impact Your Software Negotiations"
- Supplier Management & Performance Measurement Training

MEMBERSHIP

- CLA – Computer Law Association
- CAUCUS – Association of High Tech Procurement Professionals
- NAPM – National Association of Purchasing Management

Deborah Geller

8457 Ripple Road • Alexandria, VA 22314 • (703) 564-7554 • djag@hotmail.com

PROFILE: Senior public affairs executive with broad-based experience in providing government affairs counsel and strategy. In-depth experience in the healthcare industry and government compliance.

- Federal Government Relations
- State Government Relations
- Community Affairs
- Public Policy / Business Strategy Development
- Strategic Partnerships/Alliances
- Employee and Labor Relations

PROFESSIONAL EXPERIENCE:

Integrated Health Services Group, Tysons, VA (1984-present)

Vice President, Government Relations (1997-present)
Reporting to the VP of Public Affairs, directed all aspects of government affairs for a worldwide $14B highly decentralized, diversified, broad-based healthcare company.

- Restructured Federal Relations Unit (Washington, DC office) in anticipation of reform of US healthcare system.
- Reorganized State Government Relations Unit to deal with rapid change of healthcare delivery systems at the state level.
- Integrated Community Affairs Unit more fully into a $52.2 million annual contribution program.
- Facilitated team of four to shape corporate health-care reform position.
- Codirected effort to retain Puerto Rican federal tax credit during consideration of Omnibus Budget Reconciliation Acts, resulting in substantial savings.

Vice President, Federal Relations (1991-1997)

- Directed Washington office staff through a "crisis."
- Initiated reorganization and expansion of corporate Washington office to confront dramatic increase in legislative proposal affecting it's business.
- Worked with former Chairman and CEO, established liaison with senior White House staff and other members of the Executive Branch, including Cabinet Officers.

Vice President, Corporate Staff (1989-1991)
Joined the Public Affairs department upon appointment by the Vice Chairman of Public Affairs and Planning. Primary role was to provide staff support for Chairman of the Board concerning significant external commitments.

- Maintained calendar and schedule of CEO in his role as Chairman of the Business Roundtable's Human Resources Committee, and as a member of it's planning (Executive) committee.
- Assisted CEO in his role as Vice Chairman of the Business Council in planning and executing Council meetings.
- Coodinated CEO's activities and functions as member of various Boards, including the Urban Institute, the United Negro College Fund, and the Volker Commission on Public Service.

Vice President, Labor Relations Worldwide (1984-1989)
Hired by and reported to member of Executive Committee to reorganize labor relations department
and establish a consistent, business sensitive corporate strategy.

- Managed and negotiated seven successful strike settlements to reestablish the company's
  bargaining integrity.
- Developed collective bargaining parameters to insure consistency in collective bargaining
  settlements.
- Won over 10 labor union organizing campaigns.

Great Lakes Shipping Company, Chicago, IL (1980-1984)
Assistant Manager, Labor Relations Division
Senior Labor Attorney
Reported to manager of labor relations division, who was responsible for all aspects of labor
relations of a labor intensive, highly unionized work force of 111,000 employees.

- Participated in strategic planning and conduct of negotiations with US Steel workers; Great
  Lakes shipping negations with Masters', Pilots' and Mates & Marine Engineers' Benevolent
  Associations; also led a team in national Anthracite Coal Mining negotiations.
- Headed 10 arbitration attorneys who represented the company in hundreds of labor arbitration
  cases annually.

Director, Employer Relations
Reported to Group Vice President with responsibility for federal legislative and administrative
issues in the human resource area.

- Dealt with legislation leading to: ERISA, OSHA, and the amendment of the 1964 Civil Rights
  Act, to grant the EEOC enforcement power, were significant current issues during the period

---

EXTERNAL
ORGANIZATIONS:
- Vice Chairman, Board of the Public Affairs Council
- Board Member, National Foreign Trade Council
- Past Chairman, Business Roundtable Employee Relations Committee
- Past Cochairman, American Bar Assn., International Labor Law Committee
- Commissioner, NJ Public Employment Relations Commission

EDUCATION:
- L.L.M., Georgetown University Law Center, Washington, DC
- L.L.B., George Washington University Law Center, Washington, DC
- B.A., John Carroll University, University Heights, OH

Paul Bransom

123 Main Street ~ Timberwood, CA 92601 ~ 801-234-7834 ~ 801-555-3894 ~ pbransom@yahoo.com

PROFESSIONAL SUMMARY

Accomplished Lawyer with over 8 years of experience providing regulatory compliance and research. Expertise in environmental, energy and safety fields. Dynamic and persuasive, winning arguments and settling cases. Expertise in analysis, research and case preparation.

EDUCATION

Juris Doctor
Vermont Law School, South Royalton, Vermont, 1997

M.S. International Law & Policies
Vermont Law School, South Royalton, Vermont, 1996

B.S. Business Management
Penn State University, State College, PA 1993

PROFESSIONAL CAREER TRACK

Ellisworth Associates, Arlington, Virginia
Senior Regulatory Counsel, 2001 - Present
- Manage team of 8 attorneys, performing variety of energy, environmental, safety and health client services.
- Provide oversight and project management for research topics such as, state energy policy, air permitting, global climate change issues, environmental management systems, TMDL development, and underground storage tank requirements.
- Review and edit upcoming regulatory activity.

Ellisworth Associates, Arlington, Virginia
Regulatory Counsel, 1998 - 2001
- Monitored emerging state environmental regulatory activity, assessed impact on clients in oil, gas, energy, technology, chemical, and military industries.
- Advised and counseled clients on environmental health and safety compliance issues.
- Co-authored article printed in *Environmental Compliance and Litigation Strategies*, Sept 1998.
- Researched and prepared environmental audit protocols, ensuring compliance with state environmental regulations.
- Drafted and prepared memorandum of law and policy circulated to State Attorney Generals, persuading them to sign amicus brief for a pending U.S. Supreme Court case.

Professional Legal Services, Washington, D.C.
Contract Attorney, 1997 - 1998
- Analyzed and reviewed evidence for environmental criminal defense litigation.
- Reviewed documents for antitrust filings.

Paul Bransom

123 Main Street ~ Timberwood, CA 92601 ~ 801-234-7834 ~ 801-555-3894 ~ pbransom@yahoo.com

International Joint Commission, U.S. & Canada, Washington, D.C.
Legal Intern, 1996
- Authored article published in *Focus*.
- Prepared an analysis of progress to restore water quality of Mississippi River.
- Performed comparative analysis of state water laws within Great Lakes basin and existing EPA regulations.
- Researched and reported potential conflicts between international and domestic laws regarding licensing of hydropower projects on U.S./Canadian border.

Pennsylvania Environmental Protection Agency, Pittsburgh, Pennsylvania
Legal Intern, 1996
- Drafted consent and other enforcement orders.
- Researched and wrote memorandum on CERCLA liability, regulatory takings, and changes in environmental legislation.

HONORS & AWARDS

Bar Admission: District of Columbia, 2000 and Supreme Court of PA, 1997

Awarded "Best Brief" Thomas D. Grasso Court Competition, 1997

Academic Excellence Award, highest grade in Legal Process, 1997

PROFESSIONAL DEVELOPMENT

Negotiation Training, 1996

TAYLOR S. DONALDSON

199 Smithfield Court • Reston, VA 20191 • (703) 421-9065 • (703) 739-0398 • tdonald@msn.com

Certified Public Accountant with over 20 years of government, private, and entreprenurial experience with expertise in accounting, auditing, financial management and taxation

SUMMARY OF QUALIFICATIONS

♦ Effectively and accurately interpret policy and procedures.
♦ Possess proven accounting and organizational skills key to managing diverse record-keeping functions.
♦ Proficient computer skills, including Peachtree, Quicken, Excel, Word, Lotus, and various tax software.
♦ Outstanding personnel management strategies, which emphasize training and team-building.
♦ Consistently provide strategic and effective executive direction for multifaceted companies.
♦ Capable of identifying innovative methods and procedures to increase bottom-line profits.

EDUCATION

Long Island University, Brooklyn, NY
Graduate School of Business

Rutgers University, Newark, NJ
Bachelor of Science, Accounting

PROFESSIONAL EXPERIENCE

National Pharmaceutical Association, Silver Spring, MD   1999 – 2002
Chief Financial Officer
Managed all aspects of corporate financial operations, including supervision of personnel, financial planning and budgeting, cash flow management, and accurate accounting for revenues and expenditures by generally accepted accounting principles (GAAP).
➢ Developed and implemented accounting policies and procedures.
➢ Served as liaison to external auditors, including government auditors.
➢ Prepared and presented to Board of Directors on-time, accurate financial reports.
➢ Conducted financial analyses, reported trends and implications to CEO.
➢ Developed budget database and maintained balanced annual budget.

EDS, Audit, and Tax Consultant, Reston, VA   1998 – 1999
Self-Employed
Worked as a consultant to ABS, Inc. performing consulting, auditing and financial management to Department of Housing and Urban Development (HUD).
➢ Reviewed Single Audit Reports and determined deficiency, which resulted in non-compliance with OPM's administrative requirements. Recommended processes, procedures and management oversight to provide and ensure compliance.
➢ Provided training and ongoing guidance to HUD staff, ensuring full compliance to all state and federal regulations.
➢ Effectively resolved other audit findings.

Taylor S. Donaldson
Page 2

PROFESSIONAL EXPERIENCE

U.S. Department of Housing and Urban Development, Washington, DC   1990 – 1998
Senior Financial Management Analyst
Resolved complex and difficult financial issues in diverse portfolio of HUD programs. Provided technical advice and guidance. Monitored and evaluated performance of state, municipal, and not-for-profit operations to ensure compliance. Reviewed audit reports and responses to ensure timeliness and accuracy. Analyzed financial statements, Grantee Performance Reports (GPR), and fund request documents, ensuring proper transmittal or retrieval of funds. Performed financial management reviews on numerous HUD programs. Provided guidance on special budgetary reports.

- Interpreted HUD policy, regulations, and requirements and recommended appropriate actions.
- Developed and implemented financial management seminars and workshops.
- Monitored and audited grantees fiscal operations and performance in meeting financial requirements.
- Provided technical assistance to guarantees, ensuring compliance with program requirements. Resolved problems by properly interpreting existing guidance and establishing new approaches.
- Provided interpretation and implementation of new policies (OMB Circulars A-133, A-87, A-110, etc.) regulations and procedures.
- Collaborated and advised District of Columbia, local counties, and nonprofit organizations in establishing financial systems or substantially changing current systems to meet compliance.

Walton Home Loan Mortgage Company, Reston, VA   1988 – 1990
Assistant Technical Tax Advisor
Reviewed all technical tax memorandums, implemented recommended conclusions, reviewed complex Tax Research and Planning memorandums, assisted in the preparation of the Corporate Tax Return, prepared the Earnings and Profits Information Return, and the Deferred Tax Analysis (FASB 96).

Hyatt Corporation, St. Louis, MO   1985 – 1988
Section Manager of International Accounting
Prepared financial statements, financial plans, budgets, trial balances, and other necessary annual reports. Assisted corporate auditors reviewing internal controls. Partnered with CPA firms to perform annual audits. Collaborated with Foreign Sales Corporation (FSC).

OTHER RELEVENT EXPERIENCE

Edwards & Sons, Inc., St. Louis, MO, Manager of Accounting Procedures/Internal Audits.
Bluemont Instrument Corporation, Clifton, NJ, Sr. Supervising Auditor/ Regional Manager.

PROFESSIONAL LICENSES
Certified Public Accountant licensed in Missouri, New Jersey, and Virginia

PROFESSIONAL ASSOCIATIONS
American Institute of Certified Public Accountants, Virginia Society of Certified Public Accountants, Missouri Society of Certified Public Accountants

Robert F. Popov

94895 Old Dominion Avenue • Fairfield, VA 20198 • 703-500-3049 • 703-403-9958 • rpopov@yahoo.com

PROFESSIONAL SUMMARY

Dynamic and proven management analyst providing expertise in strategic and analytical planning, project management, budget development and formulation, and policy and procedure development. Track record of progressive responsibilities and promotions. Excellent communication skills, developing strategic alliances, negotiating and resolving conflicts and creating win-win solutions that contribute to successful completion of ambitious goals. Demonstrated team leader and senior advisor making quality recommendations that positively impact the organization.

PROFESSIONAL WORK EXPERIENCE

Blue Lagoon Resources, Fairfield, VA   6/2002 – Present
Chief, IRM Unit
- Direct the planning and execution of IRM program, providing full-range of supervisory responsibilities, managing and overseeing IRM projects and activities. Oversees and manages IRM program and IT portfolio management, ensuring consistent funding initiatives. Determines multiyear strategic goals and objectives. Ensures coordination and uniformity of IRM policies and operations across the organization.
- Supervise daily operations of Information Resource Management (IRM) support staff, including information technology acquisition, records management, Privacy Act, vital records, Freedom of Information Act, directives management, Section 508, and the Office of Management and Budget Information Collections and Information Quality Guidelines.
- Direct organization-wide effort responding to court mandated searches. Develop response strategy for execution by DOJ in conjunction with various Federal Courts.
- Coordinate exemption requests to court mandated freeze of all records.
- Implemented new FOIA and Information Quality tracking systems.
- Led major update process for General Records Schedule. Negotiated multifaceted implementation with NARA permitting faster implementation.
- Developed creative solutions to reduce costs associated with data storage. Challenging issues include declassification, nitrate negatives, foreign data components, copper plates, and very large electronic files.

Chief, IRM Support   10/1995 – 6/2002
- Led efforts responding to court mandated document production requirements.
- Supervise daily operations of Information Resource Management (IRM) support staff, including information technology acquisition, records management, vital records, Web operations, Freedom of Information Act, directives management, and the Office of Management and Budget Information Collections.
- Signature authority for IT acquisition process.
- As Executive Secretary for IC, successfully drove committee from inception to implementation in 30 days, including establishment of appropriate links with strategic agency groups and formation and staffing of subcommittees.
- Planned and developed infrastructures plan after comprehensive study and analysis, including conducted an IT baseline assessment analysis; collaborated in interagency IT functional analysis; developed planning methodologies and contingency positions; evaluated modeling and simulation tools and methods.

Robert F. Popov

IRM Liaison Officer   7/1993 – 10/1995
- Led efforts to modernize and update execution of public laws.
- Served as organization representative to Department Planning Group.
- Significant contributor to improvements in IRM reporting requirements, noteworthy results included streamlined IRM Review Plan, condensed, concise Strategic Plan and simplification of Section 43 and A-130 of OMB's A-11.
- Developed goals, objectives, policies and procedures coordinating information technology planning.
- Created innovative software licensing policy for organization-wide use.
- Constructed and implemented life cycle management program for successful acquisition of needed technology for scientific programs.
- Instrumental in three IRM committees that restructured and reduced paperwork for successful implementation and compliance with National Performance Review.
- Sponsored and raised funds for 10 technology demonstrations and hosted numerous forum sessions.
- Key member of Space Committee successfully developed and implemented plan to incorporate major influxes of new employees.

Staff Assistant   6/1991 – 7/1993
- Managed and oversaw planning, budgeting, technology and staffing for Information Systems Division.
- Prepared performance evaluations, staffing plans and position descriptions.
- Project coordination and project management, ensuring all project timelines were met.
- Prepared IRM Strategic Plan.
- Senior advisor (to Information Systems Council) overseeing all information systems planning, management, analysis, coordination and execution for all activities related to information technology, data administration, information storage and processing, information dissemination, security and access.
- Improved communication between management and employees by creative design and implementation of general meetings, information dissemination and team building sessions.
- Primary author of Human Resources Subcommittees Report on IRM Skills Assessment.
- Instrumental role in development and implementation of recruitment and retention program for highly skilled IT professionals.
- Participated in World Congress on Technology in cooperation with United Nations.

EDUCATION & PROFESSIONAL DEVELOPMENT

Master of Science Degree, Information Resources Management, 1999
Syracuse University, Syracuse, NY

Bachelor of Business Arts, 1985
Marymount University, Arlington, VA

PAUL MCKENZIE

10 Hudson Drive   (555) 555-5555
Tarrytown, New York   rickl2345@aol.com

FINANCIAL SERVICES / BANKING EXECUTIVE
Sales ◆ Proprietary Trading ◆ Investment Banking

Consistent top performer with a track record of successive advancement achieved through proactive leadership, generating revenues and producing bottom-line results for global leaders in the financial services/banking industry.

Expertise in the origination, investment and sales of emerging markets fixed income securities for U.S. and European institutional investors with highly profitable results that outperform emerging market equity indices. Proficient in electronic trading.

Solid network of senior-level contacts in banks, corporations and government and originated debt capital markets transactions.

SELECTED ACHIEVEMENTS

◆ Delivered $30 million in net profits for the Proprietary Trading Division of Hammond Bank Securities in 2000 and 2001 as the top contributor to the special situation equity and financing books. Instrumental in division's ranking #1 in profitability during 2001.

◆ Originated and managed several debt Private Placements for Hammond Bank's position and for clients of the financing book.

◆ Achieved top ranking in the division at Hammond Bank Securities for 3 consecutive years: #1 producer in emerging markets institutional fixed income sales, #1 producer of derivatives sales, #1 producer in Eurobond sales and #1 in structured financing. Generated $15 million in annual profits.

◆ Produced $45 million in profits over 3-year period for First Bank's Emerging Markets Division, recognized as the most profitable division within the organization.

◆ Spearheaded Eurobond syndication activity for First Bank, which became the #1 European bank involved in Eurobond underwriting over 2-year period. Participated in the syndication of 30% of all new issues – the Bank's first-ever participation in international new issues.

◆ Initiated the entire distribution of Eurobonds for First Bank, successfully cultivating relationships with over 40 institutional investors in Eurobonds and emerging markets fixed income securities.

PAUL MCKENZIE - PAGE 2

PROFESSIONAL EXPERIENCE

HAMMOND BANK SECURITIES, New York, New York   (1993-present)
Vice President / Senior Associate Director & Proprietary Trader (1997-present)

Selected to join the senior executive team in the emerging markets Proprietary Trading Division that managed U.S. $3+ billion in Bank capital. Originate and manage investments for several books: debt, equity, local currency and structured financing with a primary focus on equity investments and structured financing. Comanage U.S. $1-billion financing book of emerging markets fixed income securities as well as U.S. $100-million equity special situation book.

Associate Director – Emerging Markets Institutional Sales (1993-1997)
Managed relationships with U.S. and Latin American institutional investors and sold Brady Bonds, eurobonds, derivatives, local currency products and structured financing.

FIRST BANK, New York, New York   (1987-1993)
Emerging Markets – Senior Proprietary Trader (1990-1993)
Sovereign Debt Proprietary Trader (1989-1990)
International Banking Officer – Emerging Markets Desk (1987-1989)

Advanced rapidly through progressively responsible positions; traded Eurobonds, Brady Bonds and loans for Bank's proprietary account and Private Banking Division; negotiated sovereign debt swaps. Managed U.S. $10-million Proprietary trading line. Trained and mentored professionals new to the emerging markets desk. Established, developed and managed syndication and distribution of Brazilian eurobonds for the Bank. Built a strong distribution network with Swiss, Brazilian and U.S. institutional investors.

PRIOR ASSIGNMENTS

Consulting assignment with **LaRiviere & Company**, Paris, France, assisting with information technology and retail distribution projects for client companies. Subsequently trained in the International Trade Financing Division; participated in several European trade finance and loan syndication deals.

EDUCATION

B.S. in Financial Management
New York University • New York, New York

NASD licenses: Series 7 and 63

Diane Hatzer
567 Summit Way
Arlington, VA 22333

Phone: (703) 555-5555   Fax: (703) 222-1111   E-mail: dhatzer@erols.com

Profile: An established member of the national healthcare community with clinical nursing and public health training and practical knowledge and skill derived from experience in senior positions. Recent recipient of advanced degree in public communications and author of research project comparing two national health communication campaigns. Extensive background in organizational planning and management, communications, public affairs, and public policy.

Senior Managing Director, Clark and Curran
Washington, DC, May 1999 – August 2000

Senior member of Washington, DC worldwide public affairs/public relations agency health team.

- Developed and implemented public affairs and communications programs for health clients with a focus on midlife women's healthcare and clinical practice guideline dissemination. Furnished health expertise in connection with the launch of pharmaceutical products and medical devices.
- Provided strategic counsel and facilitation and organized advocacy coalitions for for-profit and not-for-profit health clients. Clients include pharmaceutical companies, other FDA-regulated corporations, and professional health associations.

Executive Vice President, Association of Local Health Officials (ALHO)
Washington, DC, December 1994 – March 1999

Chief executive of association with annual $6 million budget, representing the national interests of all local health commissioners. Administered office operations and supervised professional and administrative staff of 28.

- Created and implemented a new strategic plan to enhance member benefits and services and extend the visibility of public health within Congress and federal agencies and among other health organizations.
- Established ALHO as a lead advocate on public health issues including preventive services, tobacco control, HIV/AIDS, infectious diseases, immunizations, adolescent health, and environmental health.
- Enhanced working relationships with federal health agencies and private foundations, resulting in greater partnering opportunities and increased federal financial support of ALHO.
- Secured unrestricted corporate contributions from major pharmaceutical companies to establish new relationships for ALHO.
- Initiated a member marketing effort to position ALHO as an expert resource on population-based health issues. Marketing effort included use of print and broadcast media and partnering with other organizations.
- Engineered a national campaign on judicious antimicrobial usage involving major health and pharmaceutical groups. Conducted a national press conference and distributed information.

Hatzer, page 2

Executive Director, American College of Surgeons
River Ridge, IL, July 1990 – November 1994

Chief executive of organization representing 4,000 members of surgery profession. Relocated the association office, managed $3.0 million budget and recruited and supervised staff of eight.

- Increased College membership by 38 percent over four-year tenure and enhanced infrastructure.
- Reorganized national and international educational and scientific meetings resulting in a 30-percent increase in registrants and 50-percent increase in exhibitors.
- Produced numerous consumer brochures, a membership directory, and the College's first and subsequent annual reports. Helped develop the profession's first clinical practice guidelines.

Other Professional Experience

Manager, Washington Office, American College of Physicians, a Chicago-based group representing more than 50,000 physicians. Managed $1M budget and government relations staff of five. Lobbied issues regarding Medicare payment, trauma centers, peer review, and graduate medical education.
Director of Legislative Affairs, American Health Care Association, Washington DC. Representing the nation's 9,000 proprietary and not-for-profit nursing homes. Served as a registered lobbyist on federal healthcare policy, tax, and veterans' issues.
Legislative Assistant, California Office of Federal Affairs, Washington, DC. Secured funding for state-based health programs, maintained close working relationships with the California Congressional delegation, and collaborated on issues with other Governors' offices.
Professional Staff Member, U.S. Senate Committee on Veterans' Affairs. Visited the nation's V.A. Hospitals as the Committee troubleshooter, investigated issues such as Agent Orange, post-Viet Nam stress syndrome, aging, spinal cord injury, hospital staffing. Helped draft legislation on these topics.
Continuing Education Director/Member Services Liaison, American Public Health Association, Washington, DC. Organized and managed a public health continuing education program. Served as liaison for medical care, nursing, dental health, and health education sections.
Director of Federal Health Programs, American for Eye Health Association, Washington, DC. Facilitated efforts to increase optometrists' participation in federal peer review, managed care, and health planning.

Education and Certification

Master of Arts, Public Communication, 2001, American University, Washington, DC
Certified Association Executive, American Society of Association Executives
Master of Health Science, Johns Hopkins University School of Hygiene and Public Health, Baltimore, MD
Bachelor of Science, Nursing, cum laude, University of Maryland, Baltimore, MD
Registered Nurse, Lutheran Hospital School of Nursing, Milwaukee, WI

Activities

Member, Board of Directors, Community Family Services, Washington, DC
Member, Board of Directors, National Mental Health Council, Washington, DC

FERNANDO MENDENZ

4390 Eastleigh Court
Springfield, VA 22152
703-242-7436
mendezF@hotmail.com

SUMMARY

Unique blend of skills and knowledge in the areas of law and business. Professional experience in a publicly held company, in a major law firm, and in the US Court of Appeals. Domestic and international practice aided by command of the English and Spanish languages, and by familiarity with the cultures throughout the Western Hemisphere. Analytically strong, with a clear sense of key strategic issues and goals. Diligent and responsible contributor to organizational efforts. Expertise includes:

- Corporate law
- Corporate finance
- Corporate governance

- Mergers, acquisitions and divestitures
- Commercial and contract law
- International law

PROFESSIONAL EXPERIENCE

INDEPENDENT CONSULTANT – Nashville, TN   **2003 to Present**
Counsel, Mergers and Acquisitions
Provided legal assistance and support in all aspects of the negotiation and the documentation of the Company's mergers, acquisitions, divestitures, spinouts, minority investments, and related transactions. Duties and responsibilities included:

- Legal prime for over 30 different transactions, including mergers, acquisitions, divestitures, spinouts, minority investments, and related matters in the networking equipment industry.
- Responsible for all aspects of the above transactions, including asset and share purchase sale, commercial alliances, employment matters, intellectual property agreements, real estate arrangements, tax issues, etc.
- Served as the main point of contact for corporate staff, as well as managers in various corporate divisions and business units, affected by the above transactions.
- Interacted extensively with internal functional primes and managed outside counsel, both at home and abroad, towards the effective consummation of the above transactions.
- Drafted and evaluated a variety of legal agreements in a number of areas, including asset and stock purchase and sale, financing and securities transactions, commercial alliances, employment, intellectual property and real estate matters, and corporate organizational and secretarial documents.

BINGHAM DANA LLP – Boston, MA   **1997 – 1999**
Associate, Business Area
Handled all aspects of complex commercial and corporate matters, such as, debt and equity financing, mergers and acquisitions, public securities offerings, real estate transactions and general corporate maintenance matters. Member of the Entrepreneurial Services Group and the Latin America Practice Group.

US COURT OF APPEALS FOR THE FIRST CIRCUIT – Boston, MA   **1996 – 1997**
Judical Clerk for the Honorable Levin H. Campbell, Senior Circuit Judge
Studied appellate briefs and district court records, and wrote bench memos in preparation for court sittings. Reviewed and edited circulating opinions from other circuit judges. Researched factual and legal issues in pending cases. Wrote draft opinions for the judge.

EDUCATION

SUFFOLK UNIVERSITY'S SAWYER SCHOOL OF MANAGEMENT – Boston, MA
Master of Business Administration, 2003
Cumulative GPA: 4.0/4.0 (A)
Continuing education courses in mergers, acquisitions, and intellectual property

GEORGETOWN UNIVERSITY LAW CENTER – Washington, DC
Juris Doctor, 1996

YALE UNIVERSITY – New Haven, CT
Bachelor of Arts, 1993
High Honors in Political Science Major

BAR MEMBERSHIPS
American Bar Association (ABA)
The District of Columbia
The Commonwealth of Massachusetts

PRESENTATIONS

Have presented papers before the ABA and the District of Columbia Bar on updates on IRS tax guidelines for mergers and acquisitions.   2002 – 2004

ARI GELLER
123 Clean Record Way
New York, New York 10285
212-654-7635

PROFESSIONAL
SUMMARY

Senior executive with progressive experience in full range of Human Resources activities, domestic and foreign, with specialized knowledge of personnel policies and services for manufacturing and fuel industry staffing.
Strengths include:

- *Strategic Planning*
- *Organizational Effectiveness*
- *Compensation & Benefits Design*
- *Employee Communications*
- *Succession Planning*
- *Quality Initiative*

- *Reward Systems*
- *Information Systems*
- *Recruitment*
- *Labor Relations*
- *EEO/AA*
- *Policy Development*

PROFESSIONAL
EXPERIENCE

MATOTINA INC., Morristown, New Jersey
Group Vice President, Human Resources (1998 – Present)

Responsible for Human Resources function for $750-million group doing business in 117 countries with 8,500 employees and 21 plants manufacturing pharmaceuticals, healthcare products and confectionery reported to Group President. Managed domestic Human Resources programs for 20 group headquarters staff.

- Led two major reorganization of the Group: from Canada/Latin America to current configuration of Latin America/Asia/Australia/Middle East/ Africa, ensuring appropriate organization and staffing to support business objectives.
- Prepared succession plan for 30 Regional Vice Presidents and Affiliate General Managers and introduced Key Position Development Planning to ensure continuity of future management.
- Developed strategy and managed implementation of company culture to change—new creed, vision, management, values, empowerment—to drive organization forward in fast-paced, highly competitive environment.
- Participated as a team member in developing strategic and operating plans and in periodic business reviews against objectives with a 95% success rate.
- Chaired task force that designed a company-wide "pay for performance" reward system utilizing merit increases, stock options, restricted stock options, line bonuses and long-term bonuses.
- Member of Human Resources Strategy Committee of senior executives who develop strategy and design policy for domestic and international operations.
- Supported fast-growing business (15–35% CAG) by establishing a business partner concepts and implementing a total customer satisfaction approach to Human Resources.
- Reviewed and approved affiliate negotiating strategy and compensation benefit proposals with no labor actions within budget.

ARI GELLER

DAVIDSON CORP., New York City, New York (1988 – 1998)
Director, International Compensation and Policy Development (1993 – 1998)

Responsible for policy development, expatriate administration and compensation for International Operations Group, Reported to Vice President Human Resources. Administered expatriate operations for 50 culturally diverse senior executives. Managed domestic compensation program for 200 headquarters staff.

- Approved compensation, bonus and perquisite programs for 54 affiliates.
- Introduced standard salary structure system and wrote compensation manual.
- Wrote computer program for expatriate balance sheets that cut preparation time by 50% and provided for 100% accuracy in calculations.
- Chaired International Policy Committee and edited Human Resources Manual.

London, Personnel Manager (1988 – 1993)

Responsible for Human Resources function for Exploration and Production operating affiliates. Reported to the Vice Presidents of Exploration and Production.

- Developed and implemented succession plans for 50 senior level positions.
- Assessed staffing requirements and identified candidates, filling over 150 positions.
- Coordinated technology transfer to 150 local nationals ahead of schedule.
- Reviewed and approved affiliate pay and benefits budgets and headcount.
- Designed specifications for a software program that facilitated internal candidate identification, training needs and successions planning.
- Wrote affirmative action plan and obtained total compliance certification in government EEO audit.
- Maintained nonunion environment through excellent rapport with support staff, utilizing focus groups, new job posting system and informative brochures.

PRIOR WORK EXPERIENCE

- *ARCH INC.* – Singapore, Employee Relations Department Head, Sydney, Compensation and Benefits Head (1985 – 1988)
- *DD&P CO.* – Houston, Compensation Analyst, NJ, Generalist, Employee Relations Representative (1983 – 1985)
- *NYC DEPARTMENT OF EDUCATION* – NYC, Math and Physics Teacher, Computer Programmer (1980 – 1983)

EDUCATION

MBA (Management), University of Madison, Wisconsin
BS Physics, Magna Cum Laude, University of Michigan

ABRAM FRANK

411 W. 195th Street, Apt. 4B, New York, NY 10005   (212) 456-7890
jenandabe@usva.com

SENIOR INFORMATION TECHNOLOGY EXECUTIVE
& TRANSFORMATIONAL LEADER

IT Infrastructure & Organizational Design • Strategic Planning • Contract Negotiation
Productivity Improvement • Conflict Management/Resolution • Team Mentoring, Development & Leadership

Value-added Hallmarks:
Top Secret Security Clearance • Esprit de Corps Leadership Style • Marathon Competitive Athlete

CAREER HIGHLIGHTS

IBM CORPORATION, New York, NY • 2003 to Present
Executive BP, Transition Team
Recruited to manage activities of four departments across three states for a 160,000-employee division specializing in outsourcing. Currently leading major projects concurrently, encompassing:

- Conversion from current scheduling tools (Control-M, JobTrac, and Zeke) to TWS.
- Conversion from ChangeMan to SCLM.
- Providing 24/7 coverage while mentoring and motivating team extremely stressed by complexity of conversion projects and lack of human capital.
- Responding to and coordinating all audit inquiries (internal and external).
- Scheduling for batch processing on mainframe and distributed platforms.
- Tool support for ChangeMan, Endevor, and PVCS.
- Code migration for both mainframe and distributed platforms.
- Report administration/distribution for Control-M and EOS.

JEN CO., New York, NY • 2000 to 2003
Director, Data Center Operations (2001 to 2003)
Manager, Data Center Operations (2000 to 2001)
Managed four data centers (including three remotely on West Coast); with 65 employees and six managers. Controlled a $6.2MM budget, and accountable for 500 UNIX and NT servers, four large IBM mainframes, and the service restoration management department for this international financial/investment company. Key Performance Indicators:

- Increased overall productivity 21% FY02.
- Saved $457,000 in FY02 contractor fees working on insourcing mainframe batch processing project.
- Slashed consultants' fees $173,000 FY02 by renegotiating vendor contracts.
- Saved $673,000 FY04 by insourcing tape storage.
- Reorganized Data Center of the Americas (Chicago), reducing headcount from 45 to 36 due to improved efficiencies and saving $360,000 in labor costs (excluding benefits).

BIT-Z CO., St. Paul, MN • 1993 to 2000
Mastered virtually every aspect of large-scale mainframe computer operations (IBM MVS), moving through a series of key technical and supervisory assignments including:
System Operator, Job Control Specialist, Shift Coordinator, Technical Analyst.
Excelled in functioning as first- and second-level support (code migration, troubleshooting, problem resolution) for numerous systems (Payroll, A/P, A/R, Sales, and Inventory).
- Rewrote hundreds of lines to heighten efficiency of Ledger reports.
- Slashed hundreds of hours devoted to manual tasks, saving hundreds of thousands of dollars in labor costs.
- Devised and implemented automation initiative eventually used by entire IT staff in over eight regions.

EDUCATION

MA in Organizational Leadership
Penn State University, State College, PA

BA in Organizational Leadership (Management)

Regularly attend Continuing Education & Executive Development courses
Full details supplied upon request

TECHNICAL TOOLKIT

Software
MVS/XA • MVS/ESA • MVS/OS390 • TSO • Z/OS • MVS/JCL • COBOL • Control-M • ECS • Jobtrac • Infopac • FDR/ABR • TCP/IP • Tivoli • OPS/MVS • SAR • UNIX • IOF • Jobscan • Syncsort • Group 1 • EZTRIEVE-PLUS • CICS.SDSF • ManageNow • Ariba

MS OS & General Productivity Applications
Word • PowerPoint • Excel • Windows 98 / 2000 / XP • UNIX

Hardware
IBM 3033 / 370/135 / 3090 / 3590 • StorageTeck Silos • VSM1-3

AFFILIATIONS

American Federation for Computer Operations Managers (AFCOM)
United Who's Who

Suzanna Lang

1027 Strong Hollow Way ? Reston, Virginia 20194 ? (703) 712-7762 ? slang@juno.net

Accomplished project manager with expertise as analyst, fundraiser, political advisor, program director, events planner/coordinator, public relations specialist, and elected official with dynamic management, administrative, and organizational skills. Reputation for achieving results through forging cooperative alliances, implementing innovative solutions, and motivating teams to achieve ambitious goals. Comfortable and competent in military, political, and civilian environments.

PROFESSIONAL SUMMARY

♦ Proven professional trainer designing and delivering effective adult learning curriculum.

♦ Highly articulate and persuasive, *"communications skills are exceptional, always crafted and flexible to suit the situation – a rare talent."*

♦ Designed successful public relations and marketing program that resulted in the highest-ever recorded voter participation.

♦ Proactive volunteer recruiter, ensuring successful programs and initiatives.

♦ Represent Senior Congressman at community meetings, providing information and practical analysis of political options.

♦ Successful author and coauthor of numerous grant awards, including $100,000 for Delbert Child Care Center in St. Martin's, Florida.

♦ Demonstrated ability to conduct needs assessments, data synthesis, determine potential impacts of alternative strategies, and program design and structure.

PROFESSIONAL WORK EXPERIENCE

Constituent Services, District Congressional Offices   2000 – Present
Ombudsman/Passport Officer
Effectively interact with constituents, government agencies, and senior decision makers, to resolve and investigate issues and concerns. Process and advise constituents on proper passport services and application process. Represent office at community events and meetings; organize action items ensuring proper, timely completion; inform, analyze, and present resolution options.

Reach For Tomorrow   1996 – 1999
Chief Operating Officer
Coordinated and directed program assets, providing individualized instruction and educational experiences for underachieving 8th graders nationally. Promoted technology usage to increase motivation and learning and support mentoring. Developed program policies, procedures, and evaluation processes and systems. Designed and implemented effective staff training programs. Presented progress and accomplishments to senior-level DoD officials both military and civilian, corporate sponsors, and national media. Supervised the yearly recruitment of 500 students and 100 adult mentors/volunteers at six sites.

Reston Community Center, Reston, VA   1994 – 1997
Elected Member, Board of Governors
Provided strategic administration and oversight of multipurpose organization with over $3.2 million per annum tax revenues. Successfully created and implemented marketing program that increased voter awareness and understanding, resulting in highest-ever recorded voter turnout. Designed, developed, and implemented Board orientation and instruction program. Organized and oversaw national recruitment campaign for Executive Director. Developed vision and drove successful implementation of computer center for community access.

Wildund & Associates   1989 – 1994
Associate
Task Force Member and Research Associate for Ambassador Leonard Marks and the National Commission for Public Service, resulted in coauthoring of book *Public Attitudes Toward Government: Contradiction, Ambivalence, and Dilemmas of Response*, with Dr. Gregory Foster.
Collaborated in the research and development of management studies, including job assessments and position descriptions, administrative procedures and manuals, and training curricula for clients. Provided crucial assistance in extensive marketing plan and campaign that resulted in increased revenues and achievement of target goals.

University of Southern California at Edwards Air Force Base   1982 – 1982
Director, Systems Management Program
Effectively represented University, ensuring accurate, timely registration, scheduling, and academic counseling for military students. Advised and collaborated with students to provide academic curricula that met and accomplished individual goals. Resolved all scheduling, logistical, financial, academic, and professional concerns and issues, promoting and increasing student enrollments and contributing to academic successes. Liaison to Department of Veterans Affairs.

Title XX Training, California State University, Sacramento, CA   1978 – 1982
Director/Training Coordinator
Provided program development and execution of professional training programs for county staff. Determined fiscal, operational, and regulatory impact of current and pending legislation on University, state, and county programs. Created and implemented innovative, cutting edge, crossover training, enabling child protective service workers to accommodate legally mandated staffing initiatives.

Department of Health and Human Services, New York, NY   1972 – 1978
State and Community Relations Specialist/Project Officer
Selected for HEW appointment. Audited Social Security offices. Designed and implemented employee training and employee relations programs, creating awareness, strengthening skills, and improving performance. Reduced erroneous payments by $1 million. Represented Regional Commissioner in National Six State Survey, effectively reducing AFDC payment errors. Developed and conducted innovative training for administrative law judges that substantially mitigated post review reversals, saving over $3 million. Credited with reducing staffing requirements while improving administrative performance.

EDUCATION

ABD, University of Southern California, School of Public Administration
Completed all doctoral-level coursework, specialization in National Security Issues

Master of Arts, Rider College, Program for Administration

Bachelor of Arts, Montclair State College, Social Sciences and Education

PROFESSIONAL ASSOCIATIONS / AFFILIATIONS

Honorary Recruiter, United States Army
Elected Member, Reston Citizens Association
Elected County Official, Reston Community Center, Board of Governors
Member, Reach For Tomorrow, Board of Directors
Fellow, Inter-University Seminar on Armed Forces and the Society
Certified Trainer, Whole Brain Learning
Certified Ombudsman, Ombudsman Assn., Washington, DC

JEFFREY GRISS

2670 Dickerson Lane
Montvale, NJ 07645

201-555-3246   jg61@verizon.net

CAREER PROFILE

Hospitality executive with solid general management and leadership competencies with ability to drive growth, reduce costs, and strengthen bottom-line financial performance. Recognized for consistent success in developing processes, revitalizing operations, increase revenues and enhance profit performance. Participative leadership style; leads by example. Consistently successful in building consensus and drives cooperative relationships with staff. Strong communications skills.

PROFESSIONAL EXPERIENCE

GUEST SERVICES INTERNATIONAL, Washington, DC   **1980-Present**

Park Ridge Place, Park Ridge, NJ   **1997-Present**
General Manager
Full responsibility for every aspect of operations, staffing, sales, quality control, guest satisfaction, financial control, and tactical planning for this 289-room full-service hotel with 225 associates, 25 managers, 2 restaurants, 18,000 sq. ft. meeting space and annual sales of $17 million. Provide strategic direction to six Directors accountable for Sales, Operations, Finance, Human Resources and Engineering.

- Spearheaded turnaround of financial performance by taking the hotel to the top 10% of the company in financial improvement performance in 1998. Resulted in achieving the corporate Financial Excellence Award.
- Improved market share performance, which resulted in property being in top 10% of corporation. Recognized by receiving the Market Excellence Award in 1998.
- Achieved the highest Associate Satisfaction Score of 80% in 1999, the highest level in the history of the hotel.
- Received quarterly regional GM Sales Excellence Award for three consecutive years in 2001, 2002, and 2003.
- Achieved Clear Zone (above satisfactory) Guest Services Scores (GSS) for six consecutive years.
- Opened the corporation's first Irish Pub in 2001.
- Selected to serve as a training facilitator for the Northeast Region to implement new corporate Career Banding and Leadership Performance Processes.

Saddle Brook Downtown Hotel, Saddle Brook, NJ   **1993-1997**
General Manager
Recruited to lead the turnaround and return to profitability this 291-room full-service hotel and to bring the physical property up to Guest Services Standards. Provided leadership to 23 managers and 200 associates; annual sales $12 million.

- Received GM of the Year Award for Northeast Region in 1995 for exceeding sales, house profit and market share goals.
- Successful in improving house profit 25% in one year and maintaining that level through tenure in position.
- Achieved an Associate Satisfaction Score (AOS) of 82.5% in 1996, which was the highest in the history of the hotel. Hotel received AOS award for being in the top 10% of the corporation.
- Spearheaded the complete restructuring of all physical plans, including guests and meeting rooms, while maintaining the day-to-day operation of the hotel.

Stamford Guest Services, Stamford, CT   **1992-1993**
Director of Human Resources
Provided full-service HR support, including recruiting, hiring, benefits, payroll, employee relations, guidance to Executive Team and training at this 504-room hotel with 500 associates. Held concurrent responsibilities for the Loss Prevention/Security Department.

- Revitalized hotel employee development program by developing and implementing a series of training initiatives in the areas of quality, supervisory & management training, team-building, conflict management, associate cross-training program and orientation.
- Reduced Associates accidents below 1992 level by initiating safety awareness program.
- Improved hotel's success rate in unemployment cases by implementing and ensuring managers followed a standardized separation process.
- Trained employees in the Northeast Region on three-day Total Quality Management Program.

Long Island Guest Services Hotel, Uniondale, NY   **1989-1992**
Resident Manager
Responsible for all aspects of the Rooms Division in a 615-room hotel, including Front Office, Bellstand, Concierge, Housekeeping, Laundry, Gift Shop, and Security. Managed 250 associates.

- Assisted in the expansion of the hotel from a 400-room property to a 615-room conference center.

Director of Services   **1988-1989**
Managed the housekeeping, laundry, and recreation departments and 100 associates.

- Facilitated the completion of a total hotel room's renovation.

Stamford Marriott Hotel, Stamford, CT   **1984-1988**
Front Office Manager
Performed as acting Resident Manager for the last two years while in the position with responsibilities for the front office, reservations, housekeeping, laundry, and recreation.

- Exceeded profit and guest satisfaction goals while performing additional duties of Resident Manager position.

Previous managerial Hospitality Experience as Front Desk Manager and Reservation Manager from 1980-1983.

EDUCATION & TRAINING

BS, Hotel/Restaurant Management, Bryant College, Smithfield, RI
Guest Services' Executive Leadership Training: Numerous courses including the following:
    Advanced Management Skills, Human Resources Skills, Service Excellence,
    Owner Relations Training, and Revenue Management Training

PROFESSIONAL AFFILIATIONS

Secretary-NJ Lodging Association, 2002-2003
Board Member-NJ Lodging Association 1994-2003 (Received Most Valuable Volunteer Award)
Board Member-Montvale Business Association
Member of Executive Men's Golf Association, 2003

Jane Reynolds, SPHR
2243 Hopper Avenue, Wayne, NJ 07470
janereynolds@aol.com
Home: 201-345-6526
Office: 201-544-8373

SUMMARY

Versatile HR leader whose 18 years' experience range from a dot-com start-up (pre-IPO) to bricks and mortar (public and private). Manage HR with a business/marketing focus. Outstanding communicator and creative problem-solver who gets things done!

EXPERIENCE

Vice President, Homan Resources and Property Services   2001-Present
Time Warner Cable, Road Runner Division
Herndon, VA

Time Warner Cable took over Road Runner in December 2000. Annual revenues approached $600 million and division had over 500 employees in 10 states. Reporting to the President, directed the HR activities of 5 direct reports and staff of 12 in recruitment, benefits, compensation, employee relations, employee communications and property services. Company received the 2002 JD Power Associates Award for Outstanding Customer Satisfaction.
Accomplishments:
- Championed the growth in employee trust in management.
- Introduced some aspects of a large company environment into the high tech culture. For example, integrated AOL "Kudos" program with Time Warner Cable "Total Quality Service" Program.
- Led Design Team for Hiring and Recruitment for 2003 PeopleSoft HRIS upgrade.
- Acted as interim head of recruitment/staffing for TWC corporate.
- Planned company-wide implementation of BrassRing.
- Scored tops in division-wide employee opinion survey for safe/comfortable work environment free from harassment.

Vice President, Human Resources   1998-2000
Road Runner High Speed Online
Herndon, VA

A joint venture between Time Warner and MediaOne, Road Runner delivered the Internet over broadband cable at high speeds. The number of employees more than doubled to 400 in one year. At the time of takeover, annual revenues were $170 million, with location in 21 states. Directed and delivered all human resource functions. Road Runner received the 2001 JD Power Associates Award for Outstanding Customer Satisfaction.
Accomplishments:
- Developed a recruitment strategy which leverage high-tech capabilities and Internet resources. The objective was maximum effectiveness and low cost per hire. As a result, cost per hire dropped from $10,000 to $6,000.

- Designed a new print ad format in order to capitalize on the company's Website, resulting in reduced advertising costs.
- Passed SPHR certification exam in first attempt during a time period of extreme pressure and long work hours.
- Acted as beta test site for online performance tool, Performance Impact.
- In the face of major start-up challenges, successfully maintained compliance with employment regulations, avoiding lawsuits and personnel issues in an environment with many new and untrained managers at every level.
- Merged two corporate cultures by taking both into consideration in employee communications, training, policies, benefits and activities.

Vice President, Human Resources   1995-1998
Time Warner Cable-Syracuse Division
Syracuse, NY

Reporting to the President, responsible for 700 employees in 10 locations, two of which were unionized. Directed all HR functions for all business units including cable operations, advertising sales, security, home dish sales, local television production unit and call center. The cable operation served 400,000 customers with annual revenues of $130 million.
Accomplishments:

- Managed workforce of 1,000 in five states down to 400 and back up to 700.
- Created new benefits and payroll system within two weeks of joint venture between Newhouse and Time Warner Cable.
- Developed and communicated policies and compensation plans to five acquired companies.
- Motivated all locations to increase minority/female hiring, promotions, and vendor spending in order to meet EEO and Affirmative Action goals.
- Creatively marketed 401(k) and FSA Plans to workforce, resulting in the highest participation rates in the company.
- Positioned generous sick bank as an insurance policy leading to the lowest per employee sick time in the company.

OTHER WORK EXPERIENCE

Newhouse Broadcasting Corporation, acquired by Time Warner Cable, HR Manager
McCann-Erickson Advertising, New York, NY
National Governor's Association, Washington, DC

EDUCATION

MBA, Syracuse University, Syracuse, NY
MA, Media Management, Newhouse School of Public Communications Syracuse University, Syracuse, NY
BA, Pennsylvania State University, State College, PA

SHOSHANAH FRANK

633 East 35th Street
Apt 21B
New York, New York 10010

INFORMATION TECHNOLOGY / BUSINESS SYSTEMS EXECUTIVE
SPECIALIST IN TRANSLATING BUSINESS PROCESSES AND CHALLENGES INTO IT SOLUTIONS

Dynamic and results-driven IT executive offering an outstanding record of achievement creating and managing organizations to explosive growth and innovation, with a proven track record of creating and managing corporate IT divisions, driving analysis, design, development, deployment and maintenance of systems to the highest possible standards. Analytical problem solver who can immediately use extensive experience identifying business and technology opportunities and leading comprehensive systems development initiatives, quickly generating results and profits. Outstanding communication, presentation, and negotiation skills. International experience. Combination of acute business acumen with equally strong technology systems design and development capabilities. Areas of expertise include:

Systems Design & Development • Project Management
Multi-site & Offshore Development • Client Presentations / Negotiations
Executive Leadership / Team Mentoring

PROFESSIONAL EXPERIENCE

TECH COMPANY, INC., New York, New York • 2003 – Present
IT solutions provider specializing in customized object-oriented development.

Vice President – Professional Services & Advanced Solutions
Spearhead the redesign and implementation of a renewed business model toward Web enablement and legacy systems conversions. Initiate all new business relationships and strategic partnerships, retrain consultants and executives on new direction, and redesign corporate Website and marketing materials. Additionally serve as Project Manager and Systems Architect on new projects.
- Negotiated strategic alliances with IT vendors including IBM, BEA, EcoNovo, and Computer Associates.
- Established new client base and increased business revenues by effectively selling cutting-edge technology solutions to broad-based corporate clientele.

CZ SOFTWARE COMPANY, INC., New York, New York • 1999 – 2003
US-based company partnered with UK software development firm with international client base.

Managing Partner
Established a new North American corporation specializing in object-oriented consulting. Created all short- and long-range business plans, conceived and developed all marketing initiatives, initiated and secured sales, prepared all proposals and agreements, and recruited international team of technical consultants with full P&L responsibility.
- Created positive monthly cash flow within six months and cumulative net profit within nine months.
- Negotiated alliances and secured preferred vendor status with industry leaders including Oracle, IBM Professional Services, Skandia, Cargill, Lehman Brothers, Weyerhaeuser, and American Software.

SHOSHANAH FRANK
- Page 2 -

BIKE CORPORATION, Bethel, Connecticut • 1996 – 1999
$115-million manufacturer of high-end bicycles, motorcycles, 4-wheel ATVs, equipment, and accessories.

<u>Director of IS and Board Member</u>
Challenged to spearhead all enterprise IT and computer-related innovations and business applications. Led design, development, and implementation of all applications and operations for offices and automated manufacturing facilities in Connecticut, Pennsylvania, Europe, and Japan. Board of Directors member.

- Leveraged innovative technology to grow business from $3 million to over $115 million.
- Designed and developed landmark systems for manufacturing, forecasting of sales, labor, raw materials and other requirements; set up shop floor control, production scheduling, shipping, linked R&D CAD designs to BOM structures; linked IT systems to Gerber Scientific assembly line software.
- Linked AS/400s in North America and Europe, installed and implemented the CASE tool Synon/2E; developed laptop systems allowing sales reps to emulate online AS/400 systems offline at client sites.
- Innovations resulted in feature articles in IBM's annual report, CIO magazine, and other IT publications.

EDUCATION

University of Madison, Madison, Wisconsin 1995

PROFESSIONAL AFFILIATIONS

Internet Engineering Task Force (IETF)
Microsoft Developer Network - .NET Beta Tester
IBM PartnerWorld for Commercial Developers
Rational Unified Partner Program
BEA Technology Alliance Partner
Sun/Forte Early Access Program & J2EE Developer Alliance
Mensa
United States Peace Corps

Shana Levy

271 Riverside Drive
New York City, New York 10023
212-743-6544
slevy@nhp.com

Senior-level executive with extensive domestic and international experience in general management of consumer and OTC companies. Visionary leader with demonstrated success in growing sales and profits, expanding brand equities and creating new products, setting strategic direction and influencing diverse groups to perform effectively as a team.

EXPERIENCE

NATIONAL HOUSEHOLD PRODUCTS, INC., New York, NY (2001-2004)
President and Corporate Vice President
Responsible for $350-million OTC consumer business for USA and Puerto Rico. Major products included food and beverage, personal care, and kitchenware. Direct management of finance, marketing, manufacturing, legal, regulatory, R&D, sales and human resources. Managed 1,200 individuals, with an expense budget of $230 million.

- Grew sales by 16% and profit by 43% in first year, the highest level in company history. Achieved through innovative brand equity expansion, aggressive marketing, team motivation, reorganization of manufacturing / customer service, and cost / overhead reduction programs.

- Increased market share on all core businesses (26% in 2003) as well as out-performing their respective competition. Led industry in new product introductions for two years, accounting for over 38% of current company sales.

- Created innovative company vision, resulting in dynamic new strategic plan, which highly motivated and gained the commitment of the workforce.

- Initiated total company reorganization which reduced staff by 21% and expenses by 12%. Directed asset management improvements, including reductions in inventory and accounts receivable, resulting in increased cash flow.

- Established and expanded a new OTC R&D organization. Identified and secured over 30 new technologies. Introduced unique new organizational structures which redefined the marketing, manufacturing and customer service functions.

MOCHA PHARMACEUTICALS, INC., New York, NY (1991-2001)
Vice President and General Manager (1997-2001)
Accountable for all consumer and professional products for $500-million division. Selected to establish and lead new organization, which separated the division from the remainder of the US company. Directed management of marketing, finance, market research, forecasting, professional relations and new products; shared responsibility for sales, manufacturing and R&D.

- Achieved a 66% increase in sales through new product introductions, product relaunches, award-winning new, creative and improved professional programs.

- Increased profitability 270% by managing increases in sales, pricing and media support while reducing trade spending and operating cost.

- Gained significant market share, attaining its highest share in 30 years and achieving overall category leadership.

- Introduced eight major new products, primarily through expansion.

Director of Marketing (1995-1997)

Responsible for all new and established products, market research and consumer promotion in the UK, Ireland and 30 export countries. This $200-million subsidiary was one of the most visible and important units and included business in varied categories.

- Led the complete revitalization for the UK subsidiary that had historically been unprofitable. Named "Subsidiary of the Year" in 1996, has continued to be a profitable company

- Chaired a cross-functional Strategic Reassessment Study, which reorganized the division without major disruption to the business, while eliminating $21 million in overhead and expenses. Subsequently chosen to lead similar studies in four European subsidiaries.

- Directed marketing to achieve the number-one position for almost all brands; including a profitable exit. Achieved creative excellence on virtually all advertised brands, including winning several UK and international creative awards.

- Created a "top to top" program with the trade in the UK, which enabled the company to achieve excellent and profitable long-term relationships in an aggressive retail environment.

- Selected to chair a committee to determine the future organization of Europe relative to the optimization of operations, global branding and future European centralization.

Group Manager – New Products (1994-1995)

Developed and introduced new products for both the House and Personal Care divisions, including the development of four major new products from idea generation to complete national expansion.

Senior Product Manager (1992-1994)

Managed the national introduction of Widgets, the company's largest product offering with sales over $125 million. Directed initial test market, ad budget of $49 million, winner "Effe" performance award.

Product Manager (1991-1992)

Progressed through a series of developmental Product Management assignments in record time, including within the Corporate New Ventures Group, reporting to the Chairman of the Board.

EDUCATION

- New York University, New York, NY, 1993
  MBA, Marketing, minor in Finance and Accounting

- Franklin and Marshall College, Lancaster, PA, 1991
  BAA, Economics

AFFILIATIONS

- Board of Directors, American Cancer Society Foundation, New York City Chapter (2001-present)

- Board of Directors, 1992 Chairman of Marketing Committee, Non-Prescription Drug Mfg. Assn.

- Honorary Member, American Dental Association

APPENDIX

G

Sample Resumes for Select Groups

Resumes in this appendix are intended especially for specific select groups of senior-level professionals. In the following pages you will find samples for:

- Associations and nonprofit professionals.
- Retired military professionals.
- Senior-level federal government positions.
- Before and after.

Miriam Bradley, CAE
2523 34th Street NW, Apt 32
Washington, DC 20001
(202) 699-6970   E-mail: mbcae@fc.com

AREAS OF EXPERTISE

- **Board Relations**
- **Project Management/Administration**
- **Leadership/Vision**

- **Financial Management**
- **Oral and Written Communication Skills**
- **Personnel Supervision**

PROFESSIONAL EXPERIENCE

NATIONAL TRADE ASSOCIATION OF WASHINGTON, WASHINGTON, D.C., 2001-Present
Executive Director

Direct the day-to-day management of the association, reporting directly to the Board of Directors. Supervise staff of 10. Prepare and administer a $3-million budget. Oversee annual conference and exposition. Serve as media contact for organization.

* Increased NTA membership by 35%
* Cut 2002 Conference Expenses by 30% and increased overall Conference profits by 65%
* Turned NTA's Award Program from a revenue-loser to a revenue-generator
* Developed additional educational programming resulting in expanded offerings in areas not previously covered and exceeding budgeted revenue by 52%
* Planned and oversee organization's integrated marketing efforts using direct mail, e-mail, Website, newsletter, and public relations
* Facilitate and guide the work of six Board Committees, the Executive Committee, and five additional volunteer committees
* Wrote formal personnel policy handbook for adoption by Board and implemented processes and procedures

MEDIA ASSOCIATION, WASHINGTON, D.C., 1999-2001
Director, Professional Development

Oversaw daily operation of association's continuing professional program reporting directly to Vice President of Strategic Planning and Education. Supervised staff of five including Education Director, Program Managers, and Academic Advisor. Administered and monitored $3-million budget. Responded to local media requests and questions related to program.

* Reduced program expenses by 25% in one year through efficient use of resources and reduction of expenditures
* Advised and guided seven regional Boards and one National Board in implementing program policy
* Promoted and marketed association's programs through direct mail promotions, tradeshow exhibitions, articles in association media, newsletters, Website, and e-mail messages
* Worked closely with volunteers and instructors at sites all over the United States
* Recruited and evaluated 75-plus faculty/consultants at sites while emphasizing diversity
* Reviewed, updated, and revised curriculum including designing three 2 1/2-day workshops prepared exclusively for executive level professionals
* Conducted hands-on supervision of logistics at each of the seven program sites

AMERICAN BAR ASSOCIATION, WASHINGTON, D.C., 1995-1999
Coordinator

Directed day-to-day operation of ABA reporting directly to Board of Trustees. Prepared and administered budgets, approved all expenditures, oversaw management of $5.5-million endowment investment portfolios, and served as media contact for ABA.

* Established annual Board retreat and planning sessions to provide focus for yearly project priorities
* Supervised accountants in management of finances and preparation of financial statements resulting in clean audits with no reportable conditions

Miriam Bradley

* Assisted Board of Trustees in determining legislative and research priorities and coalition building
* Interacted with lobbyists of eight public interest groups to coordinate joint lobbying efforts
* Monitored federal legislation affecting state and local bar associations
* Planned monthly Board meetings, quarterly Principals meetings, retreats, special meetings, and events

ALLEGHANY COUNTY, MARYLAND, 1989-1995
Administrative Officer

Coordinated the work of 14 divisions including Personnel, Planning, Budget, Public Safety, Health, and Public Works reporting directly to the Board of County Commissioners. Prepared and administered department budgets.

* Implemented a monitoring process to assess status of all departmental projects requiring Board action
* Worked with County's financial advisor and bond counsel on presentations to bond rating agencies
* Supervised staff providing administrative support to Board
* Compiled packet of legislative priorities to present to the County's State Delegation
* Tracked State legislation directly affecting County and assisted in lobbying efforts Commissioners identified
* Served on Consultant Selection Committee and participated in determining firms to receive Request for Proposals (RFPs) for engineering, architectural, and general government projects
* Represented County in meetings with elected state and local officials including representatives of 12 cities and towns located in the County to ensure positive community relations
* Directed County's public relations effort through direct supervision of Public Information Officer
* Made Presentations and speeches to local organizations

EDUCATION

* Master of Science Degree in Public Administration, University of Connecticut (Cum Laude)
* Bachelor of Science Degree in Political Science, Journalism Minor, University of Virginia
* American Society of Association Executives, Certified Association Executive (CAE) Designation

PROFESSIONAL AFFILIATIONS

* American Society of Association Executives
* Greater Washington Society of Association Executives

JOSEPH M. SCHULZE, CAE

808 Ella Street   *Phone: 703.563.1847*
Arlington, VA 20009   *Mobile: 703.521.7481*

SUMMARY OF QUALIFICATIONS

Senior-level association executive with experience in administration and management, association governance, planning and budgeting, member services, leadership training and development, and project management. Expertise in:

- Board relations
- Membership retention and recruitment
- Product marketing
- Volunteer management

- Strategic & operational planning
- Program implementation & oversight
- Presentation and facilitation skills
- Customer service

PROFESSIONAL ACCOMPLISHMENTS

American Association of College Business Officials (AACBO), Arlington, VA
Vice President, Community & Member Services (2001 – present)
Director, Strategic Initiatives (1999 – 2001)

- Reengineered transaction-based member services department into the association's primary service area responsible for managing the member relationship
  - Incorporated marketing, community development, and volunteer management functions into one department and leveraged them to increase member access and perceived value
  - Led centralized marketing effort for all programs, products, and services, strengthening the association's brand, reducing costs, and increasing staff efficiencies
  - Oversaw the modernization and migration to a Web-based association management system, enhancing the association's ability to personalize the member experience and track member purchasing patterns
- Designed and facilitated organization-wide strategic and operational planning processes
  - Reversed two consecutive years of budget deficits to $500,000 budget surplus in first year of implementation
  - Linked board strategic planning with annual operating budget and staff performance goals
  - Increased linkages among all programs and services, enabling the creation of product lines for all major content areas driving an increase in non-dues revenues
- Developed and implemented new member recruitment and retention strategy
  - Reached 100% penetration in highly coveted university market segment
  - Achieved budgetary goal of $165,000 in annual dues revenue and membership growth in key member segments for two consecutive years
  - Refined $5 million+ annual dues collection process, reducing receivables to under $200,000, achieving an overall retention rate of 96%
- Pioneered association's community strategy
  - Developed and launched full day of customized programming and networking during annual meeting for four primary constituent groups, increasing overall participant satisfaction ratings with the event
  - Facilitated online community chats initiating association's first "pre-learning" experience linked to a live professional development event
- Directed comprehensive innovation effort for national association and its four regional affiliates designed to transform the development and delivery of services to shared membership
  - Led strategy development and implementation, project management, communications, volunteer support, and evaluation on behalf of all five associations

Olsen & Hilton, Inc., Washington, DC
Senior Consultant (1997 – 1999)

- Developed management & finance business consulting certification course. Topics included: data collection, analytical tools, communication skills, teamwork, and change management
- Assisted with the development and delivery of the first public forum showcasing the "modernization" initiatives of the Internal Revenue Service for major stakeholder groups
  - Implemented conference logistical plan and on-site management
  - Provided strategic input on curriculum and overall conference design

Association of Home Builders (AHB), Washington, DC
Director, Leadership Training & Development (1995 – 1997)
Assistant Director, Leadership Training (1993 – 1995)

- Managed comprehensive leadership development program for 800+ affiliated associations and increased attendance by 20% in first year of oversight
  - Directed two-day leadership conference held five times each year, including educational content, implementation of promotional strategies, coordination of speakers, and production of conference materials
  - Presented general sessions and workshops for volunteers on the topics of: motivating volunteers, meeting management, delegation skills, and membership development goal setting
  - Designed, produced, and promoted a variety of leadership development resources

University of Pennsylvania, Philadelphia, PA   1992 – 1993
Student Activities Advisor, University Center

California University, Los Angeles, CA   1991 – 1992
Area Coordinator, Office of Residential & Greek Life

EDUCATION

Ohio University, Athens, OH
Master of Arts: College Student Personnel

University of Pittsburgh, Pittsburgh, PA
Bachelor of Arts: Communications/Public Relations

PROFESSIONAL AFFILIATIONS

American Society of Association Executives
- **Served on Component Relations Section Council**
- **Presented at Management & Technology Conference and Annual Meeting**

Greater Washington Society of Association Executives
- **Received Superstar Award (Active Member of the Year)**
- **Chaired Membership Advisory Council**

Alexandra Frank

2154 Beacon Street, Pittsburgh, PA 15217
Office: 412-123-1234 (direct) / Wireless: 412-123-2154
Email: afrank@Earthlink.net

Experience

American Red Cross, Southwestern Pennsylvania Chapter
Pittsburgh, PA (1999-present)
Vice President for Development
Direct all fundraising for 10th largest Red Cross chapter in the United States; staff of 50 and budget of $4.5 million.

Accomplishments
- Increased donations from individuals, foundations and corporations by 75% over four years (from $1.8 million to $3.15 million).
- Expanded number of individual donors by 45% (from 1555 to 2257) primarily by conceiving and launching the "Have a Heart Campaign" to attract new donors under the age of 35.
- Persuaded William Royal Foundation to make it's first-ever grant over $100,000 to support disaster assistance training program.
- Increased development staff from 2.5 to 4; created training program that has been replicated by other Red Cross chapters to strengthen fundraising capacity of mid-level development staff.

Cleveland Museum of Art
Cleveland, OH (1992-1999)
Director of Membership and Development (1996-1999)
Director of Membership (1993-1996)
Membership Coordinator (1992-1993)
Increasing responsibility for membership and fundraising for major cultural organization.

Accomplishments
- Restructured individual membership program that increased renewal rate from 63% to 77% and increased dues revenue by 40%.
- Created corporate membership program in which 60% of Cleveland's largest companies participate, providing 25% of the museum's unrestricted revenue.
- Developed and carried out fundraising strategy that led to the museum's first grants from major foundations outside Ohio, that is, six-figure support from Ford Foundation, Pew Charitable Trusts, and Kellogg Foundation.
- Staffed and energized Board Development Committee, which historically had been underutilized but now plays a key role in the corporate membership program.

Alexandra Frank   **Page 2**

Ketchum, Inc.
New York, NY (1991-1992)
Client Services Assistant
At major public relations firm (8th largest worldwide), assisted account executives working with organizations including the Metropolitan Opera, American Express, and the New York Transit Authority. Attended firm's highly regarded two-week "PR Boot Camp" for staff new to the profession. Earned 15% performance bonus at end of first year of employment. Represented firm at job fairs at colleges on the east coast.

Education

Columbia University, B.A., Communications, 1991
Assistant Director, WNYU (campus radio station), and on-air host of
   weekly program about New York City arts and culture.
Junior year in Barcelona, Spain.

Memberships

American Association of Museums (founding member, New Audiences
   Task Force, 1997-1999).
Squirrel Hill Arts Coalition (Board of Directors, 2000-present)

Publications

"Why I Love to Raise Money – Even When They Say No,"
   NYU Alumni Magazine, April 2002

Additional Information

Extensive travel throughout Argentina, New Zealand, and the islands of
   the South Pacific.
Fluent in Spanish.
Volunteer coach of children's soccer team.

JOHN PAUL JONES, III

636 North 24th Street
Arlington, Virginia 22202
703.555.1212
jpjones1234@adelphia.net

OBJECTIVE: Executive role in logistics

SUMMARY: Leader in managing complex business activities. Expertise includes:

◆ Marketing Strategy	◆ Business Development Concepts
◆ Logistics Systems	◆ Production/Inventory Control
◆ Technology Applications	◆ Team Building and Motivation

**Business
Development**

Developed, sold to CEO, and implemented business planning modules to internal business units with annual sales in excess of $500 million. Concept included problem identification, team-building, and developed focused support from centralized functions.

Effected 20% increase in value of "partnerships" between Department of Defense agencies and industry.

Contributed to the development and implementation of "core competencies business plans," with special emphasis on the LAN and WAN applications and their documentation of the business operations.

Received approval of recommendation to use LANDSAT and its technology in the planning and tracking of long-distance hauling, resulting in more effective scheduling, documentation, and security of shipments.

**Senior
Management**

Revamped warehousing logistics, utilizing hand scanners and on-site databases, resulting in 160% throughput increase without increase in personnel.

Provided balanced leadership, guidance, and counsel throughout the transition aspects of one of the largest military logistics businesses, moderating the efforts of 40% reductions in budget and staff. Results included continual achievement of corporate-level goals and building and even more effective business units.

Negotiated data exchange processes with Pacific Rim countries, eliminating third-party considerations and reducing approval cycles by as much as 25%.

Installed commercial practices into government operations, developing training program that shortened cycles by as much as 60%.

Implemented downsizing strategies in an organization with three international bargaining units and four nation bargaining units without lost time or strife.

Eliminated two levels of supervision using the combination of selective hiring, team-building, and separation incentives.

John Paul Jones, III   **Page 2**

Communications

> Created atmosphere for motivation, teamwork, and the attainment of individual and group goals through effective, open communication, enunciation of vision, and personal visitation.

> Successfully worked with elected officials and their staffs to support organizational changes affecting the community. Successfully defended unpopular yet necessary changes.

> Took Six Sigma concepts, designed and successfully implemented comprehensive quality programs relevant to the business.

> Introduced Performance Business Councils for each business unit. Within the year CRM surveys showed between 15 and 40% improvements.

Human Resources

> Introduced Six Sigma concepts to the Human Resource function, starting with Recruitment.

> Created development program to bring the Human Resource function into the strategic planning orbit of the organization.

> Increased Employee Referrals from 12% to 32% through effective communications, and establishing lunch meetings between operational managers and recruiters.

> Tasked the HR function with developing quarterly communication program for the operation Whereby each business unit meets with senior management to review past performance, next quarter's goals, measurement criteria and responsibilities. Senior management responds in terms of committed support. First year's review shows retention of all key personnel and voluntary turnover to 5%.

MILITARY EXPERIENCE:

> **United States Army**
> 1976 to Present
> **CEO (Commanding General)**, 11th Infantry Division.
> **Deputy Director of Operations**, Office of the Deputy Directory of Operations and Plans.
> **COO (Deputy Commanding General)**, 2nd Infantry Division.
> Earlier leadership positions include Brigade Commander and Company Commander.

EDUCATION:

> **M.B.A.,** University of Chicago, Chicago, IL
> **B.A.,** Chemistry, University of Illinois, Champagne, IL
>
> Army War College, Carlisle, PA
> Command and General Staff College, Ft. Leavenworth, KS

JOHN PAUL JONES, III

1636 North 24th Street
Arlington, Virginia 22202
703.555.1212
jpjones1234@apelphia.net

PROFILE

Senior leader who accomplishes tough goals and expanded missions with static staffing, constrained budgets, and restricted material availability. An innovative manager of large and small-line organizations, and high technical staff organizations. Solid, reliable, and a quick study leader whose reputation for high standards of performance based on clear and open communication encourages subordinates to excel. A team-builder who finds complex, emotional, and high visibility problems a challenge met and resolved through teamwork and consensus-building. Career U.S. Army officer.

REPRESENTATIVE ACHIEVEMENTS

- Planned, coordinated, and directed all U.S. military operations and training throughout Latin America.
- Developed and maintained excellent working relationships with national governments and their militaries, U.S. State Department, and U.S. Corporations operating in Latin America.
- Developed and successfully implemented strategies with foreign leaders to achieve mutually established goals.
- Coordinated Department of Defense preparation and response of military resources to support various states during disaster relief and other emergencies.
- Represented Army leadership in daily dialogue with subordinate field commanders.
- Led recreational business with annual sales exceeding $30 million with each unit profitable allowing quality improvements throughout entire business component.
- Developed multimillion-dollar initiative to "jump-start" the Army's exploitation of space -based capabilities.
- Designed product package and marketing strategies to use in marketing new technologies to senior leadership.
- Initiated, planned, and executed special programs to effect solutions in high-stress environments. Achieved projected goals at minimum cost.
- Successfully negotiated transforming Army reserve components into smaller, mission-oriented units.

ORGANIZATION AFFILIATION

United States Army
1976 to Present
CEO (Commanding General), 11th Infantry Division.
Deputy Director of Operations, Office of the Deputy Directory of Operations and Plans.
COO (Deputy Commanding General), 2nd Infantry Division.
Earlier leadership positions include Brigade Commander and Company Commander.

EDUCATION

M.S., Information Systems, California Institute of Technology
B.S., Chemistry, University of Chicago
Army War College with concentration in Strategic Planning
Command and General Staff College

JOHN PAUL JONES, III
1636 North 24th Street
Arlington, Virginia 22202
703.555.1212
jpjones1234@adlephia.net

PROFILE

Extensive background in executive leadership of large, dynamic, multicultural organizations with progressive, people-oriented skills. Excellent record of performance in effectively orchestrating multi-unit, multi-disciplined organizations to perform at levels that set standards to emulate. Strong budget management of six- to seven-figure budgets, operational turnarounds, and demonstrated performance at maximum levels from existing staff and resources. U.S. Army.

SELECTED ACHIEVEMENTS

♦ Planned, coordinated and led all U.S. military operations and training throughout Latin America, developing excellent working relationships with national governments and militaries, the U.S. State Department, as well as the overseas operating units of U.S. Corporations.

♦ Selected to direct deployment of forces in support of Bosnia.

♦ Developed a multimillion-dollar initiative to "jump-start" the Army's exploitation of space-based capabilities, designing the product package and marketing it.

CAREER HISTORY

US Army   **1976 - Present**
CEO (Deputy Commanding General/Commanding General), 1st Infantry Div.   2000 - Present
Finalized its conversion to mechanized while maintaining total mission readiness.
♦ Conceived design, implemented and led realignment activities involving training, teamwork cohesiveness, utilizing latest information technology and personal involvement.
♦ Introduced new techniques in field reporting and accountability.
♦ Instituted state-of-the art logistics planning for Division relocation.

CEO (Brigade Commander) 7th Brigade, Light Infantry, 15th Infantry Div.   1996 - 2000
Developed and implemented new troop and equipment mobility techniques.
♦ Insured quality performance and safety; solved competitive and communications issues.
♦ Called for redesign and implementation of airlift technologies and techniques.

Fourteen years senior level leadership experience coordinating, integrating, and partnering diverse, individually focused organizations, successfully achieving major objectives. Developed, implemented, and managed models for inter-service groups, enabling goals to be met within controlled budgets. Well-versed in corporate level restructuring while meeting preestablished conditions with restricted staff and budget. Frequent testimony before Congressional Committees.

EDUCATION

MBA, University of Pennsylvania, Wharton School of Business, Finance Major, Philadelphia, PA
B.S., University of Missouri, Civil Engineering, Columbia, MO
Harvard JFK Senior Management Program, Boston, MA
Army War College with emphasis in International Strategic Studies, Carlisle, PA
Command and General Staff College, Ft. Leavenworth, KS

Ralph H. Ossier

9374 Stoutwell Place ~ Oak Hill, VA 20171 ~ W:703-512-7032 ~ H:703-698-5439~ rossier@erols.com

SSN: 123-45-6789	Veterans Preference: N/A
Federal Status: Current Career Employee, GS-0201-15	Citizenship: U.S.
01/1992 – Present	

Vacancy Announcement Number: DEU-SES-04-0201
Position Title: Deputy Assistant Secretary of the Navy

PROFESSIONAL SUMMARY

Dynamic, visionary Human Resources professional with 25 years of successful, productive and innovative federal service. Expertise in federal human resource management, including program management and assessment, policy evaluation, development and implementation, and congressional and legislative processes. Unique background of successful service as a Reagan political appointee and career employee in a domestic agency and the Department of Defense, in the field and at headquarters levels and at strategic, managerial, and tactical levels. Significant achievements designing and implementing policies, programs, and reforms to improve government service.

EDUCATION

Graduate DoD Defense Leadership and Development Program (DLAMP)

Master of Science, National Resource Strategy, 1999
National Defense University, Washington, DC 20319

Bachelor of Arts, English, 1973
California State University, Fullerton, CA 92634

Arcadia High School, Phoenix, AZ, 85018, 1977

PROFESSIONAL WORK HISTORY

Office of the Deputy Under Secretary of Defense	01/2002 – Present
Civilian Personnel Policy, Washington, DC	Hours: 50+/week
Director, Congressional and External Affairs, GM-0201-15	Salary: $120,000/yr

Supervisor: Stewart Blackwell 703-698-5309 May be contacted
Principle advisor and liaison to the Deputy Under Secretary of Defense (DUSD), Civilian Personnel Policy (CPP) on legislative strategy.
Develop and direct program and strategy to define, coordinate, package, promote, and enact major legislation and appropriations initiatives for DoD civilian human resources management.
Ensure advancement of enterprise management solutions involving Department and Administration leadership and critical Congressional public service interests.
Develop and recommend strategies to clarify and promote DoD initiatives on civilian human resources management.
Effectively draft and respond to media, public, and Congressional inquiries.
Developed innovative legislative strategy that aligned human resource proposals with national security requirements that gained key Senate support and provided basis for fiscal year 2004 effort.
Designed 2004 legislative package of personnel management flexibilities that became key part of Secretary's transformation proposal.
Orchestrated and produced overnight draft testimony for DUSD (CPP) on critical Senate testimony. Efforts recognized in substantial bonus for year and later direct cash award from the Under Secretary of Defense.

Ralph H. Ossier 123-45-6789
Announcement DEU-SES-04-0201

Office of the Secretary of Defense	01/1992 – 01/2002
Civilian Personnel Policy, Washington, DC	Hours: 50+/week
Chief, Civilian Training, Education, & Career Development Policy	Salary: $116,000/yr

GM-0201-15   Supervisor: Bob Wright 703-444-9023
Develop, coordinate, and evaluate human resources management policies and programs.
Research, evaluate, and implement state-of-the-art practices in public and private sector training, education, career development, retraining and executive development for improved defense initiatives.
Successfully collaborated to develop first comprehensive civilian program of leadership development—the Defense Leadership and Management Program.
Designed four-day briefing for South African defense ministry on DoD civilian leadership development initiatives.
Led effort with defense acquisition community to adapt and apply a RAND-designed system for strategic planning of the 130,000-person acquisition workforce.
Extracted workforce capabilities and competencies from Departmental transformation roadmap.
Developed "retraining bounty" for surplus employees that became law.
Developed and enhanced institutional relationships with key functional communities (acquisition, intelligence, information technology, and financial management).
Recognized with selection to Industrial College of the Armed Forces and substantial bonus.

U.S. Air Force, Randolph AFB, TX	01/1990 – 01/1992
Chief, College Recruitment GM-0201-14	Hours: 45+/week
Supervisor: Melvin Duggin (retired)	Salary: $68,400/yr

Developed highly competitive presence on college campuses, proactively recruiting new talent.
Significantly improved college recruitment program.
Revitalized program and reshaped office into team-based representatives for functional, organizational, and diversity accounts across Air Force achieving recruitment targets and overcoming obstacles.
Changed recruiting requirements process in coordination with major command customers, developed professional recruitment materials, started first comprehensive training program for civilian recruiters.

U.S. Air Force, Washington, DC	04/1998 – 01/1990
Chief, Legislative Program GM-0201-14	Hours: 50/week
Supervisor: Gerald Finley 202-731-2964	Salary: $64,000/yr

Directed AF civilian personnel management legislative program.
Performed project management for all special projects, ensuring accuracy, timeliness, and quality.
Served as legislative advocate, strategic planning assistant, and chief speechwriter.
Executed strategy resulting in enactment into law of last move home benefit for the Senior Executive Service.
Collaborated in development of landmark USAF strategic human resources plan.

U.S. Office of Personnel Management, Washington, DC	02/1985 – 04/1988
Deputy Director, Congressional Relations	Hours: 55/week
Supervisor: Suzanne Smith 202-552-8345	Salary: $55,000/yr

Performed legislative strategy development for three agency directors.
Lead strategy that resulted in lifting of two-year congressional ban on pay-for-performance rules. Successfully negotiated without compromise GAO review of sensitive agency draft on comparable worth.
Closely engaged in entire range of human resource policy and legislative issues from recruitment to retirement.

U.S. House of Representatives, Washington, DC	04/1983 – 02/1985
Post Office and Civil Service Committee	Hours: 55/week
Committee Assistant	Salary: $32,000/yr
Supervisor: Smithy Jonas (deceased)	

Served ranking member on Compensation Subcommittee.

Ralph H. Ossier 123-45-6789
Announcement DEU-SES-04-0201

Planned and promoted legislative initiatives and reforms to improve civil service.
Developed strategic alliances and relationships to further program agendas and reforms.

U.S. House of Representatives, Washington, DC   04/1979 – 04/1983
Legislative Assistant   Hours: 60/week
Supervisor: William Walters (retired)   Salary: $28,000/yr

Served as legislative aide, executive assistant, caseworker, and grants development person (developed small business federal grants guidebook).
Developed strategies and materials promoting legislative and regulatory programs in support of congressional district citizens.

PROFESSIONAL DEVELOPMENT

Legislative Issues Seminar, 2002

Managing Public Information and Mass Media Communications
Georgetown University, 2001, 3 credits

Management Control Systems
George Mason University, 2000, 3 credits

Management Information Systems
George Mason University, 1999, 3 credits

Chester J. Smithfield

6112 Sugarland Crest Circle • Chester, VA 23832 • (804) 456-7200 • (804) 392-0394 • csmithfield@yahoo.com
SS#: 123-45-6789 • Citizenship: U.S. • Veteran's Preference: 5-Point Preference

OBJECTIVE: Director of General Aviation Security, SW-0340-02/02

ANNOUNCEMENT NUMBER: TSA-04-7142B25

PROFILE

Experienced Airport Director with over 6 years' demonstrated ability to manage and coordinate all airport activities and operations. Track record of progressive responsibilities and achievements, including directing and implementing airport projects, developing policies and procedures and providing strategic direction and planning. Develop and manage airport security planning, programs and procedures.

Skilled in managing complex construction projects, developing and securing state and federal grants, and providing oversight of all administrative functions. Fiscal responsibility for grants management and annual budget. Successfully achieved self-sufficiency in 1977 and have obtained funding for 17 state and federal projects totaling over $6.6 million.

Strong team manager, coaching for performance improvements, directing for successful completion of all tasks, developing talent, and motivating to exceed Airport goals and objectives. Expertise in customer relations and developing customer loyalty. Demonstrated track record of establishing customer goals and exceeding expectations to delight Airport customers. Proficient negotiation and conflict resolution skills and creating win-win solutions.

EMPLOYMENT HISTORY

Sugarland County Airport, Virginia   40+ hours/week
Airport Director   Nov 1995 to Present
Supervisor: Fred Dixon (804) 123-0987   Salary: $xx,xxx/year
Direct and manage staff of administrative, technical, and mechanical employees providing oversight and direction of all airport operations and activities. Coordinate an average of 6 annual projects, including securing funding, training and assigning personnel, developing plans and providing project management. Maintain all state and federal programs. Ensure compliance with all state and federal regulations, FAA, VDA, Environmental regulations, and Airport Rules and Minimum Standards. Consistent record of fiscal profitability, ensuring revenues exceeds operational expenses.
Accomplishments:
- Completed construction of 20 new T-hangers.
- Collaborated and completed Airport Marketing Plan and Rate Analysis study.
- Developed and initiated new policies and procedures streamlining processes and improving organizational efficiencies.
- Developed the Airport Emergency Action Plan.
- Wrote and implemented numerous agreements and documents, including Tie Down Lease Agreement, T-Hanger Lease Agreement, Tie Down Rules and Regulations, Construction Safety and Compliance for Airport Operations Area, Airport Advisory Board Annual Summary, and T-Hanger Rules and Regulations.

- Updated and completed the Airport Policies and Procedures Books, Airports OSHA and Certification Training Book, Money Matters, Airports Financial Accounting Code Book, Customer Service Plan, Airport/FBO Contingency Plan, and FAA 6-Year Capital Improvement Funding Plan.
- Successfully obtained funds for 17 state and FAA projects totaling over $6.6 million.
- Initiated and developed TQM processes such as flowcharting all Macro/Micro processes.

Green-County Regional Airport, Kentucky   40+ hours/week
Airport Manager   Nov 1994 to Nov 1995
Supervisor: Susan Pritchard 405-712-9034   Salary: $xx,xxx/year
Provided oversight and management of large, limited 139-certificate airport, including grounds management, projects management, administrative oversight, and day-to-day direction and supervision.

Pulseside Town Department of Public Safety, New York   20+ hours/week
Public Safety Officer   Jul 1991 to Jul 1992
Supervisor: James Brown 212-708-5534   Salary: $xx,xxx/year
Performed routine patrol of town parks, beaches, office buildings and facilities. Enforced all town codes, issuing summons for infractions and responding to complaints.

United States Army, Fort Rucker, Alabama   40+ hours/week
Warrant Officer   Feb 1990 to Dec 1990
Supervisor: Sam Mitchell 312-873-0577   Salary: $xx,xxx/year
Graduated Warrant Officer School Class 90-121. Earned Honorable Discharge.

Air West Heliport, New York   40+ hours/week
Heliport Director   May 1987 to Dec 1989
Supervisor: Robert Mitchum   Salary: $xx,xxx/year
Oversaw daily operations of diversified high volume heliport.

PILOT CERTIFICATIONS

Second Class Medical Certificate, Commercial Pilot-Rotorcraft Helicopter, Instrument Rotorcraft Helicopter-Airplane, Private Privileges-Airplane Single Engine Land, Advanced Ground Instructor

AWARDS & HONORS

2001   Sponsored and coordinated Virginia Aviation Specialty License Plate
2000   Virginia Airport Operators Council/Special Recognition
1998   Virginia Aviation Award – Airport Manager of the Year

EDUCATION & PROFESSIONAL DEVELOPMENT

Bachelor of Science, Aviation Management, 1986
American University, Washington, DC

FAA/AAAE Advanced & Basic Airport Safety and Operations Specialist School 1994, 1995, 1996, 1997
Vice Presidential Airport Visit Security Coordinator, 1995
Aircraft Firefighter Familiarization Trainer School, 1998
School of Quality and Continuous Improvement, 2000
Virginia Department of Aviation Airport Security Task Force, 2002
AAAE National General Aviation Airport Security Task Force, 2002

PROFESSIONAL ASSOCIATIONS

Member – American Association of Airport Executives (AAAE)
Member – National Business Aircraft Association (NBAA)
Member – Southeast Chapter, Airport Managers Association (SAMA/SEC)
Treasurer – Virginia Airport Operations Council (VAOC)
Member – Virginia Aviation Business Association (VABA)

Joseph T. Harriss

501 Tulson Street, • Salt Lake City, Utah 84101 • (801) 601-3584 • (801) 304-0926
E-mail: joseph@m.cc.utah.edu

Social Security Number: 246-78-9023   Federal Status: N/A
Citizenship: U.S. Citizen   Veteran's Preference: None

OBJECTIVE:

Director, Sensors ES-0301-01/06 Announcement Number: SES-02:51
Department of Defense, Office of the Secretary of Defense, Assistant Secretary of Defense

PROFILE:

Highly accomplished and recognized Ph.D. Executive with extensive background in sensor technology, including developing policies, interoperability, and architecture matters. Achievements in modeling and characterization of chemical and biological detections systems, novel chemical sensors, high throughput combinatorial screening technologies, and embedded piezoelectric sensors. Patent pending research in infrared sensing technology, a novel concept in characterizing and modeling chemical and biological sensors, and novel concepts in breath monitoring. Ongoing research includes characterization of chemical and biological agents in air and water. Secret Clearance.

EDUCATION:

Case Western Reserve University, Cleveland, OH
Ph.D. Electrical Engineering and Applied Physics, 1972

Princeton University, Princeton, NJ
Master of Science, Electrical Engineering, 1967

Polytechnic Institute of New York, New York, NY
Bachelor of Science, Electrical Engineering, 1965

PROFESSIONAL CAREER HISTORY:

University of Hatfield, Snowbend, UT	1985 – Present
Supervisor: Mary Ellen Purvis (801) 340-9578	Salary: $80k/yr
Professor, Department of Science and Engineering	1985 – Present
Chairman, Department of Science and Engineering	1985 – 1988
Associate Director, Microanalysis Lab	1988 – Present
Director, Center of Excellence	1987 – 1989

Selected Professional Committees:

Chairman, College of Engineering Council	2001 – Present
Chairman, Departmental Accreditation Committee	2002 – Present
Utah Governor's Task Force on Defense Conversion	1985 – 1988
Utah Governor's Task Force on the Information Highway	1985 – 1988

➢ Oversaw and managed significant departmental growth during period of general budget declines.
➢ Conceived and implemented state-sponsored Center for Excellence in Advanced Materials.
➢ Research: Adaptive non-linear systems models for chemical and biological detectors. Test system for obtaining data for point and standoff detector models. Incorporation of noise, uncertainties, and correlations in simulation of sensor performance, combinatorial techniques for drug recovery, and detector design. Piezoelectric embedded sensors for materials analysis and fabrication control, piezoelectric chemical, and biological vapor generators.
➢ Designed and taught advanced courses in VLSI Fabrication Principles, Gallium Arsenide IC Processing, Micromachining, and Case Studies in Materials Selection together with core courses such as Basic Materials, Thermodynamics, and Materials Processing Laboratory.

Joseph T. Harriss

PROFESSIONAL CAREER HISTORY, Continued

England Institute of Technology, Cambridge, MA   1994 – 1997
Supervisor: Peter Haddock (617) 340-0048   Salary: $90k/yr
Visiting Professor
➢   Developed novel piezoelectric cure monitor and property estimator for composite materials.
➢   Developed chemical field effect transistor arrays using cyanoplatinate and calixarole polymeric layers.
➢   Developed novel high throughput screening technology.
➢   Served on the multi-agency, multi-institutional program in "Next Generation Manufacturing."
➢   Taught graduate courses in Thermodynamics and Introduction to Programming in C and undergraduate courses in Materials Processing Lab and Quantum Chemistry.

Sands Research Institute, Reno, NV   Summer 1985
Supervisor: Harold Manfred (617) 394-0783   Salary: $90k/yr
Science Advisor
➢   Developed SDI propellant diagnostics program.

Smithfield University, Boston, MA   1982 – 1985 Supervisor: Dr. Phili
Damon   Salary: $70k/yr
Professor, Electrical, Computer, and Systems Engineering
Chairman, Department of Electrical, Computer and Systems Engineering   1982 – 1983
➢   Conducted research in control of small-scale energy generation and utilization in rural areas.
➢   Developed fabrication technology lab in silicon microelectronics technology.
➢   Conducted research in reactivity control in energetic materials using electric fields modeling of nonlinear microwave components.
➢   Initiated Personal Computer-Based Instrumentation Program.
➢   Designed and taught numerous courses, including VLSI Fabrication, Advanced Semiconductor Devices, and Semiconductor Device Fabrication Laboratory, together with core courses in electronic and digital circuits.

Polytechnic Institute of New York, Brooklyn, NY   1980 – 1982
Supervisor: Stewart Jones (617) 549-0213   Salary: $65k/yr
Chairman & Professor
➢   Developed departmental programs in solid-state electronics and energy technology.
➢   Stimulated 50% increase in research volume.
➢   Collaborated to provide oversight and coordination of NYC Board of Education Science Fairs through department.
➢   Research: photovoltaic module reliability predicators, synthetic fuel technology, and integrated energy delivery systems.
➢   Introduced personal computers into instructional laboratories.
➢   Installed database and office automation program for department.

Colorado State University, Fort Collins, CO   1974 – 1980
Supervisor: Elizabeth Sommers (970) 459-1429   Salary: $32k/yr
Associate Professor, Tenured
Assistant Professor of Electrical Engineering   1974 – 1977
➢   Principal Investigator for research programs in fossil fuels, novel solar cells, hybrid solar systems, radiation catalysis, natural resource ores, and measurement automation.
➢   Discovered indium tin oxide on silicon solar cells, achieving 140 efficiency on 20 cm2 polycrystalline silicon.
➢   Discovered phase transitions in oil shale.
➢   Conceived and implemented DA/DTA/electrical impedance materials characterization technique.
➢   Pioneered use of Ion Beam sputtering to fabricate active electronic device structures.
➢   Codiscovered room temperature molten salt electrochemical solar cell.
➢   Taught circuit theory, semiconductor device physics, and integrated circuit technology.

Joseph T. Harriss

PROFESSIONAL CAREER HISTORY, Continued

Electronics Journal, New York, NY   1973 – 1974
Supervisor: Allen Dixsom (212) 553-0782   Salary: $18k/yr
Components Editor
➢   Concentrated on new devices, optoelectronics, and passive component technology.
➢   Reviewed manuscripts for potential book and magazine publishing.

ENTREPRENEURIAL AND CONSULTING ACTIVITIES

CEMOB LLC, Cambridge MA   1996-1998
Performed contract research for DARPA on micromachined inlets for bio detectors.

Ellis Inc., Salt Lake City, UT   1990-1995
Provided consulting on propellant safety to minimize technical risk for defense contractors. Modified Best Manufacturing Practices.
Primary Client: Willis Willoughby, Undersecretary of the Navy for Acquisition.

FEIC Inc., Reno, NV   1985 – 1992
Provided consulting in energy conversion, propellant systems, and program development assistance.

DIMAS Corporation, Boston, MA   1983 – 1985
Oversaw development of PC instrumentation products and customer software products.
SIED Corporation, Fort Collins, CO   1978 – 1982
Provided consulting on energy technology.

PUBLICATIONS:

Over 120 published articles and writings, including "Software Architecture for Integrated Test & Evaluation of Chemical/Biological Sensors" and "Criteria for the Design of Chemical Sensors."

HONORS & AWARDS:

Numerous invited papers and chaired sessions at conferences.
NASA Achievement Award – Invention of Indium Tin Oxide on Silicon Solar Cell

PROFESSIONAL ASSOCIATIONS:

Institute of Electrical & Electronic Engineers, Association of Old Crows, American Chemical Society, National Defense Industrial Organization, American Defense Preparedness Association – Utah Chapter

Mark Williams
3135 Appledore Court, Falls Church, VA 22043
Tel. (703) 440-7645 E-mail: mwilliams@msn.com

SUMMARY

Organizational development consultant with successful track record initiating, planning, and implementing improvement strategies and programs for private, public, nonprofit and government organizations. Expertise includes:

- Strategic Planning & Alignment
- Executive Coaching
- Leadership Development
- Process Improvement
- Project Management
- Team Building

- Change Management
- Organizational Effectiveness
- Performance Management
- Career Progression & Development
- Employee Surveys & Assessments
- Cultural Diversity Integration

Facilitate organizational alignment around strategic business vision and objectives. Design, develop and implement executive retreats and leadership development programs. Refine performance management systems including career progression models to enhance employee retention and development. Facilitate and coach individuals and teams to improve collaboration, effectiveness and productivity. Integrate cultural diversity. An award winning new business developer. Results improve overall organizational effectiveness, productivity and profitability.

Organizational Strategic Planning, Alignment & Process Improvement

- Coach executives and management teams to define their corporate vision, mission and values.
- Facilitate alignment of corporate objectives throughout the organization through partnering with and coaching leaders, managers and their teams.
- Consult on the design and implementation of integrated corporate diversity plans.
- Successfully lead business units and divisions through organizational restructuring processes.
- Consult technical engineers through ISO 9002 certification and systems life cycle redesign.
- Examine core business processes, and system designs for structural and process improvements.

Results: Focused organizations, enhanced corporate culture and integrated diversity. Established clear organizational directives. Opened lines of communication. Improved overall commitment to corporate objectives. Improved organizational process, procedures, efficiency and productivity. Accomplished results through virtual off-site teams. Facilitated the first hospital in the U.S.A. to receive ISO 9002 certification for their Technical Systems Management Department. Improved ability to meet customer and stakeholder expectations.

Performance Management

- Design and implement process and systems to enhance performance.
- Institute 360 degree leadership feedback profiles for executives and managers.
- Develop position descriptions
- Lead teams to successfully design, develop and implement career progression models.
- Revise performance appraisals to encompass objective task, behavioral and developmental assessments that supported the organizational objectives.
- Develop and implement balanced score card processes and measures.
- Oversight of reward and recognition programs that reinforced desired behaviors.

Results: Opened communications between managers and employees. Provided guidance and structure for career progression. Provided management with tools to coach, develop and assess employee's performance. Lead team of 15 to design, develop and implement a career progression model. Improved resource utilization, employee morale, satisfaction and retention.

Leadership Development

- Design, develop and implement leadership development programs that progress from understanding one's self as an individual, to team leadership to gaining a corporate leadership perspective.
- Incorporate the executive team dialogues and general managers to co-facilitate to solidify their commitment, support, involvement and self-learning in the program.

- Coach executives, vice presidents, senior managers and mangers in strategic planning, team building, management, communication, conflict management and interpersonal skills.
- Lead the corporate charge to become a "Fortune 100 Best Company to Work for in America."
- Implemented 360 leadership feedback assessments and facilitate succession planning initiatives.

Results: Designed, developed and implemented an extremely successful leadership development program which received accolades from the highest level. The program transformed managers into corporate leaders and created candidates for leadership succession. It instilled leadership competencies, aligned the organization around corporate objectives and ignite corporate commitment. It opened minds and doors and created life-changing experiences for participants.

Teambuilding
- Consult and partner with division, department, business unit managers and team leaders to design initiatives to achieve the desired business results.
- Facilitate teambuilding sessions for divisions, departments, business units and work groups.
- Establish goals, measures and action plans.
- Follow-up initiatives through regular meetings using action registers to monitor progress.

Results: Successfully transitioned work groups to team based operations. Improved intra-team and cross-functional cooperation, collaboration and trust. Established accountability and ownership for results.

Training and Development
- Design and conduct needs assessments via individual interviews, focus groups, phone interviews, Web-based employee surveys. Analyzed assessment results and wrote executive summaries and management reports including recommendations.
- Incorporated date from needs assessment to design relevant active learning scenarios for self-discovery and experiential learning.
- Develop and implement Train-the-Trainer and Facilitator Training workshop including training manuals, material and multimedia kits.
- Design, implement and analyze results of course evaluations for continuous improvement.

Results: Transferred team and leadership skills and competencies to team members that improved communications, interpersonal relationships, personal development, morale, employee satisfaction, productivity and retention.

PROFESSIONAL WORK HISTORY

President, Snyder & Associates, Fairfax, VA	1998-Present
Director, Organizational Development and Training, BTG/Titan Corp., Fairfax, VA	2000-2002
Senior Consultant, Human Management Services (HMS), Arlington, VA	1996-1998
Senior Consultant, ERIS Enterprise Inc., Columbia, MD	1994-1996
Training & Development Coordinator, Navy Federal Credit Union, Vienna, VA	1990-1994
President, Snyder & Associates, Fairfax, VA	1989-1990
Senior Account Representative, Control Data Corporation, Washington, DC	1985-1989

EDUCATION AND CERTIFICATIONS

B.A. Counseling Psychology, University of Florida, Gainesville, FL
Master Social Work, Large Systems Administration, Barry University, Miami, FL
Organizational Development Certification, Georgetown University, Washington DC
Myers Briggs Type Indicator and FIRO-B Certification, Otto Kroeger Associates, Fairfax, VA
ISO 9000, BSI Auditor/Lead Auditor Course, CEEM Inc. Fairfax, VA

SELECTED PRESENTATIONS

Medical Device and Invitro Diagnostic Manufacturing Industry Conference, New York, NY
State of Maryland, Department of Transportation, Annual Conference, Emmitsburg, MD
ASQ 52nd Annual Quality Congress, Philadelphia, PA
Clemson University, Professional Development and Leadership Seminars, Washington DC

(Before)

ALLEN T. WILLIAMS	3378 Coolidge Road Shrewsbury, NJ 07702 Home: (732) 530-9654

** SUMMARY

Results oriented, with excellent organizational skills and attention to detail. Superb written and verbal communication skills. Able to resolve conflict, prioritize workload, meet stringent deadlines and work as a team builder. Capable of directing projects in a high pressure atmosphere. Office skills include Microsoft Word and Excel.

** WORK EXPERIENCE

Sept. 1995-present   Division Manager/Vice President-Logistics
CEDENT LOGISTICS, INC., New York, NY

General Manager. Establish, design and manage the new division engaged as an out-source specialist. Directed all customer and supplier activity; recruited and trained the personnel; researched and direct marketing and sales, manage inventory controls and reports, including P&L.

1991-1995   Vice President
BURRELL MORTGAGE GROUP, New York, NY

Vice President Sales, Operations and processing; Systems administration.

1989-1991   General Manager
MORELAND CO., INC., New York, NY

Manage the administration and service operations of this specialty repair company. Restructured operation to improve profit and create a team environment. Duties – Sales Manger, Operations Manager, Customer Service Manager, Call Center Manager, Customer Support Manager, and Systems Administrator.

1984-1989   Division Manager
FARRELL MOVING SYSTEMS, New York, NY

Manager, Household Goods moving department. Reorganized the accounting department procedures, streamlined the data entry system. Established a system of scheduled sales appointments, call reporting and commission management. Duties: Director of Household Goods Sales, Operations Manager, Customer Service Manager, Call Center Manager and Customer Support Manager.

** EDUCATION

Bachelor of Science, major in Business Administration
Fordham University, New York, NY, 1975

(After)

ALLEN T. WILLIAMS
3378 Coolidge Road
Shrewsbury, NJ 07702
Home: (732) 530-9654 • Cell: (732) 530-1900 • ATWMS@comcast.net

---

EXECUTIVE PROFILE

General Management … Sales … Operations … Customer Support

18+ years of experience managing all core business functions and delivering consistent revenue growth in start-up, turnaround, and high-growth environments. Achievements in financial systems, expense control, sales, marketing, business development, and administration. Expertise in analyzing and streamlining product delivery systems to maximize productivity, quality, and efficiency. Adept negotiator.

SELECTED ACCOMPLISHMENTS

♦ **Restructured and revitalized nonperforming sales organization at Cedent Logistics, Inc. and developed successful start-up venture which grew 10% per month in revenues.**

♦ **Negotiated and captured major outsourcing contract for Cedent Logistics, Inc.; grew account from zero to $250K per month while achieving a 50%–60% profit margin.**

♦ **Designed, executed, and managed call center operations for a key account at Cedent Logistics, recognized by client for 100% order processing accuracy and on-time service delivery.**

♦ **Improved efficiency, streamlined functions, and restored failing operation at Moreland Co., Inc., achieving a consistent, profitable growth record annually.**

♦ **Established and launched the profitable Home Loan Division for real estate sales operation of Burrell Mortgage Group.**

♦ **Turned around operations at Farrell Moving Systems and boosted revenues from $300K to $5M within 18 months, instituted strong financial controls/reporting process, implemented creative marketing strategies, and improved service quality through staff training.**

♦ **Effectively expanded Farrell Moving Systems to become an agent of Mayberry Transit Company and led operations to rank #9 in sales out of 600 agents nationwide within 3 years.**

♦ **Initiated and closed the largest, most sensitive sales contract in Mayberry's history for a Chinese exhibition.**

PROFESSIONAL EXPERIENCE

<u>**Division Manager/Vice President-Logistics**</u>
CEDENT LOGISTICS, INC. • New York, NY • 1995-present

• Recruited to restructure and turn around declining operation of multimillion-dollar international transportation company. Manage entire division with P&L accountability for all sales, marketing, operations, inventory control, administration, and human resources. Led development of new start-up venture and captured new business which tripled profits.

(After)

ALLEN T. WILLIAMS • Page 2

Vice President
BURRELL MORTGAGE GROUP • New York, NY • 1991-1995

- Selected to spearhead and direct start-up of new Home Loan Department of multimillion-dollar organization serving the real estate industry. Designed and implemented sales and market development strategies contributing to business growth and success. Managed entire loan administration activities and staff.

General Manager
MORELAND CO., INC. • New York, NY • 1989-1991

- Restored profitability to $15M international specialty auto repair, race car design, and building organization (Porsche cars) and assumed full P&L accountability for all sales, customer service/ support, call center, human resources, and systems administration. Instituted inventory controls, enhanced productivity and efficiency while reviving employee morale and dramatically improved service level to an all-time high resulting in continued profitability. Positioned company for its successful sale in 1991.

Division Manager
FARRELL MOVING SYSTEMS • New York, NY • 1984-1989

- Revitalized and expanded operations of $15M computer and trade show mover to include household goods. Rebuilt entire finance/accounting function, instituting financial controls and reporting system. Instituted service-oriented culture through staff training and development, which enhanced service quality and customer satisfaction, as well as eliminated claims. Innovated marketing strategies, including new telemarketing program to drive forward revenue growth.

EDUCATION

Bachelor of Science – Business Administration
Fordham University • New York, NY

(Before)

CARLOS MENDOZA
688 Brousard Drive
Fremont, CA 94538
510.384.9932   mendoza@aol.com

Objective: A senior level Management position utilizing both my management skills and technical exposure to increase revenues and significantly contribute to the bottom line.

Employment History

KOLL CORPORATION, SAN JOSE, CA (1999-PRESENT)
VICE PRESIDENT OF BUSINESS DEVELOPMENT

Assisted in successful acquisition of software division of major software firm. Responsible for marketing and business development. Created the first marketing plan and delivered all objectives to date. Guided initial company strategic plan development and executed multiple partnerships.

RENAUD, INC., Dublin, CA (1996-1999)
SENIOR VICE PRESIDENT OF SALES & MARKETING

Created a sales, sales support and marketing group for the subsidiary. Responsible for reengineering focused technology solutions sales in large call center and customer service departments of several vertical markets. Hired team in 3 months creating pipeline of $45M in less than 5 months.

AMERITECH, San Jose, CA (1990-1996)
VICE PRESIDENT OF SALES & GENERAL MANAGER
VICE PRESIDENT OF SALES

Responsible for worldwide revenue for this provider of HR, payroll and financial applications. Managed sales, sales support, RFP, telemarketing and contracts. Produced revenue at plan while expenses kept below plan. Increased sales to $7.5M in first year after product release.

KIRLIN ENTERPRISES, Irvine, CA (1987-1990)
DIRECTOR OF SALES & MARKETING

Reported to the President of this leading voice processing solutions firm across multiple markets. Complete responsibility for direct, distribution and federal sales channels. Managed staff of 25 producing $16M, $21 M and $25 M, respectively, during my tenure. Used sound sales management skills to achieve revenue plan while also controlling expenses and providing margin contribution.

Education

M.B.A.   University of California
B.S., Marketing   University of Chicago

(After)

CARLOS MENDOZA
688 Brousard Drive • Fremont, CA 94538
510. 384.9932
Mendoza@aol.com

SALES & GENERAL MANAGEMENT EXECUTIVE
Technology Industry

Demonstrated track record of achievements in building and leading top-performing sales organizations, both domestic and global. Innovative strategic thinker successful in revitalizing sales staffs and operations delivering consistent and sustainable revenue growth. Strong qualifications in general management, P&L management and negotiations. Expertise:

• **Strategic Sales Planning**	• **Sales Training & Development**
• **Team-Building & Leadership**	• **Multi-Channel Development**
• **Budgeting & Forecasting**	• **Account Relationship Management**
• **Compensation & Incentive Planning**	• **Consultative Solutions Selling**

EXPERIENCE & RESULTS

KOLL CORPORATION, San Jose, CA (1999-present)
VICE PRESIDENT OF BUSINESS DEVELOPMENT

• Selected to join board of directors and retained to provide management structure and strategic direction to marketing and business development organization of company with 50 employees. Achieved all objectives and currently remain as board member.

♦ *Led strategic plan development, recommended/provided sales staffing strategies, strengthened accounting/reporting, improved morale and communications, and created all new sales collateral.*

♦ *Initiated successful acquisition of Integral's financial software division and instrumental in forging multiple business partnerships.*

RENAUD, INC., Dublin, CA (1996-1999)
SENIOR VICE PRESIDENT OF SALES & MARKETING

• Recruited to create and direct sales organization for first systems integration subsidiary of Renaud, providing customer service/call center technology solutions to national firms in various vertical markets. Company merged with two other technology divisions resulting in closure of operation.

♦ *Recruited and trained staff of 17 in sales, marketing and sales support in just 3 months, meeting plan goal.*

♦ *Designed and executed effective sales strategy generating pipeline of $45+ million within first 5 months.*

♦ *Assumed marketing responsibilities within 60 days of hire. Revitalized struggling department and revamped all public relations and collateral material.*

AMERITECH, San Jose, CA (1990-1996)
VICE PRESIDENT OF SALES & GENERAL MANAGER (1993-1996)

• Senior executive directing worldwide sales organization with 27 employees for client/server provider of HR, payroll and financial software products. Concurrent assignment as division general manager with full P&L accountability and leadership of 25 sales, software development, customer service, and sales support staffs.

• *Revised compensation plan attracting higher caliber of sales talent and rebuilt sales team in just 4 months.*

• *Grew sales from $2.5 million to $7.5 million in first year by creating energetic success-oriented environment.*
Restructured division, reducing staff and expenses while achieving planned revenue objectives.

(After)

CARLOS MENDOZA • 510. 384.9932 • Page 2

VICE PRESIDENT OF SALES (1990-1993)

- Provided strategic sales planning and solid management direction to direct and indirect sales groups in U.S. market for leader of voice processing solutions. Grew company revenues through strong leadership.

- *Delivered 38% cumulative sales growth (from $18 million to $25 million) over 3-year period.*
- *Developed and managed successful multi-distribution channels producing 40% of overall revenue.*
- *Created Federal government sales group and closed $5-million contract; account remains viable today.*
- *Devised new compensation plan, performance system, pricing strategies, and configuration methods.*

KIRLIN ENTERPRISES, Irvine, CA (1987-1990)

DIRECTOR OF SALES & MARKETING

- Created and led sales, sales support and marketing group of 20 in company's first venture promoting packaged image solutions across several vertical markets. Active on speakers' circuit on image processing technology.

- *Built high-performance team and drove sales growth from $2 million to $25 million in only 2 years.*
- *Succeeded in penetrating financial and utility markets for the first time in company's history.*
- *Captured six high-profile accounts generating a combined $7 million annually.*

EDUCATION

M.B.A. • University of California • Irvine, CA

B.S. Marketing • University of Chicago • Chicago, I

INDEX

About the Authors

Marshall A. Brown

Marshall A. Brown, CPCC, is a certified career and life coach and founder of Marshall Brown & Associates. Marshall has always had a passion for helping people find ways to live more fulfilling lives. He channeled his interest and energy into a successful career in human resources, specializing in building innovative career services centers for association management professionals.

Marshall is known for his personalized and focused approach to getting people on the right career and life track. Over the years, many clients have come to him without a clear articulation of who they were, what they were looking for, and the compelling reasons why someone should hire them.

As a result, Marshall gives his clients the tools to create compelling self-promotional presentations—resumes that stand out from the crowd and get candidates in the door. This book reflects his successful work with hundreds of job candidates. His coaching clients also benefit from accurate assessment tools, networking training, and job search targeting. Organizational clients come to Marshall for targeted staff improvement programs and online career center enhancements.

Marshall is the Board President of the International Coach Federation-D.C. Chapter and Past President of the D.C. Chapter of the Association of Career Professionals, International. He is an active member and volunteer leader for the American Society of Association Executives and the Center for Leadership Development.

He writes a monthly career column for *Association Trends* and has published articles in leading association magazines and newsletters. His speaking engagements have attracted hundreds of association and business professionals around the country.

Marshall has a bachelor's degree in Psychology from the University of Pittsburgh and is certified by the Coaches Training Institute. He grew up in Pittsburgh and now lives in Washington, D.C. with his cocker spaniel. Franklin. Marshall enjoys spending time with friends who appreciate his upbeat and positive approach to life and engaging sense of humor. He enjoys all kinds of traveling—from exotic trips abroad to long weekends at the Delaware seashore. The youngest of three, Marshall has two older sisters—who let him spoil all six of his nieces, nephews, and their spouses—one great-nephew, and one more on the way!

For more information contact Marshall at marshall@mbrownassociates.com or go to *www.mbrownassociates.com*.

Annabelle Reitman, Ed.D.

A career management consultant with more than 30 years' experience in career counseling and higher education career center management, Annabelle Reitman works with a diverse clientele, from young professionals to early retirees, either in workshops or individual consultations. Her specialty is helping people create focused and targeted resumes, projecting an ideal professional image for job search and marketing purposes. Dr. Reitman conducts short-term career coaching helping people set career priorities and develop an individualized professional niche, enabling them to move towards the next step in their career pathway.

She has been a lead career coach at the American Society for Training and Development's (ASTD) International and Technowledge Conferences and an author of their Web-based Career Q&A Column. She coauthored *Career Moves: Take Charge of Your Training Career NOW!* (ASTD Press, 2001), and authored *Take Charge of Your Career* (ASTD Press, 2003). Dr. Reitman is a contributor to the annual *Training and Performance SourceBooks*, edited by Mel Silberman (Active Training Publications). She writes career management articles for Web-based publications; print newsletters; magazines, including ASTD's *T&D Magazine* and their OD and Leadership Network's online newsletter; *dcjobnetwork.com*; American Society of Association Executives (ASAE) online newsletter, *Global Links*; and Association of Career Professionals International (ACP Int'l). For more than 20 years, Dr. Reitman has presented at professional meetings and conferences.

For the past two years, she has served on the Board of the Washington, D.C. Chapter, Association of Career Professionals International (ACP Int'l). Dr. Reitman is a past president and copresident of the ASTD Metro Washington, D.C. Chapter.

Dr. Reitman received her doctorate and master degrees in Higher Education Administration from the Teachers College, Columbia University, and her bachelor's degree in Sociology from Brooklyn College, CUNY.

For more information, contact Annabelle at AnReitman@aol.com.